THE TRAUMA RESPONSE

TREATMENT FOR EMOTIONAL INJURY

THE TRAUMA RESPONSE

TREATMENT FOR EMOTIONAL INJURY

Diana Sullivan Everstine

Louis Everstine

W.W. NORTON & COMPANY • NEW YORK • LONDON

NORTON PROFESSIONAL BOOKS

The text of this book was composed in Elante.
Composition by Bytheway Typesetting Services, Inc. Manufacturing by
Haddon Craftsmen, Inc.

Library of Congress Cataloging-in-Publication Data

Everstine, Diana Sullivan, 1944–
    The trauma response : treatment for emotional injury / Diana
Sullivan Everstine, Louis Everstine.
        p.   cm.
    Includes bibliographical references and index.
    ISBN 0-393-70123-9
    1. Post-traumatic stress disorder—Treatment.   2. Psychic trauma.
I. Everstine, Louis, 1993– . II. Title.
    [DNLM: 1. Stress Disorders, Post-Traumatic—therapy.   WM 170
E93t]
RC552.P67E84   1992
616.85′21 — dc20
DNLM/DLC
for Library of Congress   92-49171   CIP

W.W. Norton & Company, Inc., 500 Fifth Avenue, New York, N.Y. 10110
W.W. Norton & Company, Ltd., 10 Coptic Street, London WC1A 1PU

2   3   4   5   6   7   8   9   0

Acknowledgments

Recognition of the trauma response has had its own evolutionary process, from awareness of the emotional reactions produced by war, to those caused by natural disasters such as floods and earthquakes, to the results of accidents and domestic strife. It is a matter of some irony that only in recent years was recognition made of the fact that the victims of crimes are equally traumatized. In California, for example, it was not until the 1970's that legislation was passed providing state aid for crime victims, as well as those who are witnesses to crimes. With state funding, victim-witness assistance programs were established in each county to dispense these funds; they are used to defray health care costs incurred by citizens whose lives are directly altered by crime.

In Santa Clara County, the Victim-Witness program is administered by the local chapter of the National Conference of Christians and Jews, whose executive director, Lilian Silberstein, is a pioneer in this field of service. She was ably assisted by program director Mike Hyllested and analyst Patricia Evans. We have provided psychotherapy services by referral from this program since it began and take pride in helping a small sample of its vast population of beneficiaries.

In addition to therapy for victims of crime, we work in the forensic field as evaluators of emotional injury in civil cases. We have been fortunate to collaborate on a number of these cases with, among others, attorneys Richard Gregg and Richard Alexander of San Jose, and attorneys Peter Neumann and Lawrence Semenza of Reno.

We have taken our views on the trauma response to several European countries, where we have encountered workshop and conference audiences eager to learn. We have been made especially welcome in Holland, thanks mainly to inspiring collaborations, in Utrecht, Rotterdam, and Ghent in Belgium, with Dr. Hermann Vergouwen and Bert Van Luyn, our genial hosts. At the psychiatric hospital in Amersfoort, we conducted a seminar at the invitation of Dr. H. J. Dalewijk and Dr. Klaus Schmitt.

In Norway, on two occasions we were guests of psychologists Bjorn Reigstad and Knut Sørgaard to present workshops at the Nordland Psykiatriske Sykehus in the city of Bødo. In France, we have had the good fortune to participate in the seminars of the training institute P'SOMATICS in Antibes, with our friends Catherine Mesnard and Dr. Anne Ancelin-Schuztenberger.

In 1989, we were invited to Mexico City to speak at the First Seminar in Emergency Psychology of the Red Cross of Mexico. Our hosts were Dra. Elisa Pallares and Humbelina Casso, and through them we met Gerardo Gally, director of Editorial Pax of Mexico, who is publishing our books in Spanish. From the Red Cross disaster workers, we learned a lot about their work with survivors of the earthquake in 1985. In Mexico as well, we have collaborated with Dra. Helen Castro, Dr. Jorge Llanes, and Dra. Dalila Yussif de Esposito. Much of this book was written in the hospitable ambience of Las Mañanitas in Cuernavaca, manager Rubén Cerda presiding.

The validation project for the Everstine Life Stress Index (see Chapter 3) is guided by Dr. Murray Tondow and Dr. Robert Broenen of Behaviordyne, Inc. Many of the data are being provided by Dr. Stuart Greenberg of Seattle, to whom we are especially grateful.

This book was transformed from lined paper to typescript by Adele Johnson and Barbette Mylar. Vicki Telfer helped to compile the references. Along this journey, our Virgil was Margaret Farley, our editor at Norton. Many thanks.

Contents

Preface

"Life is what happens to you when you've made other plans."

—Anonymous

"Trauma" is an all-purpose term for what we feel when our lives are turned upside down. The Greek root, "traumat-," means "wound," and the connotation of a cut or a bruise or a fracture or a bullet hole provides an apt metaphor for the subject of this book. It deals with shocks to the system, lacerations of the spirit, soul damage. Life being what it is, sources of trauma are plentiful. Imagine that trauma is felt by everyone whose loved one has died. It is said that, in our country, a woman is raped every six minutes. In 1991, it was reported that, of the marriages contracted in America during the 1980's more than half had already ended in divorce. And we live in a world in which, since records have been kept, there has never not been a war somewhere. Every emergency is to some degree traumatic, and clinicians are beginning to understand that every trauma is an emergency.

The purpose of this book is to help clinicians identify, measure, and treat emotional trauma. It is generally intended for professionals who work in the mental health field, namely psychologists, psychiatrists, nurses, social workers, and marriage, family, and child counselors. But many other care-givers encounter trauma victims, need to know their states of mind, and will strive to help them if they can. In this category are police officers, firefighters, emergency medical technicians, general practice nurses, emergency room physicians, and those who work on disaster relief teams. More-over, a worker in just about any kind of social agency may one day open the office door to someone who has just experienced a traumatic event. Others who might wish to understand and assist trauma victims include attorneys, judges, probation officers, teachers, guidance counselors, and the clergy.

If at any moment the world can be divided into those who need help and those who are able to supply it, this book is written for those who are lucky enough to care.

PART ONE

An Introduction to Trauma

CHAPTER I

Trauma as Aftermath

PSYCHOLOGICAL TRAUMA occurs in the wake of an unexpected event that a person has experienced intimately and forcefully. From the perspective of this book, trauma is a response, a reaction, the answer to a question. For example, it may be a person's reaction to someone's death, to being injured, or to becoming the victim of a crime. It is useful to distinguish between the *event* as cause and the trauma itself as effect. In this view, an event in itself is not traumatic. A person must experience the event before trauma can be said to have occurred. The more intense the person's experience of the event, the greater may be the trauma. Hence, there can be many degrees of trauma, from mild to severe.

Because the primary cause of trauma *is* the death or injury-causing accident or crime, the many complicating factors that may accompany such an event are best categorized as secondary causes of trauma. These complicating factors can be real or imagined; in either case, they probably would not, taken alone, have produced trauma. As one example, an injury victim may have to wait for a long time in an emergency room before receiving treatment; ordinarily, such a wait by itself would not have a traumatic effect, although it might arouse strong emotions. But, in the context of the total catastrophe, it may serve to add "insult to injury." Another example would be the case of a person's being seriously hurt in an automobile accident (traumatic event), in which the other driver was later found to have been drunk (complicating factor). In some instances, these secondary sources of trauma may serve a diagnostic purpose; it may be possible to rule out trauma or identify recovery from trauma when the person places more emphasis on the secondary cause than on the traumatic event itself.

3

POTENTIALLY TRAUMATIC EVENTS
OR EXPERIENCES

Any one of hundreds of events that occur in a person's life could produce a traumatic reaction. Even so, it is possible to identify some of the most common sources and categorize them by type. Table 1.1 identifies 12 major categories containing 40 such events.

This by no means exhausts the full range of trauma-producing life events. Many other events can affect people adversely, such as when a police officer must shoot someone in the line of duty or when a reporter must view the mangled victims of a plane crash. The list was drawn to be most useful in its general application. Moreover, these 11 categories are not mutually exclusive: two or more of them may be combined in a specific case. A woman could be seriously injured in the course of being raped and, as a result of the assault, could suffer additional loss when her husband is unable to understand her despair. Or, a man who was injured in an automobile accident may later learn that a friend or family member was killed in the same accident; further, because of lost time from his job, he could lose an opportunity for promotion in his work. And these serial traumas may have more than an additive effect. They might interact in ways that would *multiply* their impact upon the victim.

There is a wide variation in the apparent strength and intensity of events as listed in Table 1.1. On the surface, there is no comparison between the death of a spouse and being refused promotion. Yet it is human nature to apply personal values in judging practically any life event. Hence, trauma is assigned a value by each person who experiences it, and the definition of its impact is unique to the individual. In effect, trauma is in the eye of the beholder. For that reason, to assign arbitrarily a certain weight to a tragic outcome such as dismemberment or "loss of consortium," as do insurance companies and civil courts, is as incorrect as it is heartless. For the same reason, it is essential for the therapist to know not only what happened to a client, but also what that experience meant to the client.

In summary, the list of potentially traumatic experiences and events provides a foundation for the diagnostic process. If one or more of these has happened in a person's life, it is valid to raise the question of whether or not trauma has occurred. The more that are combined, the greater the likelihood that trauma is present. No matter what has happened, the significance attached to the event by the person involved is the key to measuring traumatic effect (see Chapter III).

HISTORICAL BACKGROUND

The effects of trauma upon the psyche have been well documented, by writers and scientists alike, for many centuries. Samuel Pepys described his

TABLE 1.1
Potentially Traumatic Events

Natural Disaster
  earthquake
  flood
  fire
  landslide
  volcanic eruption
  tornado, hurricane

Physical Assault
  being mugged
  being beaten, battered
  being kidnapped, held hostage

Sexual Assault
  rape
  molestation

Property Loss
  burglary
  theft, robbery

Physical Loss
  severe illness
  accidental injury
  self-inflicted injury[a]
  unplanned pregnancy

Violent Agency
  causing death willfully (as in war)
  causing death accidentally
  causing injury accidentally

Loss by Death
  death of spouse
  death of child
  death of parent
  death of close friend
  death of close relative
  death of colleague at work
  death of beloved pet

Loss of Relationship
  end of love relationship
  end of close friendship

Bearing Witness to Tragedy
  seeing a loved one or friend killed
  seeing a loved one or friend seriously injured

Portent of Danger
  being threatened with bodily harm
  being the target of a credible death threat

Threatened Loss
  learning that a loved one or friend is terminally ill
  disappearance of a family member

(*continued*)

TABLE 1.1
Potentially Traumatic Events (Continued)

Loss of Status
  being fired
  being demoted
  being refused promotion
  bankruptcy
  public humiliation

---

[a]In some cases of attempted suicide the only surprise, on the part of
the attempter, is having survived. This, too, can produce trauma.

intense emotional reaction to having observed the London Fire of 1666.
Then and later, traumatic events were thought to produce a disruption of
the nervous system that led, in turn, to behavioral changes. In the late 19th
century, this conceptualization was replaced by the notion that response to
trauma resembled the symptoms of hysteria then being described by Char-
cot, Breuer, and Freud. In accord with changing fashion, this interpretation was later supplanted by one in which the symptoms caused by trauma
were classified among those in the general category of "neurosis."

Once trauma reactions were labeled as neurotic symptoms, they were
then linked, in psychoanalytic theory, to unconscious conflicts with their
origin in childhood. As noted by Mendelson,

> Freud himself expressed doubt that objective danger alone can give rise to a
> neurosis without the participation of the deeper unconscious layers of the
> psychic apparatus, or that a frightening experience can of itself produce
> neurosis in later life. (1987, p. 50)

Clearly, this idea that trauma merely lays bare hidden layers of neurotic
conflict tends to diminish the importance of a traumatic incident in a
person's life.[1] Placing emphasis on the "emotional vulnerability" of a per-

---

[1]The mental health profession is notorious for mystifying the public by its faddish
jargon, as illustrated by the following observation. Writing for *The New York Times*,
Martha Weinman Lear described her visit to a recent convention of the American
Psychiatric Association:

> . . . nowhere in any of this . . . is there ever talk of "neurosis" . . . in five days . . . I never
> once heard the word, and am told that it does not even appear (except in parentheses
> for historical continuity) in psychiatry's bible, the revised third edition of the *Diagnos-
> tic and Statistical Manual of Disorders* . . . (1988, pp. 30, 31).

Having spent the better part of a century trying to "cure" neurosis, the profession
has chosen to make it disappear.

son *before* he experienced the event opens the way to the opinion, held by some, that what is observed in a trauma victim after the event is merely a sign that a "preexisting condition" was already in effect. The practical implications of this opinion will be discussed both in Chapter XI ("Trauma in the Workplace") and in Chapter XII ("Trauma and the Law").

World War I taught us that the experience of surviving modern warfare can be profoundly traumatic, as witness the many authentic cases of "shell shock." The same syndrome was referred to as "war neurosis" during World War II, but even then it was not met with much compassion. To some, such as Fairbairn (1943), the reaction was thought to be caused by a failure of conscience that led to dereliction of duty. This epitomized the view that those who claim to suffer from the effects of trauma may be malingering, a topic that will be addressed more than once in this book.

More recently, clinicians have developed a sensitivity to the vicissitudes of trauma that Freud could not have anticipated. For example, we observe that women who undergo hysterectomies can show signs of emotional trauma (Kaltreider et al., 1979), that persons who must search for dead bodies after a plane crash (Taylor & Fraser, 1982) or deal with mass suicide-such as the one at Jonestown (Jones, 1983) can develop these symptoms. We have learned that children who are forced to witness acts of violence involving a parent (e.g., murder, rape of the mother, suicide of a parent) may suffer catastrophic psychological injury (Pynoos & Eth, 1985). And we are aware that children are exceptionally vulnerable to traumatic effects from many sources, such as when their homes are destroyed by flood (Newman, 1976) or in a case in which children were held hostage for days in a partially-buried school bus (Terr, 1983). Clearly, this house of human frailty has many mansions.

Specific examples of the devastating aftermath of various kinds of events abound, but the point is not made by accumulating case histories. The fact is that one's ego must contend with any environmental stimulus that comes along. Sudden stimuli must be dealt with swiftly and painful stimuli must be met by a healing force. This is true no matter what the person's "condition" before the event and whether or not the person was emotionally "vulnerable" in advance. In short, anyone can be traumatized, from the most well-adjusted to the most troubled. For a clinician, it is the person's mode of responding that is the salient fact.

THE CONCEPT OF STRESS

The phrase "post-traumatic stress" has entered common usage, generally in reference to a specific phenomenon within the broad category of stress.

What is "stress"? The concept rose to prominence in the psychology and psychiatry of the 1950s, largely through the work of the endocrinologist Hans Selye (1950). For Selye, stress was the causal factor in certain otherwise inexplicable physiological changes, especially hormonal imbalances, that in many cases preceded organ malfunction or organ breakdown. This observation led to the view that, with many psychosomatic disorders (e.g., peptic ulcer, hypertension, some skin disorders), the prior experience of stress is a critical factor (Kaplan & Kaplan, 1967). When Holmes and Rahe produced their pioneering instrument for measuring stress, the Social Readjustment Rating Scale (1967), its premise was that high levels of stress would lead eventually to physical illness. This revelation of stress as a causal factor in internal physical changes was certainly heuristic, but it scarcely anticipates the way in which the concept is currently being used.

What has occurred in recent years is the generalization of a causal factor into an effect on its own — stress as an outcome instead of part of a process. Consider that a person can sue for damages related to stress itself, as opposed to suing over an illness in which stress was a contributing factor. The larger implication is that stress is now construed mainly as a psychological phenomenon, not a physiological one. What began in the endocrine system now resides in the realm of thoughts and feelings.

When a term that has descriptive usefulness in generalized beyond its early referents, it can become distorted and overworked. It can be made grandiose, as in statements like "stress is life and life is stress" (Figley, 1983, p. 5). It can be made trivial, as in "Stress is a fact of life, a natural and expected aspect of emotional and social development" (McCubbin & Figley, 1983, p. 228). Or, when used in so many contexts that its meaning is exhausted, it can be treated as something ineffable: "Stress is stress" (McCubbin & Figley, 1983, p. 222). Further, when a concept is stretched out of shape, it can be used indiscriminately, especially when it passes from the language of science into common parlance.[2] A cartoon in a recent issue of *The New Yorker* shows people walking along a city street, carrying briefcases, their faces contorted in a rictus of anguish resembling the figure in Edvard Munch's famous painting, *The Scream*. In the caption, one person says to another, "I suppose one could say that stress is an inescapable part of the human condition" (14 October 1991, p. 82).

A result of this trend in the lay usage of the term is that "stress" now connotes an inner state as ubiquitous as hunger or fatigue. It's convenient

---

[2]This carefully printed sign was observed in the office of a law enforcement officer in Stockton, California:

"Stress": the confusion caused when one's mind overrides the body's basic desire to choke the living shit out of some asshole who desperately needs it.

for people to refer to "stress" as a precipitating factor in nearly every type of personal problem; that is, as a precursor to the development of a psychological symptom. In addition, people use the same word to refer to a collection of symptoms, as when a person is said to be "stressed out." This kind of devaluation of the concept must be taken into consideration by the mental health professional, so that one's meaning is clear when the term is used. Caution is the order of the day when a word is employed so broadly as to refer to any emotion from malaise to Angst. For clarity of thinking, it will be helpful to *narrow* the use of the term and prevent its further expansion.

WHAT IS TRAUMA?

It may be that, by taking over the concept of stress (or at least the term in its original meaning) as a useful label for what a trauma victim is feeling, trauma theorists have succeeded in muddling the issue. If we limit the definition of "stress" to a state similar to the one referred to by "tension" and use the terms interchangeably, we may be able to see each phenomenon in a sharper light. To be tense (physically and/or emotionally) is a recognizable condition: we know when we feel it. The same is true for "having stress" or "feeling stressed." We can experience this state (by either name) at any waking moment. It can be the result of a host of causal factors and, in one context, refers to something very like extreme frustration.

In any case, stress is not *necessarily* the product of a traumatic event. (Unless we say, misleadingly, that the setting of the date for a final exam that we must take was a "traumatic event," even though we feel considerable stress as the date approaches.) Certainly, the subject of a "stress management" course is not normally the result of that kind of event. In fact, what is referred to as "job stress" mainly concerns *pressures* that are felt in a person's work environment. Therefore, if stress can be produced in the absence of a traumatic event, perhaps what the concept describes is a condition qualitatively different from a traumatic reaction. Should that be the case, use of the concept in an explanation of trauma is misplaced.

In our view, an alternative conceptualization of "trauma" is worth examining. What is internally perceived as trauma is a manifestation of impaired mechanisms of defense. Under normal circumstances, the person is stabilized and protected by an integrated system of defenses such as repression, denial, rationalization, etc. These processes have acquired, through time, a certain flexibility of adaptation to meet the demands of a wide range of life events and experiences. This quality of resilience has proven useful in deflecting many assaults on the person's sense of integrity and in promoting recovery from emotional wounds. As an example of the latter, the rejected lover can draw upon a well-established capacity for rationalizing by declaring that the other person "wasn't right for me"; here, the traumatic event was the moment of rejection. The family of a soldier who is missing in action can deny its feelings of loss for years, sustained by any rumor that the loved one could be found alive; the traumatic event was the announcement that the soldier was missing. In every sound, a hostage hears the approach of the phantom rescuer; being taken and being held hostage can be seen as serial traumatic events.

When something happens in a person's life that threatens the natural balancing system, psychological symptoms may soon appear. Experiencing a traumatic event is that quality of threat taken to an extreme. In some cases a person's mechanisms of defense may have been relatively weak before the event occurred, or the event itself has rendered him inoperative—crushed him as it were. As we intend to show, it is not necessary to postulate an intervening state such as stress as a means either to diagnose or to treat the effects of trauma. In effect, whatever happens to a person after a traumatic event is not "stress" in the usual sense of the word. Instead of thinking that someone possesses more stress or a new category of stress following the event, we shall mount trauma in an entirely different frame.

TRAUMA DISORDER

When psychological symptoms emerge after a potentially traumatic event has occurred, most people draw the conclusion that a "post-traumatic stress disorder" (PTSD) has developed. It should be noted that "disorder," in this context, is the medical conception of a pathological state. As defined by the *Diagnostic and Statistical Manual of Mental Disorders (DSM-III-R)*,

> The essential feature of this disorder is the development of characteristic symptoms following a psychologically distressing event that is outside the range of usual human experience. . . . (APA, 1987, p. 247)

Note that, in this definition, the phenomenon "stress" is not defined. The term "distressing" is the equivalent, according to one thesaurus, of ". . . misery . . . affliction, grievance, tribulation, trouble, annoyance, vexation, perturbation, aggravation . . . misfortune, adversity" (Rodale, 1978, p. 315). None of these terms reflects what Selye had in mind.

Increasingly, the public is becoming aware of the label "PTSD" and is trying to comprehend its significance. An article by Charles Krauthammer exposed the practical aspects of its recent application to criminal justice:

> The 17-year-old girl stole another girl's leather jacket, then shot her dead. Her attorneys argued that rather than go to prison she should get therapy in Wisconsin's juvenile system. Why? Because she suffered from post-traumatic stress disorder (the Vietnam-era name for what in World War I was called

"shell shock" and in World War II "combat fatigue"). No, she was not a soldier, but had picked up the disorder, which made her unable to control her violent urges, growing up amid the poverty and brutality of the inner city.

The good news is that a Milwaukee judge . . . rejected the argument. The bad news is that our legal system has been so degraded by pseudo-psychiatry that such absurdities can even be attempted. (11 February 1992, p. 7B)

This comment reveals that observers of the contemporary scene are beginning to recognize both the debasement of the term and the bankruptcy of the concept to which it refers.

In this book, we endeavor to move beyond the disease model of psychological affliction, to formulate a different way of looking at trauma syndrome. By looking away from the pathological aspects of a symptom or set of symptoms, we can see that trauma is by no means a "disorder" in the way that the term is used to refer to a breakdown of the personality. By contrast, the *symptom* can be viewed as an element of a response pattern whose purpose is not to prolong or exaggerate or destroy, but rather to heal. Instead of seeing the person's reaction to a traumatic event as abnormality revealing itself, one can consider it an outward sign that a homeostatic process has begun. This process is intended to restore equilibrium to the person's emotional life. In that sense, the trauma has set in motion the person's own internal coping functions. Those functions consist of a pattern of responding that is unique in every instance.

When, by rejecting the disease model, one is freed from the constraints of traditional thinking about trauma new dimensions come into focus. For instance, in medicine, a clear distinction is made between illness and injury. An illness can be caused by a wide range of different factors, from invasion by bacteria or a virus to a genetic weakness, poor diet, or aberrant life-style. Its onset is often perceived as sudden, but in hindsight prodromal signs are usually detected (e.g., one may say, "He must have been coming down with it for weeks" or "The disease was incubating for months."). An illness can be systemic, as in cancer, and its course will in many cases by unpredictable — witness the common cold.

By contrast, injury presents a different medical picture. Unless self-inflicted, an injury is normally unforseen by the person who suffers it. With the exception of the usual risk-takers, injury is not the result of poor hygiene or careless habits; i.e., the victim is not guilty of failing to "take care of" himself or herself. An injury is, in most cases, organ-specific, becoming systemic only when left untreated. Injury implies the need for immediate attention, isolation of the organ, surgery or treatment and sometimes both. Again, in most cases recovery follows a predictable course — providing that a correct diagnosis is made, followed by an appropriate intervention.

In the context of our present subject, the parallel between an intervention for psychic trauma and emergency medical care can be instructive. When injury occurs, the body is usually capable of activating some homeostatic functions that serve to limit the spread of effect, as when swelling and pain both protect and discourage further use of a fractured arm. This system of "damage control" is mirrored by the protective devices that are employed by the psyche when it is assaulted by a potentially traumatic event. And just as we can see the industrious effort of the body to send white corpuscles to an injured organ as a primitive attempt to heal the damage, so we can see a trauma symptom like hypervigilance as a process by which the mind reminds itself to avoid any new, potentially traumatic event.

Our perspective on trauma incorporates this physical injury analogy. As will be seen in the chapters to follow, we do not ignore the possibly concomitant presence of psychological illness or the possible contribution of a prior illness to the person's reaction to a recent traumatic event. Naturally, a physical illness could begin simultaneously with the occurrence of a physical injury, although seldom are people that unlucky. A more likely situation would be one in which the course of a long illness is punctuated by the occurrence of injury.

Neither of these situations can be ignored by the treating physician/ therapist. In the present context, we encourage the identification of underlying psychological complications in the treatment of emotional injury. A suggested format for collecting information about the injured person's psychological history, including possible continuing or previously concluded episodes of illness, will be presented in Chapter III on assessment.

By emphasizing the healthy, restorative functions of a reaction to trauma, it is possible to take a new route to effective treatment. The term "post-traumatic stress disorder" is replaced, here, by "trauma response." A framework for this change in approach is shown in Figure 1.1.

The second diagram in Figure 1.1 implies that a specific event in a person's life may or may not produce a traumatic effect upon the person. The term "response" is used to connote the nonpathological aspects of what *DSM-III-R* calls "disorder." The best reason for making this shift in conceptualization is that any treatment *solution* can be misguided if the *problem* is misdiagnosed.

CONCLUSION

In review, the concept of stress is not useful to an understanding of the aftermath of a traumatic event. To the extent that it adds an extraneous variable to the equation, it may cloud understanding. A crucial difference

PTSD MODEL

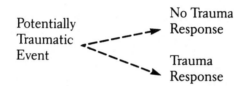

RESPONSE MODEL

Potentially
Traumatic
Event

No Trauma
Response

Trauma
Response

Figure 1.1

between stress as it affects people in ordinary circumstances (such as when a person is facing a crucial examination or dangerous surgery or the prospect of financial loss) and the trauma experience is that with trauma a specific event has already occurred. For that reason, the trauma reaction is event-specific, and helping the person to recover from trauma must take into account the personal *significance* of that event. Moreover, the quantitative differences between experiencing stress and living through the consequences of a traumatic event are obvious. Certainly the ordinary pressures and conflicts of everyday life are pushed aside by the occurrence of a traumatic event. In effect, trauma is a psychological emergency. If therapy was already in progress when trauma occurred, that course of treatment must give priority to guiding and ameliorating the trauma response. In short, recovery from trauma takes precedence over all other therapeutic concerns.

Figure 1.2 adds the treatment process to the response model. In this diagram, "recovery" means restoration of the person to the level of his or her adjustment prior to the occurrence of the event (being "made whole") and, preferably, more than that. The guiding principle in this respect is the adage, "That which doesn't kill me makes me stronger."

Working with trauma victims is not the easiest form of clinical work, and the content of therapeutic sessions is often appallingly grim. A clinician should beware of his negative thoughts about people who develop symptoms following a traumatic event; in other words, bias may intrude upon

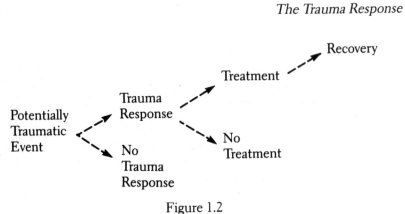

Figure 1.2
From Event to Recovery

one's objectivity. Even so, when the reaction to trauma is envisaged as part of a restorative process and not as abnormal behavior, a new incentive to helping the victim recover is gained. In any sphere of psychotherapy, it is a simpler task to aid a natural process than to cure a disorder.

CHAPTER II

The Phenomenon of Trauma

M OST PEOPLE have little preparation for or knowledge about traumatic processes. In the minds of many, a traumatic experience and its ensuing symptoms are associated with weakness, cowardice, hysterical exaggeration, or outright malingering for financial gain. Because of this lack of understanding by the general public—not to mention some members of the helping professions—many trauma victims hide their thoughts and feelings because they are ashamed of them. We have found this to be true both of those who have been physically injured and those who have not. Even so, those who were severely injured, disabled, or disfigured are often the most reluctant to admit to psychological symptoms. This is probably because they see their very survival as an act of will. They may feel that their minds represent the only faculty that has remained intact; thus, to reveal emotional problems would mean a loss of competence in every sphere.

Finding a way to cut through this reluctance to admit emotional pain is one of the clinician's major tasks in the early going. When working with someone who denies symptoms, we suggest utilizing an indirect tactic such as acknowledging that the victim may have none of these symptoms or feel none of these feelings, but adding that most people who have been through a similar event do. We say that, as clinicians, we would like the person to know about the normal reactions to trauma, just in case he or she *should* experience them. We then describe the trauma phenomenon and how most traumatized people respond. With the person who has been severely injured physically, inclusion of counseling or psychotherapy as a part of the medical treatment plan is a means of making it more acceptable to the victim.

THE TRAUMATIC PROCESS

In schematic form, Figure 2.1 (adapted from Everstine and Everstine, 1983, p. 168) describes the thoughts and feelings that are experienced by most people in sequence after a traumatic event, from onset of the event to onset of the trauma response.

A dominant quality of the antecedents to trauma is the person's lack of preparedness. Even professionals such as police officers and fire fighters are often surprised by the emotional sequelae to traumatic events. The most immediate sensation is disbelief. Thoughts such as "This can't be

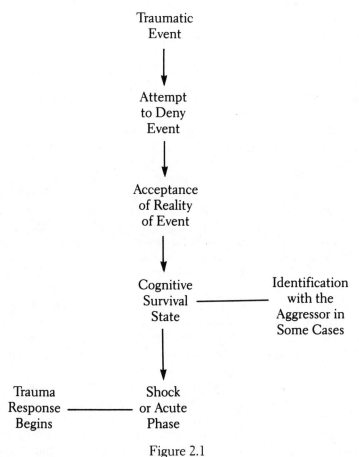

Figure 2.1
Traumatic Process

real," or "I must be dreaming," or "This must be some horrible joke" intrude. The person may start doing some uncharacteristic or seemingly foolish activity in an attempt to deny the reality of the trauma. Many traumatized people feel ashamed, later on, about having had such thoughts or behaving the way they did; they may need help in gaining a perspective on the "logic" of the denial mechanism. Some victims, particularly those who were seriously injured, actually have no memory of the event. This may be due to physical trauma (i.e., head injury), emotional trauma, or both. Some may eventually remember what happened to them, while others may never experience the memory. "Losing" a segment of time is very frightening for most people, and they may require help in accepting this kind of loss; others, by contrast, may be relieved to have no conscious memory of the event.

After the period of shock and denial, the cold reality of the event takes hold. The person goes into a cognitive survival state, in which every thought is focused on staying alive. The many perceptual distortions that occur have their purpose but can also be a source of terror to the traumatized person. For example, when one enters the cognitive survival state, time is distorted. During a car crash, glass flies slowly and people seem to move as though under water. The person who dives to avoid bullets in a robbery feels as though he or she were diving in slow motion. Seconds seem to be minutes and minutes become hours as the mind struggles to gain additional time to cope with the overwhelming sequence of events. Traumatized people may angrily wonder why help took so long in coming when, in fact, it took only a short time: A trauma victim's perception of time is virtually never accurate.

Other perceptual distortions are common; for example, loud sounds such as gun shots are muted to popping noises. Traumatized people rarely feel the full pain of their injuries during or immediately after the event. Some go into a dissociative state and experience themselves as leaving their bodies. Some feel as though the event were happening to another person. A seriously injured man, who was trapped in an overturned vehicle, said that he heard his anguished cries as though another man had been screaming.

Many traumatized people are bewildered when they reflect how emotionless and coldly logical they were in a moment when they could have faced death. Others are ashamed and disgusted at things they did to survive. The clinician should be prepared to find that some victims of protracted violence may be in a state of "identification with the aggressor" and may speak well of, or actually defend, their assailants. This phenomenon occurs frequently in cases of family violence, as well as with hostages and in some cases with political prisoners, as described below.

IDENTIFICATION WITH THE
AGGRESSOR[1]

This is a complex process in which the traumatized person's critical faculty breaks down in such a way that his or her ability to think in the abstract and to assess relationships properly is impaired. The victim then creates, or is induced to create, a new construction of reality in which a distorted form of relationship occurs.

Identification with the aggressor develops as follows. A victim is attacked or captured by an assailant. The victim comes to believe that the assailant intends to kill him or her. The person is not killed but only wounded or is merely kept captive. In the concrete logic of the cognitive survival state, the victim concludes that the assailant could have killed him or her, but chose not to. Nevertheless, since the attacker clearly meant to do so originally, it could happen at any moment.

With the passage of time, the victim begins to think, "Because the assailant changed his [her] mind about killing me, the fact that I have been spared means that I owe my life to this person; further, because he [she] could kill me at any time, I owe my future existence to this person." Expanding on this assumption, the victim may reason, "Because the assailant holds over me the power of life or death, he [she] must be a powerful person; powerful people must be obeyed; and, if I obey, some of that power may attach itself to me. Finally, since those who may be seeking to rescue me have not yet arrived, they must be powerless indeed."

This deluded mode of thinking is neither crazy nor stupid when seen in context. The victim of assault has few resources at his or her disposal in the initial, acute phase: The scope of the person's thought processes is constricted, the range of vision myopically shortened. Insight and abstraction are luxuries that the mind cannot afford when locked in a struggle to survive. In addition, the longer the assault is extended in time, the more isolated is the victim from sources of new information that could stimulate fresh ways to conceptualize the situation. When isolated from outside information, a victim can only obtain information from the assailant, however false.

As more time passes, a victim of repeated attacks or prolonged captivity becomes increasingly dependent upon the perpetrator for the everyday necessities of life. In effect, the person's survival and comfort depend on the whim of the assailant, who can manipulate hunger and thirst, pain and relief, darkness and silence, which gains him or her even stronger psychological control. Through this unending maze of abuse gropes the victim,

---

[1]Similar phenomena, variously labelled "Stockholm syndrome," "brainwashing," and "learned helplessness" are beyond the scope of the present subject.

certain after a while that he or she will never escape and has been abandoned by those who should, long ago, have intervened. Identification with the aggressor takes on the harsh light of necessity.

It must be reiterated that the phenomenon described here occurs not only in cases of kidnapping, hostage-taking, or with political prisoners, but even in traumatic situations that are of short duration. For instance, the victim of a violent crime such as rape or battering may also experience a form of identification with the aggressor, and this response to trauma could manifest itself within minutes of the initial assault. Moreover, children who are the victims of physical or sexual abuse often exhibit another form of the same reaction, which has been called "accommodation syndrome" (Summit, 1983). This form of identification with the aggressor is, in fact, thought to be a causal factor in perpetuating the crime of abuse (i.e., a child who was abused or witnessed abuse grows up to become an abuser as well).

When people are repeatedly traumatized, such as those who are taken hostage, those who suffer chronic family violence, the victims of kidnapping, or the survivors of war atrocities, they may actually be trapped in the cognitive survival state for long after the events have ceased. In such extreme instances, it may take a long time (as much as a year or more) for the clinical stabilization process to be completed before the person can enter the usual kind of psychotherapy process. Stabilization in these severe cases can be painstakingly slow, but it should never be considered time wasted. In addition, stabilization may be delayed by a myriad of diagnostic and/or surgical procedures that, although medically necessary, can have the effect of reinforcing traumatic effects. An example would be that of a burn victim who must undergo a series of skin grafts, followed by months of reconstructive surgery. (The subject of stabilization is discussed in depth in Chapter IV.)

THE HOSPITAL EXPERIENCE

Medical professionals need to be more aware of how procedures applied after a traumatic event can have the unfortunate effect of keeping the victim in a cognitive survival state. They are often unaware that this problem can manifest itself when additional medical procedures must be carried out a considerable period of time after the event occurred. In such situations, medical staff may be bewildered by, or annoyed at, their patient's difficult behavior; they fail to see that being anesthetized (akin to being knocked out) or having surgery performed at the sites of the original wounds very nearly amounts to a second traumatic event.

A psychotherapist can help to prevent this inadvertent infliction of trauma upon trauma in several ways. One is to teach relaxation techniques to the victim as a means to reduce anxiety, and/or self-hypnosis techniques to lessen pain. A secondary benefit of learning these skills is that the client acquires a sense of mastery because he or she is *participating* in his or her own medical care. When a person assists in his or her own treatment, he or she has a "stake" in the recovery that treatment seeks to achieve.

Some formerly traumatized people return to a trauma state, feel physically ill, or have a flashback at the very sights and smells of a hospital. We have encountered victims who, much later, were reluctant to visit their friends or relatives in hospital because they felt that returning to such a place would be overwhelming. Most of them were embarrassed about feeling this way and would concoct excuses for not going to the hospital because they feared being seen as weak or foolish.

TYPICAL INITIAL REACTIONS

Unprofessional psychological literature and lay thinking abound with the notion that a person can control his or her own destiny or "karma" by positive thinking, by "affirmations," or by "living the good life." These are among the many superstitious maneuvers that many people use to immunize themselves from facing their own vulnerability to trauma and loss. Sadly, this popular form of rationalization only serves to focus blame on the trauma victim. The assumption is that if a terrible thing has happened to someone, the person has lost control. Cautioning people to avoid risk-taking behavior and seeing to it that a traumatized person takes proper steps to prevent being re-traumatized should be clearly separated from the above-mentioned myths. A more detailed discussion of issues pertaining to risk-taking will be presented in Chapter IV.

Many traumatized people believe that they could have magically prevented the traumatic event from occurring or that the event was some form of punishment for past wrongs or misdeeds. Questions pertaining to the causes of an event or blame for it need to be sensitively explored, even if it was patently *not* the person's fault. A therapist cannot assume that the victim feels blameless. The question may need to be raised many times before a client will feel safe enough to reveal his or her true thoughts about this issue; the thoughts themselves may be fairly primitive or irrational. At the very least, most trauma clients go through a period of "If I only had done this or that, it wouldn't have happened." A therapist could open an inquiry about the causality of a traumatic event by saying: "Some people have thoughts or feelings about why things like this occurred to them." The therapist may add that it is quite natural for a person to want to know why such a terrible thing happened.

Even if a victim vehemently places the responsibility elsewhere, one cannot assume that the victim does not secretly blame himself or herself. A clinician should be particularly suspicious of unresolved self-blame or guilt in cases in which a victim seems to be arrested in the depressive phase of recovery, because a cornerstone to rebuilding a client's psyche, so that the person can leave this phase of trauma recovery, is self-acceptance. Through self-acceptance, a client can become a survivor and not a "bad" person who is being punished for past misdeeds. Each one of us has asked "Why me?" and it is only natural for trauma victims to do so as well. It is a therapist's task to ensure that the person does not draw the conclusion "It was my fault" or "This is my punishment."

Related to this initial reaction is the fact that many traumatized people feel somehow "marked" by fate or destiny. This may be particularly true if the person has had the bad luck to have been struck by more than one traumatic event in his or her life. Such thinking may result in generalized anxiety reactions or phobias. In some instances, a hint of stimuli that are reminiscent of the event may cause a person to reexperience the trauma or feel as though he or she is about to be traumatized once again. As with the magical thinking about guilt that was described above, many traumatized people know that such thinking is illogical. For that reason, they may be reluctant or embarrassed to reveal such thoughts to a therapist.

A clinician will eventually be called upon to help the traumatized person recover a sense of territorial integrity. The territorial issues resulting from losses that occur in one's home or work environment are usually obvious to the victim, but those who suffer from *bodily* injuries may require the therapist's help to bring these issues to light, because they are so primitive. In many cases, territorial wounds of this kind will be expressed by statements such as "I don't feel whole anymore," "I feel as though I've been broken into little pieces," or "The slightest thing happens and I fall apart." (In cases in which no physical injury occurred, such statements may reflect symbolic territorial injuries.)

Fundamentally, territorial concerns may also be expressed by people as feeling uncomfortable when touched or when close to others, or when they find themselves in places where there is no clear exit. For example, an extreme form of territorial injury associated with trauma is that of Vietnam veterans who, years later, cannot sit with their backs to a door; they may be unable to allow anything to cover their ears, such as stereo headphones or carmuffs; or they may be unable to sleep in a place where others are moving around them.

It is significant that evidence of lasting trauma of this degree may be observed in veterans who lead successful professional lives and have good family relationships. One can never expect that, because someone is successful in various spheres of life, he or she may not, at the same time, suffer from the pain of past trauma. Unfortunately, there is a popular misconception that, if someone is truly traumatized, the person will be nonfunctional or an emotional cripple. This is by no means the typical case.

When working with a trauma victim, a therapist will also need to help the person reestablish a "relationship" with his or her environment that is neither counterphobic nor phobic. Children first experience this quality of relationship during the developmental stage of the "terrible twos," when they first discover the powerful word "no" and use it. And, if all follows as it should, the child becomes an adult who feels confident of having some control over what happens to him or her. If fate is kind and the person does not encounter trauma, ideas about how much control he or she has over the environment become quite entrenched in the person's construction of reality. We assume that words like "yes" and "no" and phrases such as "I will" and "I won't" actually possess certain power. The problem with such a construction is that it is based upon fantasy and a modicum of good fortune, not on ordinary life. When trauma strikes, in one horrible moment the foundation for this construction is swept away.

At the traumatic moment, the person confronts his or her own vulnerability and eventual mortality. This encounter is that much worse if the trauma was at the hands of another person; worse still if the action of the other was intentional, because a victim will have to come to terms with the idea that another human being was capable of inflicting such harm or pain. The situation will be further compounded if the event was caused by someone known and trusted. In the latter instance, the victim's world view may be shattered, and the result could become an existential crisis. It is one of the tasks of the therapy process to help trauma victims rebuild confidence in their ability to assert themselves and to take charge of what happens in their lives.

Many traumatized people quickly generalize the helplessness of the cognitive survival state into other aspects of their lives, namely those in which they may need to influence or control the actions of others: they now feel powerless to do so. Or, conversely, they may impute some form of retaliatory motive to anyone who may attempt to exert influence or control over them. It usually requires considerable working-through before traumatized people are able to establish a reasonable balance of forces within themselves concerning issues of influence by others, as well as an ability to have a controlling effect on the world around them.

FUNDAMENTALS OF TREATMENT

Strategies of treatment for the trauma response are the subject of Chapters IV, V, and VI. Here, some general considerations are worth noting. Above all, the trauma response requires specially designed treatment methods.

The problem is that if each person's response to a traumatic event is unique, how can we find techniques that will work when, for example, we are trying to help a rape victim on Monday and the survivor of a plane crash on Tuesday? We find an answer in conceptualizing the very symptoms that we observe in trauma victims as steps toward recovery itself. In short, the symptoms are both the reason for treatment and the key to treatment success. In therapy, they are transformed into the coping behavior that will lead the person back to his or her starting point, before the traumatic event occurred.

Consider that with most types of problems that a therapist is asked to solve causal forces are key elements. For example, in family conflicts it may be necessary to reverse the factors that led to conflict, before resolution can be achieved. When alcoholism has led to marital strife, it must be dealt with and removed as a cause before the spouses can improve their relationship. In this instance, treatment seeks to remove a symptom by altering its cause. By contrast, trauma symptoms are caused by a traumatic event. In the vast majority of cases, that event is not likely to occur again in the victim's life, or at least the likelihood of imminent repetition is small. The "best part" about a traumatic event is the fact that the event itself has come to an end; it's not "over and done," but it has ceased for now.

The foregoing is not intended to suggest that therapy with trauma victims is easy work. On the contrary, trauma work is difficult *because* the causal force that led to the problem is so irrevocable. The therapist may succeed admirably in helping a victim to achieve remission of symptoms and in paving the way to recovery, but the traumatic event still takes a place in the person's history that cannot be erased. A clinician may enable the trauma client to come to terms with what has happened, but it would be too much to expect that the person can ever forget. Towering above the valley where the work of therapy occurs is the mountainous *event*.

For treatment to proceed efficiently, each one of myriad critical elements of the event, as well as characteristics of the victim, must be factored into the equation that will produce recovery. The next chapter presents an analytic schema for organizing these factors.

CHAPTER III

Assessing the Trauma Response

IDENTIFYING THE TYPE and extent of traumatic effects is not as simple a diagnostic question as it may seem. Some severely traumatized people appear not to be suffering because of their use of defense mechanisms such as repression and denial. Others are emotionally "flat" and constricted because they utilize obsessive-compulsive defenses. Some people may not be consciously aware that they *were* traumatized because of a dissociative process. Others simply may be unable to articulate what happened to them or describe their emotional states during or after the traumatic events. Still others may make a conscious effort to hide their emotional states because they are fearful or ashamed of being perceived as psychologically "weak."

In a hospital emergency room, there are many instruments and procedures that can be used to find out how much physical trauma a person has suffered. For psychological trauma, few such methods exist in the emergency room; moreover, in the past, few have been available even to clinicians in general practice. This chapter offers some recommendations for techniques that will fill this need. After an assessment of the injury caused by the traumatic event has been completed, a course of therapy can begin or a course already begun can achieve a fresh start, with new routes suggested by the results. The therapist will want to answer another important question: What was this person like before it happened? The usefulness of baseline data about the person will be addressed in this chapter as well.

FIRST STEPS IN ASSESSMENT

A major characteristic of the traumatic event is its sudden occurrence; seldom is a warning given. After an event has run its course, the trauma response takes over and its own dynamic processes are set in motion. There is little time or energy for reflection, for taking stock. Every effort is expended to survive and to move on. The clinician strives to enter this realm of confusion, to make sense of what is happening with the victim, and to formulate an intervention strategy. Clearly, this is the place for thorough study of the victim's present status. It may be that there is no more appropriate occasion, in clinical practice, for making an incisive evaluation of current level of adjustment and personality functioning than when working with a client who has experienced trauma.

We have found that the short, structured interview is a good place to start. Some trauma victims cannot sustain a full-hour assessment session because their trauma defense mechanisms take over. If this happens, a clinician will get inaccurate information and, needless to say, begin the evaluation in the wrong way. If the therapist suspects severe trauma, it may be wise to begin by asking the victim to provide some basic demographics in a paper-and-pencil format or by using a self-report instrument that was developed in our clinical practice, the ETRI (see below).

Our experience is consistent with that of Mollica (1988, p. 302) who found that severely traumatized people respond well to objective data-collection instruments, because they can simply check symptom descriptions or descriptions of stressors, without having to describe them orally. Many victims are not capable of providing an oral inventory of their feelings in the early stages of the trauma response. In short, structured questionnaires may yield more accurate information from severely traumatized people than direct questioning. Victims have a tendency to deny symptoms, not because they don't have them but because they would rather not talk about them or are ashamed of having them.

Psychological Testing

Sooner or later in the process of assessment with a trauma victim—but certainly not until the shock phase has ended—it may be useful to administer one or more psychological tests. Our favorite battery of suitable tests includes predominantly personality measures, but some indication of current intellectual functioning should be obtained. Table 3.1 presents a preferred battery of tests. The list in Table 3.1 can be abbreviated or augmented by other tests as time and resources permit.

FROM SYMPTOMS TO DIAGNOSIS

Once the current level of adjustment has been established by means of psychological testing, it is possible to examine the elements of trauma themselves. After finding out which aspects of the personality are functioning well and which are not, one must find out what impairment, if any, can be attributed to the intervention of the traumatic event. This kind of

TABLE 3.1
Recommended Tests

- PROJECTIVES
  Rorschach
  Thematic Apperception Test
  Draw-a-Person Test
  Sentence Completion Test

- INTELLIGENCE AND NEUROLOGICAL FUNCTIONING
  Bender Gestalt Test
  WAIS-R
  WISC-R or WIPPSI-R (children)

- OBJECTIVE INVENTORIES
  MMPI
  CPI
  Self-Analysis Inventory (anxiety)
  Personal Assessment Inventory (depression)
  Coopersmith Scale (self-esteem)

---

injury assessment must be approached sensitively and not conducted too soon, precisely because it is trauma-specific. As such, it may arouse memories of the event that have already been somewhat repressed.

One approach to measuring the injury that was caused by a traumatic event is to inventory the symptoms that the person has experienced since the event occurred. This is a relatively nonintrusive vantage point for gathering information, because it only requires the victim to identify certain feelings or thoughts that he or she may already have conveyed to friends and relatives in countless ways.

Trauma symptoms can be organized, roughly, into three major types (*DSM-III-R*, APA, 1987, p. 250):

1. persistent reexperiencing of the trauma; referred to as "intrusion";
2. avoidance of thoughts about the trauma;
3. a state of increased arousal or "vigilance."

Of course, to reexperience the trauma and to avoid thinking about it is a paradox — both can't happen at the same time. What does happen is that the person *alternates* between one and the other: One minute there are intrusive thoughts that remind the person about the traumatic event, and the next minute the person goes through a mighty struggle to drive those thoughts away and "forget all about it." Both of these states require the expense of tremendous psychic energy. And either one, in its turn, can be accompanied by symptoms in the third category, namely "increased arousal." Clearly, this is chaos. To measure these crosscurrents is a bit like trying to get a pulse rate from an octopus—you don't know where to start.

Another key factor is the perception of a given symptom by the person who is experiencing it. The same is true of physical hurts and sensations. One man's chest pain is another man's heartburn. A sprained ankle means many things to many people in terms of how they react to it. That's why an instrument intended to measure a psychological symptom should be sensitive to the *impact* that the symptom has made upon the person's ability to cope; in other words, how much trouble has the symptom caused in the person's life?

In the course of relating her recent history, a woman client revealed that her father had died suddenly, only six weeks before. Noting that this event occurred just a week or two before the woman had sought treatment, the therapist expressed his condolences and said, "This must have hurt you very deeply." Without hesitation, she laughed and said, "Not a bit. I hated the bastard." In later sessions, it became clear that only after her father's death was she able to consider entering therapy and that, all things considered, she looked upon his loss as a source of her liberation. Now she could begin to come to terms with her problems and remake her life.

A third dimension to trauma measurement is the *persistence* of a symptom through time since the traumatic event occurred; in effect, how long has the trauma response been going on? It's logical to believe that a symptom that keeps coming back (or won't stop) is more significant than a symptom that happened only once. And just as it can be said that the greater the impact of a symptom the more severe the trauma, it can be said that the longer the reaction has persisted the more severe the trauma.

To summarize, we need to know specific details of the reaction, in the form of symptoms, that a traumatic event has caused; next, we need to know what effect the reaction has had on the victim; and finally we need to know how long this effect has lasted. In short, the ideal test for the trauma response will combine an estimate of *intensity* with an estimate of *duration*.

EVERSTINE TRAUMA RESPONSE INDEX (ETRI)

The Everstine Trauma Response Index is an instrument expressly designed for finding out whether or not a person has suffered psychological trauma. In cases in which a potentially traumatic event has occurred, it measures the extent to which the person has been affected by it. ETRI is intended to describe this response, both qualitatively and quantitatively. Further, as will be discussed in more detail in Chapter IV, an instrument of this kind can enhance therapy by giving the victim a definitive description of symptoms or trauma-related behaviors, thus helping the victim to find words and phrases that lend some structure to amorphous, chaotic thoughts.[1]

ETRI shares a conceptual background with various scales, surveys, and inventories conceived to measure stress (e.g., Holmes & Rahe, 1967; Sarason et al., 1978). Instruments of this kind do not measure stress directly, but instead collect information about whether or not the test subject had experienced a potentially stressful event. A typical format requires the person to read a list of such events (e.g., death of a spouse, divorce, being fired from a job) and check those that have happened to him or her recently. In this regard, the instruments measure the presence or absence of possible stressors.[2]

Background of the ETRI

In 1979, Horowitz et al., published a study that made use of an instrument they had devised called the "Impact of Event Scale." They focused on two key categories of reaction to traumatic events, "intrusion" and "avoidance"; as introduced above, the former consists in thoughts or feelings that seem to force themselves upon a trauma victim, and the latter refers to attempts by the victim to deny or minimize the impact of the event. The Impact of Event Scale is comprised of eight items dealing with avoidance and seven items dealing with intrusion. This instrument, while useful, falls short of being comprehensive enough for current use. In recent years, our understanding of the trauma syndrome has deepened considerably, and the resulting definitions that evolved into the one given in *DSM-III-R* have complex elements that are not measured by the Impact of Event Scale.

Currently, attempts are being made to adapt the Minnesota Multiphasic Personality Inventory (MMPI, MMPI-2) to assess the quality and extent of post-traumatic reactions. While the MMPI is an extremely valuable instrument for measuring a wide range of personality dynamics from the normal to the abnormal, it is not ideally suited for this adaptation, for the following

---

[1]The test described here is primarily intended for adults, although it has been successfully administered to adolescents as young as thirteen. A version for children aged eight to twelve is planned.

[2]On reflection, it can be seen that Holmes and Rahe *defined* "stress" as what happens to a person if one or more of the events on their list had occurred in his or her life. In that sense, they were defining an effect by its cause.

ETRI

EVERSTINE

TRAUMA RESPONSE

INDEX

LOUIS EVERSTINE, Ph.D., M.P.H.
Affiliated Psychologists
Palo Alto, California

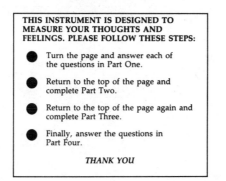

> **THIS INSTRUMENT IS DESIGNED TO MEASURE YOUR THOUGHTS AND FEELINGS. PLEASE FOLLOW THESE STEPS:**
>
> ● Turn the page and answer each of the questions in Part One.
>
> ● Return to the top of the page and complete Part Two.
>
> ● Return to the top of the page again and complete Part Three.
>
> ● Finally, answer the questions in Part Four.
>
> *THANK YOU*

PART ONE

A frightening thing happened to you.
AFTER the event occurred
(Please check the box if it applies):

PART TWO

For each box that you checked, please indicate how
UPSETTING the experience was for you:

	NOT VERY UPSETTING									EXTREMELY UPSETTING

		NOT VERY / EXTREMELY
1.	Did you lose a lot of weight?	0 1 2 3 4 5 6 7 8 9 10
2.	Did your friends treat you differently because of what happened?	0 1 2 3 4 5 6 7 8 9 10
3.	Did you feel angry?	0 1 2 3 4 5 6 7 8 9 10
4.	Did you lose confidence in your work?	0 1 2 3 4 5 6 7 8 9 10
5.	Was your temper short with family members?	0 1 2 3 4 5 6 7 8 9 10
6.	Did your emotional state change without warning?	0 1 2 3 4 5 6 7 8 9 10
7.	Did you feel guilty that it happened to you?	0 1 2 3 4 5 6 7 8 9 10
8.	Did you have trouble in remembering things?	0 1 2 3 4 5 6 7 8 9 10
9.	Did you stay away from social gatherings?	0 1 2 3 4 5 6 7 8 9 10
10.	Did you lose trust in other people?	0 1 2 3 4 5 6 7 8 9 10
11.	Did you feel sad?	0 1 2 3 4 5 6 7 8 9 10
12.	Did you try to avoid thinking about what happened?	0 1 2 3 4 5 6 7 8 9 10
13.	Did you question whether or not life was worth living?	0 1 2 3 4 5 6 7 8 9 10
14.	Did you experience nightmares about what happened?	0 1 2 3 4 5 6 7 8 9 10
15.	Were there times when you didn't know what to do next?	0 1 2 3 4 5 6 7 8 9 10
16.	Did you have difficulty in sleeping through the night?	0 1 2 3 4 5 6 7 8 9 10
17.	Did you feel "numb" or unable to relate to other people?	0 1 2 3 4 5 6 7 8 9 10
18.	Were you afraid to return to the place where it occurred?	0 1 2 3 4 5 6 7 8 9 10
19.	Was your temper short with people at work?	0 1 2 3 4 5 6 7 8 9 10
20.	Did you feel like crying when you thought about what happened?	0 1 2 3 4 5 6 7 8 9 10
21.	Did you feel "jinxed" or "marked" in some way?	0 1 2 3 4 5 6 7 8 9 10
22.	Did you feel threatened by forces beyond your control?	0 1 2 3 4 5 6 7 8 9 10
23.	Did your sexual desire decrease?	0 1 2 3 4 5 6 7 8 9 10
24.	Did thoughts about what happened keep returning?	0 1 2 3 4 5 6 7 8 9 10
25.	Did you feel that you must be on your guard?	0 1 2 3 4 5 6 7 8 9 10
26.	Did you change your life-style because of what happened?	0 1 2 3 4 5 6 7 8 9 10
27.	Did you feel that others couldn't understand what it was like?	0 1 2 3 4 5 6 7 8 9 10
28.	Were there times when you had trouble falling asleep?	0 1 2 3 4 5 6 7 8 9 10
29.	Did you sometimes feel that it was happening again?	0 1 2 3 4 5 6 7 8 9 10
30.	Did you feel punished for something that you didn't do?	0 1 2 3 4 5 6 7 8 9 10
31.	Did you have trouble in concentrating?	0 1 2 3 4 5 6 7 8 9 10
32.	Did people who know you comment that you had changed or seemed different?	0 1 2 3 4 5 6 7 8 9 10
33.	Did you gain a lot of weight?	0 1 2 3 4 5 6 7 8 9 10
34.	Did you feel waves of emotion sweeping over you?	0 1 2 3 4 5 6 7 8 9 10
35.	Did you "block" when you tried to think about what happened?	0 1 2 3 4 5 6 7 8 9 10

X Y Z A

X ☐   Z ☐

Y ☐   A ☐

PART THREE

In the case of each upsetting experience, please indicate how long you felt upset: AT LEAST:

WEEKS	MONTHS	YEARS
1 2 3	1 2 3 4 5 6 7 8 9 10 11	1 2 3 4 5
1 2 3	1 2 3 4 5 6 7 8 9 10 11	1 2 3 4 5
1 2 3	1 2 3 4 5 6 7 8 9 10 11	1 2 3 4 5
1 2 3	1 2 3 4 5 6 7 8 9 10 11	1 2 3 4 5
1 2 3	1 2 3 4 5 6 7 8 9 10 11	1 2 3 4 5
1 2 3	1 2 3 4 5 6 7 8 9 10 11	1 2 3 4 5
1 2 3	1 2 3 4 5 6 7 8 9 10 11	1 2 3 4 5
1 2 3	1 2 3 4 5 6 7 8 9 10 11	1 2 3 4 5
1 2 3	1 2 3 4 5 6 7 8 9 10 11	1 2 3 4 5
1 2 3	1 2 3 4 5 6 7 8 9 10 11	1 2 3 4 5
1 2 3	1 2 3 4 5 6 7 8 9 10 11	1 2 3 4 5
1 2 3	1 2 3 4 5 6 7 8 9 10 11	1 2 3 4 5
1 2 3	1 2 3 4 5 6 7 8 9 10 11	1 2 3 4 5
1 2 3	1 2 3 4 5 6 7 8 9 10 11	1 2 3 4 5
1 2 3	1 2 3 4 5 6 7 8 9 10 11	1 2 3 4 5
1 2 3	1 2 3 4 5 6 7 8 9 10 11	1 2 3 4 5
1 2 3	1 2 3 4 5 6 7 8 9 10 11	1 2 3 4 5
1 2 3	1 2 3 4 5 6 7 8 9 10 11	1 2 3 4 5
1 2 3	1 2 3 4 5 6 7 8 9 10 11	1 2 3 4 5
1 2 3	1 2 3 4 5 6 7 8 9 10 11	1 2 3 4 5
1 2 3	1 2 3 4 5 6 7 8 9 10 11	1 2 3 4 5
1 2 3	1 2 3 4 5 6 7 8 9 10 11	1 2 3 4 5
1 2 3	1 2 3 4 5 6 7 8 9 10 11	1 2 3 4 5
1 2 3	1 2 3 4 5 6 7 8 9 10 11	1 2 3 4 5
1 2 3	1 2 3 4 5 6 7 8 9 10 11	1 2 3 4 5
1 2 3	1 2 3 4 5 6 7 8 9 10 11	1 2 3 4 5
1 2 3	1 2 3 4 5 6 7 8 9 10 11	1 2 3 4 5
1 2 3	1 2 3 4 5 6 7 8 9 10 11	1 2 3 4 5
1 2 3	1 2 3 4 5 6 7 8 9 10 11	1 2 3 4 5
1 2 3	1 2 3 4 5 6 7 8 9 10 11	1 2 3 4 5
1 2 3	1 2 3 4 5 6 7 8 9 10 11	1 2 3 4 5
1 2 3	1 2 3 4 5 6 7 8 9 10 11	1 2 3 4 5
1 2 3	1 2 3 4 5 6 7 8 9 10 11	1 2 3 4 5
1 2 3	1 2 3 4 5 6 7 8 9 10 11	1 2 3 4 5

PART FOUR

Please PRINT Your Name:

LAST	FIRST

☐ Male   ☐ Female

Current Marital Status:

☐ Married   ☐ Single

☐ Divorced   ☐ Widowed

Number of Children Who Live with You at Present: ☐

Number of Children Who Do Not Live with You at Present: ☐

Present Occupation (Please check one):
Full-Time Job ☐   Homemaker ☐
Part-Time Job ☐   Unemployed ☐

Your Date of Birth:

Month	Day	Year

Age

Today's Date:

Month	Day	Year

Date of the Event:

Month	Day	Year

Type of Company or Organization: _____

Title of Position: _____

Are you a: Smoker? ☐   Non-smoker? ☐
Do you drink: More than you would like ☐   In moderation? ☐   Very little? ☐   Non-drinker ☐

Were you the victim of:

A violent crime? ☐   A natural disaster? ☐
An accident in the home? ☐   An accident at your work? ☐
An accident in a vehicle? ☐   A product that malfunctioned? ☐

Were you physically injured? Yes ☐   No ☐

If you were physically injured, did you have to:

Stay in a hospital? ☐   How long?_____   Present time ☐
Visit a physician or clinic? ☐   How long?_____   Present time ☐
Did you have psychotherapy
or counseling? ☐   How long?_____   Present time ☐

reasons: (1) only 49 of 566 MMPI items appear to have relevance to symptoms purported to have been caused by stress (Keane et al., 1984); (2) the items themselves do not pertain directly to stress resulting from a *traumatic event*; and (3) because the MMPI elicits only "true" or "false" answers, it has no capability to measure the *impact* that the referent of a "true" response has had upon the person who is taking the test.[3]

In summary, a valid test for trauma should be one that measures:

1. the full range of symptoms comprising the trauma response;
2. the degree to which these reactions to trauma have affected the person who experienced them (i.e., their impact).

One other component that was lacking in every previous effort to measure the response to trauma is the factor of the persistence of a response through time. In short, the onset of a symptom has been measured but not its course. As argued above, it is reasonable to conclude that a response to trauma that the person has made again and again (or without ceasing) since the traumatic event happened is more significant than a symptom that occurred only once. Further, if the greater the amount of upset aroused by a symptom the more severe the trauma, then it follows that the longer this reaction has persisted, the more severe the trauma.

What Is Being Measured

ETRI is administered on the premise that a potentially traumatic event has occurred in the life of a person who takes the test. In that respect, it follows the approach of *DSM-III-R*, in that no distinction is made *a priori* concerning what kind of event may have occurred. The *DSM-III-R* description, "outside the range of usual human experience," is intentionally broad. On those terms, the existence of trauma is considered to be shown by the presence of a reaction or reactions that could only have been elicited by a "distressing event" or would have been exhibited only in mild form under normal circumstances.

The 35 questions that comprise ETRI are listed in Table 3.2. They were written with the aim of eliciting information about salient points of the *DSM-III-R* criteria. For example, "unpredictable explosions of aggressive behavior or an inability to express angry feelings" (APA, 1987, p. 248) is reflected in these ETRI questions:

---

[3]It is an unfortunate accident of history that most studies linking MMPI results to traumatic reactions have been done on Vietnam veterans, as was the work of Keane et al.

#5: Was your temper short with family members?
#19: Was your temper short with people at work?

Both questions carry the implication that the behavior referred to is of recent origin or is in some way different from the person's ordinary pattern of behavior.

The identifying criteria for PTSD in *DSM-III-R* begin with the category of persistent reexperiencing of the trauma ("intrusion"). ETRI incorporates this type of symptom with the following questions:

#14: Did you experience nightmares about what happened?
#20: Did you feel like crying when you thought about what happened?
#24: Did thoughts about what happened keep returning?
#29: Did you sometimes feel that it was happening again?

The second category, avoidance of thoughts, is reflected by these questions:

#2: Did your friends treat you differently because of what happened?
#9: Did you stay away from social gatherings?
#10: Did you lose trust in other people?
#12: Did you try to avoid thinking about what happened?
#13: Did you question whether or not life was worth living?
#17: Did you feel "numb" or unable to relate to other people?
#18: Were you afraid to return to the place where it occurred?
#21: Did you feel "jinxed" or "marked" in some way?
#23: Did your sexual desire decrease?
#27: Did you feel that others couldn't understand what it was like?
#35: Did you "block" when you tried to think about what happened?

The third category, increased arousal, is reflected by these questions:

#3: Did you feel angry?
#5: Was your temper short with family members?
#8: Did you have trouble in remembering things?
#15: Were there times when you didn't know what to do next?
#16: Did you have difficulty in sleeping through the night?
#19: Was you temper short with people at work?
#25: Did you feel that you must be on your guard?
#28: Were there times when you had trouble falling asleep?

#31: Did you have trouble in concentrating?

#32: Did people who know you comment that you had changed or seemed different?

Several other questions represent aspects of the *DSM-III-R* category labeled "associated features" (p. 249), as follows:

#4: Did you lose confidence in your work?

#6: Did your emotional state change without warning?

#11: Did you feel sad?

#26: Did you change your life-style because of what happened?

#33: Did you gain a lot of weight?

In addition, ETRI incorporates several questions designed to elicit information on subjects not included in the *DSM-III-R* criteria:

#1: Did you lose a lot of weight?

#7: Did you feel guilty that it happened to you?

#22: Did you feel threatened by forces beyond your control?

#30: Did you feel punished for something that you didn't do?

#34: Did you feel waves of emotion sweeping over you?

The latter represent commonly expressed feelings of people who have been victims of obvious trauma.

As presently utilized, the *DSM-III-R* criteria serve the clinician as a kind of checklist. Having completed an evaluation of the client, whether by interview or psychological testing or both, the clinician will match his or her findings to each of the three categories listed above. In doing so, a weighting procedure is followed in which a prescribed number of symptoms in each category must be present for the diagnosis to be assigned.

1. reexperiencing the traumatic event: at least one out of four specified types of symptoms must be present;
2. avoidance of thoughts: at least three out of seven specified types must be present;
3. increased arousal; at least two out of six types must be present (APA, 1987, p. 250).

If the categories above are labeled X, Y, and Z respectively, it can be seen that the *DSM-III-R* requires one X, three Y's, and two Z's for trauma to be present. A formula for the *DSM-III-R* definition of "trauma" (T) is:

T = X + 3Y + 2Z. Suffice it to say that this sort of mathematical manipulation is seldom carried out in practical situations.

ETRI attempts to reach the same destination by a different route. Each ETRI question carries equal weight, thus permitting the total score to have some utility in describing whether or not trauma has occurred. But ETRI goes much further by adding a quantitative estimate of the *degree* to which a certain reaction has affected the person.

Finally, a key provision of the *DSM-III-R* rules for assigning a diagnosis of post-traumatic stress disorder is that the symptoms observed (in categories X, Y, and Z) must have been present for at least one month. This factor of the persistence of a reaction through time, with one month as a minimal criterion, is accounted for in ETRI, as noted in the following section.

Description of the Instrument

ETRI is a paper-and-pencil, self-report questionnaire consisting of 35 questions and two self-rating scales (Table 3.2). The instrument measures the response to an event according to these dimensions:

1. number of symptom questions answered affirmatively (Part One)— total possible score is 35;

2. the extent to which the experience of a particular symptom, indicated by an affirmative answer to one of the 35 questions, has made an impact on the person; this is measured by a rating scale of how "upsetting" the experience was for the person (Part Two)—this scale has a zero point as well as points one through ten, with ten indicating the highest degree of intensity;[4]

3. the length of time that has elapsed since the upset that was caused by a symptom began and the present (i.e., when the questionnaire is being filled out); this is measured by a rating scale (Part Three) that is calibrated by weeks (up to a month), months (up to a year), and years (up to five years)—in this scale, responses indicating that an upsetting symptom has lasted for one, two, or three weeks are *not* scored; scoring begins with the one-month category and is calculated by months throughout (e.g., a symptom that has persisted for a year and a half is scored as 18 months; two and a half years is scored as 30 months; the maximum score is 60 months/five years).

---

[4]Some trauma reactions are not felt as especially disturbing or upsetting. When a question is answered affirmatively but the answer on the rating scale is zero, the answer is only counted in the first dimension of measurement (Part One) and not carried forward to the other dimensions.

The three ETRI dimensions of measurement are designed to be combined in this way: Each of the 35 symptom questions that is answered affirmatively is then rated on the 10-point scale of how upsetting the experience was for the person. This yields an *intensity* score that can vary up to a maximum of 350 (35 symptoms times 10). In the next step, the person rates the upsetting experience on a scale of the time during which he or she felt upset by the experience. For example, a symptom may have lasted for two years since the event occurred and hence would be rated at 24 months on the dimension of *duration*. The *duration* score can vary up to a maximum of 2,100 (35 symptoms times 60 months). In this scoring process, the dimensions of *intensity* of the symptom and *duration* of the symptom are combined into a single score reflecting the total impact of the traumatic event. How this is done is described fully in the section on "Determining the Index" below.

Administration of the Instrument

In most cases, a client can complete ETRI within 15 to 20 minutes. The questionnaire is given with the instructions that it be filled out in private and that the questions be answered honestly and fully. In Part Four on the back of the form, the person is asked to enter personal data. Key information that will be obtained from Part Four includes the date when ETRI is being filled out and the date when the event in question occurred. Another type of useful information yielded by Part Four concerns the person's medical or psychotherapeutic history since the event.

Part Four asks for the client's name, but if it would be inappropriate to require this information, a code number can be assigned. Details of how the code number will be linked with the person's name, how this linkage will be stored, and under what conditions it can be disclosed, should be discussed with the client in advance. No matter what procedure is followed to protect confidentiality, it should not be implemented until the client has given informed consent (Everstine et al., 1980).

Because ETRI is a multipurpose questionnaire intended to record people's *reactions* to many kinds of traumatic events, exact details of the event in question are not required on the form. It is expected that they will be available from numerous other sources and can be linked to the completed ETRI by name or other identifiers. A brief, general, checklist of types of potentially traumatic events is included in Part Four.

Scoring the Results

Details of the tabulation procedures for ETRI are provided in a Manual for Administrators (Everstine, 1989). When scored, the test yields answers to these questions:

1. Did the person suffer trauma?
2. If so, what effect did it have on the person?
3. If there was an effect, how long did it last?

In respect to the first question, ETRI provides a single score that is simply the number of items checked out of the total of 35. In addition, it enables the scorer to calculate whether or not the three *DSM-III-R* criteria for trauma have or have not been met.[5] The second question is answered by calculating the *intensity* value described above in this section, namely on a scale of one to ten. The third question is answered by calculating the *duration* measure described above in this section, namely on a scale of one month to 60 months.

Determining the Index

The relative impact of trauma on the person is represented, in ETRI, by the Trauma Response Index. This index (R) is calculated by multiplying each one of the person's intensity scores times the corresponding duration score and summing the total, as in the formula $\Sigma i_{35}(I \times D)$. As intensity increases the Response Index increases; further, as duration increases the Response Index increases. Because 35 items can be checked, with each rated at an intensity of 10 and each rated as having a duration of 60 months, the total possible value of R is 21,000 ($35 \times 10 \times 60$).

In review, ETRI is a self-report questionnaire that identifies the existence of psychological trauma and measures its effects upon the person. It is based on the concept that the victims of trauma are not suffering from a "disorder" but instead have been forced to cope with a catastrophic interruption in their lives. Each person will react uniquely, and this pattern of responding will be a key element in any treatment that leads to recovery. ETRI quantifies the impact of trauma by combining a measure of the intensity of the response with a measure of its duration, yielding a Trauma Response Index that carries face validity. Accumulation of normative data will permit individual cases to be compared and contrasted.[6]

---

[5]Responses to other questions, such as those addressing "associated features" and subjects not included in the *DSM-III-R* criteria, are tabulated in column "A" of Part One.

[6]A Spanish version of the test, "Indice Everstine de Respuesta al Trauma," is being studied by *Dra. Helen Castro* in Mexico City as a project of Unidad de Atencion a Victimas, Servicios a la Comunidad, Procuraduría General de Justicia del Distrito Federal.

FURTHER EXPLORATIONS

There is much more that we need to know about the trauma experience, as well as the event that caused it. And because some of this information lies at the heart of the person's feelings of loss and confusion, these subjects must be broached cautiously. Some trauma clients can be asked about facts of this kind on first meeting, but with others the questions will have to be interspersed through later sessions. The purpose of collecting these data is to inform the preparation of a treatment plan for his or her client, but the clinician will want to avoid upsetting a client in the process. The following is a general description of what is needed.

The degree to which a victim's body was injured or penetrated has a significant role in determining how severely the person was traumatized emotionally. One should also consider whether or not the person believes himself or herself to have been disfigured or permanently damaged, physically, by the traumatic event. Psychologically, to the extent that a person believes that he or she has suffered physical damage, the person *is* damaged.

Traumatic events of human agency or intention are among the most difficult to recover from, because they can raise extremely complicated social-psychological issues. Further, traumatic events caused by known and trusted persons or institutions can be far more harmful than those inflicted by strangers or unknown entities, the reason being that they call into question the victim's ability to trust as well as his or her competence in choosing safe persons or institutions. For example, the parents of a child who has been abused at a school or day-care center of their own choosing may feel more traumatized than if the child were accosted by a stranger: Naturally, the parents chose the school or day-care canter as a safe place for their child and what has happened impugns their judgment as well as the ability to protect their child.

Further, if the traumatic event robbed the victim of his or her role or vocation or sense of worth, e.g., brought an end to a career or prevented the person from functioning in his or her customary family role, the reaction to trauma will be more severe. The location of the traumatic event also can have a significant effect: for example, when it happens in the home, a place that is supposed to be nurturing and safe. Whatever the location, if the victim must, of necessity, return there soon, the fear of doing so followed by the actual return could heighten traumatic intensity. Finally, the effects of trauma can vary according to whether or not being a survivor of the traumatic event is a source of pride or of humiliation, as when people in San Francisco wore sweatshirts proclaiming, "I Survived the Quake of '89" within days of the earthquake. By contrast, there are no sweatshirt slogans for the survivors of rape or other violent crimes.

TRAUMA ANALYSIS PROTOCOL

The Trauma Analysis Protocol is a method for organizing information in the development of a treatment plan. The plan should incorporate both dynamic and systemic issues that the victim must come to terms with on the way to recovery. It enables the clinician to create a therapy that is both structured and specific to the victim's trauma response. The questions that comprise the Trauma Analysis Protocol are listed in Table 3.3.

Questions About the Event

When formulating a treatment plan for a victim, the clinician needs to know how long ago the traumatic event took place. Generally, recent trauma is more accessible to direct clinical intervention because the traumatized person and significant others may be less likely to have developed maladaptive coping mechanisms or trauma-reactive pathological behavior. In respect to recent trauma, a primary focus of treatment will be helping the victim to activate appropriate defense mechanisms. Such a course of treatment can be fairly short, ranging from six months to a year and a half, depending on the severity of the trauma. Treatment will primarily utilize direct behavioral and cognitive techniques to alleviate the traumatic symptoms, combined with dynamically-oriented counseling to help the client to complete the trauma response and build or rebuild healthy defenses.

In a case in which the traumatic event occurred more that two years ago, the clinical picture could be complicated if the client has developed maladaptive defenses. If this has happened these maladaptions will have to be unscrambled by the clinician before a victim can be led to develop healthier modes of interacting. Methods of treatment for the traumatized adult are the subject of the next chapter. Cases in which the trauma has been buried for many years are discussed in Chapter VI.

A child who was the victim of a traumatic event in the past may have been in the midst of a different developmental stage from the current one, a fact that makes it difficult to sort out problems that were created then from problems that the child may obviously be having now. A typical example is that of the child who was traumatized during the latency period and is being treated for a delayed response to trauma after the onset of puberty. It is hard enough to deal with the issues of adolescence without having to resolve unfinished business from a stage that seems, at least to the child, "ancient history." The treatment of child victims is the subject of Chapter VIII.

When creating a treatment plan, a clinician must consider the systemic issues that pertain to the origin of the event. In general, people may have an easier time in adjusting to injuries that were not of human origin or, if

TABLE 3.3
Trauma Analysis Protocol

Questions about the Event:

1. *Timing:*

   Did it happen:

   (a) within the past two years?

   (b) two years or more ago?

   In the case of a child victim, did it happen:

   (a) during the current developmental stage?

   (b) during a prior stage?

2. *Origin:*

   Was the agent that caused the event:

   (a) a person:
      i. known to the victim when the event occurred?
      ii. known and trusted by the victim?

   (b) more than one person:
      i. known?
      ii. known and trusted?

   (c) a political or military group?

   (d) an animal or act of nature or environmental force?

   (e) a mechanical or chemical or other man-made entity?

3. *Intent:*

   If the event occurred by human agency, was there intent to harm?

4. *Stigma:*

   Was the event one to which a social stigma is attached (e.g., incest, the Vietnam War, an accident due to the victim's own negligence)?

5. *Warning:*

   Was there warning prior to the occurrence of the event?

6. *Potential Vulnerability:*

   What is the probability that the victim will reencounter the source of the traumatic event in the near future?

(continued)

TABLE 3.3
Trauma Analysis Protocol (Continued)

Questions about the Victim:

1. *Status:*

   When the event occurred, was the person:

   (a) alone?

   (b) one of two or more victims?

   (c) in the company of a large group?

   (d) a witness to someone else becoming a victim?

2. *Impact:*

   To what extent is the victim aware that the event had a traumatic effect?

3. *Perceived Threat:*

   Did the victim believe that he or she might be maimed or killed?

4. *Reactions of Others:*

   Do significant others acknowledge that the victim was traumatized by the event?

5. *Traumatic History:*

   Had the victim been:

   (a) a victim of a similar type of traumatic event in the past?

   (b) a victim of a different kind of traumatic event in the past?

6. *Clinical History:*

   Had the victim:

   (a) received treatment for previous trauma?

   (b) suffered from a diagnosable psychological condition prior to the traumatic event:

      i. treated?

      ii. untreated?

---

they were, were not intentionally inflicted. When trauma originates in the environment ("acts of nature"), the principal issues raised concern the person's fate or destiny, and often these can be worked through by means of philosophical dialogue. By contrast, when the trauma was intentionally inflicted, it can reshape (or, in the case of a young child, shape) the victim's whole world view, as well as damage the dynamic forces that comprise the self. Traumatic injury of this origin may change the psyche of the trauma-tized person for life.

Social stigma needs to be taken into account when treating a trauma victim, because, if the client has endured a traumatic event that is socially misunderstood or castigated, this complication will inevitably find its way into therapy. From a systemic standpoint, a client will need to develop appropriate strategies for dealing with those who have applied the stigma. At a deeper level, issues such as being "marked," shamed, outcast, or some-how made different must be addressed. Eventually, issues pertaining to self-image and self-esteem need to be carefully worked through, so that the client does not develop a defensive or self-deprecating trauma response.

A therapist must also consider the real possibility that some victims will encounter a similar (or reencounter the same) situation in which they were traumatized; for example, it was part of his or her job or the event happened in the midst of an aspect of daily life that is unavoidable such as driving a car or going shopping. The therapist may wish to employ a cognitive/behavioral technique such as desensitization to alleviate this kind of apprehension, so that the client does not develop a phobic or counterphobic reaction.

The clinician can also help a victim to achieve a sense of mastery in this context, by encouraging him or her to think proactively. That means devel-oping strategies for coping with future instances in which the person will likely encounter a situation similar to the one that produced trauma. By this process, a therapist can assist the traumatized person in ways such as giving a clear message that he or she is worth taking care of, and that the victim is competent and capable of doing something to make things better, so that he or she does not feel so vulnerable at the hands of fate.

Finally, in cases of severe trauma, the clinician may have to help a client accept the fact that he or she may not be able to return to the activity or profession in which the traumatic event occurred. This can be a painful, but necessary, process because the victim must grieve yet another loss.

Questions About the Victim

Was the victim alone or part of a group? If a victim was traumatized with another person or as part of a group, how does he or she feel about the behavior of the other(s)? Is the person wiling to work with the other victim (or victims in a group), to reexamine what happened?

Clinicians need to be particularly sensitive to those who witness trau-matic events. Many are as much affected by witnessing the event as is the actual victim, because they have experienced the impact of the event without the protection of the defenses that are available to the victim.

While the victim concentrates on survival, the witness to the event must cope with his or her inability to do anything about it. The traumatic impact of such an experience is particularly damaging to children; this will be discussed further in Chapter VII.

In many cases of trauma, the victim himself or herself may not define the event as traumatic. This is most likely to occur when the event was one of intrafamilial violence such as physical abuse or incest. Denial of the impact of trauma is also very prevalent in occupations such as the military service, police work, and fire fighting, in which trauma and tragedy are met on a regular basis. People in these occupations tend to encapsulate and minimize their feelings. There is also considerable encouragement, within their respective professions, for people to deny traumatic impact.

When these persons seek treatment, they rarely do so for an actual trauma or for traumas suffered in the past. They are outwardly concerned about other matters and see no connection between their present problems and a possibly traumatic event. Some enter therapy because spouses or supervisors insist that they do so. Hence, it will be the therapist's task to uncover any relevant hidden trauma in a manner that the client can tolerate. Such a process requires great skill and sensitivity, because these reactions may be wrapped in a mantle of denial or dissociation. The lingering wound may be complicated by a long-festering sense of helplessness or humiliation. And because a victim's *persona* is so threatened by revelations arising through this process, the person may withdraw from treatment before the clinician has been able to intervene.

The perceived lethality of an event can have marked significance on the severity of trauma. If the person thought, even for an instant, that he or she could be permanently injured or killed by what was happening, the resulting terror can be deeply felt and persistent. For some people, this perception is delayed, coming as a kind of "aha" phenomenon hours or days later, when they realize, "I could be dead." Some dwell on this morbid thought long afterward. For many, of course, it is the first time they have had such an intimation of mortality. Certain people will incorporate it merely as a chastening experience; others will feel dragged prematurely to a new level of maturity. Therapy must rest on an estimation of where the client belongs on this spectrum.

An additional complicating factor that should be dealt with when formulating a treatment plan occurs when people who are significant to a traumatized person do not accept the event as having been traumatic. If the victim recognizes the event as traumatic and the others do not, it will be necessary for a therapist to help the client realize that he or she holds a different perception of the situation than do the others. This approach may be difficult, because it may mean that the client will lose or have to alter close relationships. Chapter IX provides strategies for dealing with this contingency.

A client's history of trauma or its absence is a key component of trauma analysis. If the victim has been traumatized before, his or her response to the recent event may be heightened or complicated in some way. This of course will be further complicated if the client has denied or encapsulated a trauma response experienced in the past. Even though we believe that the trauma response is frequently over-pathologized, we recognize that many trauma victims have preexisting psychological conditions that will affect the present reaction and the ensuing course of treatment. Nevertheless, it is wise not to assume hastily that underlying pathology exists, because normal traumatic responses can masquerade as pathology. A fuller discussion of this point is found in Chapter IV. The best policy is to treat the trauma, and if an underlying condition exists it will surface; then, treatment of the latter can be interwoven into the plan.

PART TWO

Treatment for Adult Trauma

CHAPTER IV

The Stabilization Phase

MORE AND MORE, clinicians are called to the scenes of traumatic events or asked to see people shortly after such events have occurred. It is well established that early intervention and clinical follow-up can play a significant role in lessening the severity and duration of the post-traumatic response (Lindy, Green, Grace, & Titchener, 1983, 1986; Mollica, 1988). Our own experience, as well as that of Vail-Williams and Polak (1979), indicates that short-term "crisis intervention" efforts or "critical incident debriefing" groups whose primary focus is catharsis are seldom effective in reducing the severity of the trauma response. In fact, we find that some traumatized people view these "intrusive" techniques as another source of trauma, and avoid psychotherapy afterward.

When first considering working with traumatized people, a clinician needs to be keenly aware of personal biases toward fate and causality, and to examine how he or she has been taught to cope with loss and suffering. A therapist must be able to accept the fact that there are truly innocent victims of fate, even though some people "tempt fate" or "set themselves up" to be victims. In no other field of clinical practice does a therapist experience his or her own vulnerability as acutely as when treating trauma survivors. Save for a stroke of luck, the clinician could have been driving the car that was struck in the intersection, could have been living in the town ruined by flood or earthquake, or could have been the person who was robbed at gunpoint. Only when a therapist is clearly in touch with his or her own mortality can he or she focus effectively on the reality of the traumatized person.

The first step in treatment of a traumatized adult is for the therapist to enter the shattered reality of the victim and see it through the victim's eyes, while maintaining a clinical perspective. To do this, the clinician needs to be secure within himself or herself, as well as supported by colleagues. This inner security will enable a therapist to help the trauma victim regain a sense of emotional control. Immediately after a traumatic event, a person's cognitive and analytical faculties are usually in a state of disarray; often the victim functions solely at a primitive, instinctual level. For this reason, he or she may be acutely "tuned in" to the perception of feelings such as fear, disgust, or blame on the therapist's part, even though the person may not be able to voice this sensibility at the time. One consequence of such a development could be that the client will simply "fade away." In some cases, the client may not be able to articulate clearly why he or she is leaving therapy.

STEPS TOWARD RECOVERY

One of the primary roles of a clinician who treats trauma victims is to facilitate the traumatized person's entry into the recovery process, a natural psychological passage that is similar to grief. Further, one must assist the person in moving through the various stages of this process in such a way that he or she does not become arrested or blocked in one of the stages. Figure 4.1 presents a general schema for the normal sequence of experiences on the way to recovery (adapted from Everstine & Everstine, 1983, p. 168).

As noted above, much of theory in psychotherapy is rooted in models of pathology, i.e., maladaptive behavior or interactions. Many traumatized people exhibit behavior such as anxiety, depression, or even paranoia, but these symptoms are *reactive* to the trauma and not necessarily the result of underlying pathology. In fact, anxiety, depression, and paranoid or hypervigilant thinking are in many cases quite understandable, when one considers what the victim has experienced. Even so, many traumatized people are embarrassed by their feelings, and by using the pathology model a clinician runs the risk of re-traumatizing someone or driving the victim away from therapy, by confirming the person's worst fear that he or she has been made crazy by the event.

As an illustration of this point, some seriously injured or disfigured victims develop a trauma-reactive form of paranoid thinking. Their injuries have caused them to be hospitalized for long periods of time, isolated from mainstream society. Next, they undergo long periods of rehabilitation at home or in an extended-care institution. When they emerge, they have been out of touch with day-to-day, "normal" life for a long time. Simple tasks that the average person takes for granted, such as getting on a bus, going shopping, or going out for a meal, become complex and difficult for

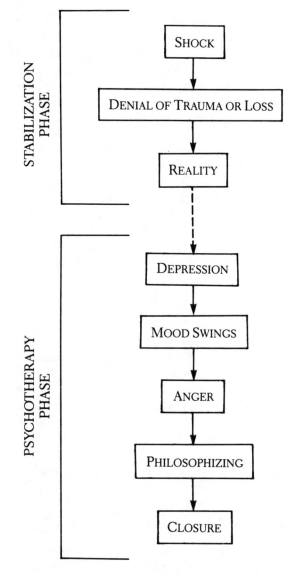

Figure 4.1
The Recovery Cycle

those on crutches or in wheelchairs or those who have obvious disfiguring scars. People stare; the world becomes a hostile obstacle course on which they cannot compete. They begin to see themselves as being in a battle of some kind with the privileged, "normal" world. Such a viewpoint is not the product of a delusional system. It is the reality of disabled or disfigured people, into which fate has cast them. If a therapist is to help these people find their way out of this angry, cloistered place, he or she must first see the world from their perspective, trying not to mistake their reality for pathology.

We do not deny the existence of significant pathology in trauma victims, but if a clinician begins treatment by looking for the manifestations of illness, he or she usually will miss the mark. If there was preexisting pathology, it will surface as the client proceeds through the recovery process and can be dealt with as a part of the course of treatment. In fact, treatment of the person's underlying pathology will be a *necessary* condition for complete recovery; nevertheless, this must wait until after stabilization has occurred and the victim has entered the psychotherapy phase (see Figure 4.1 above).

EARLY INTERVENTIONS

Many traditional clinical intervention strategies are not appropriate when working with acutely traumatized persons. The problem is that these approaches are based upon an assumption of pathology or maladaptive behavior on the part of the client that is not appropriate in most acute trauma situations. In fact, in many traumatic situations, the person's behavior may be quite appropriate—even adaptive—given the circumstances.

Another reason that these approaches are not appropriate to the acute stage of trauma is that they require a higher level of intellectual functioning than is possible for traumatized people at this stage. For example, the "reflective" technique, often taught as a crisis intervention strategy, employs a level of abstraction and cognitive reasoning that is beyond the acutely traumatized person. This reflective approach will only add to the fears and frustrations of someone who is acutely traumatized, by demonstrating how much his or her thinking is impaired. This can be a terrifying "double bind" for the victim because, as a result of that same cognitive impairment, he or she will not be able to *explain* being incapable of reflection. In such instances, a traumatized person will become anxious, confused, or will merely "shut down."

Above all, the use of methods designed to induce catharsis is contraindicated in cases of acute trauma. These methods encourage a victim to "let go" and to "vent" his or her feelings, at a time when the person is struggling

became clear that the woman was in too much pain to hear someone speaking in a normal voice, the therapist spoke in a louder voice each time she repeated the phrases, "I am a doctor. You are hurt. You are in a hospital. You are safe now." She kept repeating the phrases until she was sure that the woman could hear and understand what was being said; this took a few minutes. Then the therapist interspersed other phrases among the original ones, such as, "I'm a doctor. You are in pain. Doctors will help you. You are in a hospital. You are safe now. Look at me. You are safe in a hospital."

Eventually, the victim focused on her as she repeated the same phrases, each time inserting more information. Then the clinician sat next to the woman as she continued to rock back and forth on the table. Eventually, she was able to put her arm around the woman's shoulders and gently move her backward so that she was lying down on the table. While this happened, the therapist continued saying the phrases rhythmically, adding that the doctors needed to examine her to help her. Then she asked the woman to say the phrases, "I'm in the hospital. I'm safe." When the woman had repeated them several times, it meant that her frame of reference had been sufficiently altered from the cognitive survival state to one that enabled her to permit a doctor to touch her. Eventually, she was able to repeat, "I'm in the hospital. The doctors are taking care of me."

Throughout the examination, the clinician made sure that the victim looked at her, while she held the woman's hand and talked to her reassuringly. The purpose was to keep the victim outside the cognitive survival state long enough to permit the medical staff to examine her. This constant contact with the therapist prevented the woman from having a flashback to the traumatic incident that would have forced her into cognitive survival again.

Both examples demonstrate the necessity of entering a traumatized person's frame of reference. The second case illustrates that severely traumatized people can be out of touch with their surroundings; they can be either so flooded with emotions or in so much pain that someone attempting to help them must literally cross a barrier to chaotic thinking without adding further trauma. The key, in both cases, was to "join" the victim and then to direct him or her into doing what needed to be done. One may wish, in some cases, to raise the volume of one's voice to penetrate pain or confusion, but this should be done gradually. An exception occurs in *very high risk* cases when quick action needs to be taken to prevent further harm, or when events have accelerated out of control so that someone is in imminent danger.

When the situation is volatile, a therapist must act swiftly and decisively to "break through" to the traumatized person; often, making a very loud, startling noise can accomplish that. Next, the clinician should speak in a loud voice (or even yell), but with a hypnotic tone; the aim is to match the clamorous intensity of the victim's reality. For example, when a seriously injured man who needed immediate medical attention was fighting with emergency workers, a therapist slammed a metal pan down on an adjoining table; then she shouted, in a loud, rhythmic voice, "Chest hurts . . . chest hurts bad . . . look at me . . . chest hurts . . . look at me . . . chest hurts . . . breathe slowly . . . chest hurts. . . ." While shouting, she grabbed hold of the man's hand so tightly as to cause pain. In rhythm with his breathing, she continued to shout, "Chest hurts . . . breathe slowly . . . hold my hand . . . breathe slowly." Then she slowed the cadence of her commands. In a matter of moments, the therapist had broken through the man's formless terror and escalating pain and had refocused his attention so that he could breathe normally. She was then able to induce him to cooperate with the medical staff.

When clinicians intervene in cases of severe trauma, it is important to be cognizant of the fact that traumatized persons, especially during the acute stage, may not be totally aware of their surroundings and may not realize who the helping professionals are. Hence it is wise, in these acute situations, to make sure that the person knows who you are and what your role is, so that your very presence does not add to the chaos. Medical practitioners, in particular, should consider the fact that some necessary medical procedures may be similar enough to the traumatic experience to cause the victim's trauma to intensify.

For example, in the case of the elderly woman described above, the medical staff needed to touch her and, eventually, have her lie down in order to suture her many wounds and treat her gynecologically. Her first perception of these procedures was that people were holding her down again, just like the men who had repeatedly beaten, raped, and sodomized her. In this flashback, she believed that she was being attacked: She had no idea that she was in a hospital. The lesson to be learned is that medical procedures implemented after a traumatic event should be done with considerable caution, to ensure that the victim recognizes the surroundings and is cognizant of what is being done.

As noted above, trauma victims' thought processes are concrete on the one hand and suffused with emotion on the other. Hence their ability to *absorb* information is very limited. The clinician should, therefore, not be hesitant about repeating himself or herself until quite sure that the intended message has been received and understood by the victim. During this initial, acute stage, a clinician can have only limited expectations about what acutely traumatized people are able to retain. He or she should be prepared both to repeat what was said and to write significant information down for the person to review, as an *aide memoire*, at a later time. Trauma victims, especially those who have any form of head injury, simply do not recall much (if anything) that is told to them during the acute stage. For example, we placed a large card in a prominent place in the hospital room of a young woman who had been in a very serious auto accident; the card bore the message that her husband and son were safe at home and that everyone in the car had survived. Many victims awaken alone (or fade in and out of consciousness) in a strange hospital room; they know they are injured, but have no clear recollection about what has happened to themselves or anyone who was with them. Such an experience adds to trauma and only serves to deepen the person's sense of helplessness.

When possible, it should be arranged that a trauma victim will not have to regain consciousness alone in a dark room. And because of the common experience of short-term memory loss in such situations, the person may need to be told about his or her medical status, and that of any other victims of the same event, more than once. Nevertheless, it is unfair to assume that nurses will be there each time the patient regains consciousness to convey this information, because of the demands of their duties. Victims can therefore be given basic information relating to trauma in writing, and this applies even to those who are being released to return to their homes. Added to this can be a standard description about traumatic reactions and their duration, including what symptoms may occur.[1]

In our experience, even mild concussive syndrome is accompanied by psychological symptoms that can be very frightening and, by themselves, traumatize. If victims do not know what symptoms are the natural components of traumatic reactions, they may think that they are losing their minds. Hence, insufficient information can serve to make a traumatic situation even worse. Table 4.1 presents a sample document that can be used to inform clients about trauma responses and what to expect. (For the parents of traumatized children, a different sample document is presented in Chapter IX.)

Communicating with acutely traumatized people can be a delicate process. Because they are overwhelmed, what one says to them should be as uncomplicated as possible. Questions posed should be of the sort that can be responded to by yes, no, or one-word answers. In this way, the clinician will obtain the information that he or she needs and the victim will experience a sense of competence. Open-ended or complex questions such as "How do you feel?" or "Tell me about your feelings" should be avoided during this acute period, because responding requires a level of analysis

---

[1]Following a traumatic event, traumatized people often have a very strong wish to return to their normal activities. This usually stems from their need to feel a sense of control in their lives, as well as a desire to prevent the experience from intruding any more than it already has. In this situation, a clinician should assess how much of his or her regular activities a trauma victim can realistically do. The client can then be encouraged to attempt to resume as many ordinary activities as is reasonable, and can be dissuaded from attempting activities that may aggravate trauma.

TABLE 4.1
Information on Reactions to Traumatic Events

An emotional reaction to a traumatic event such as the one you have just experienced is quite natural. Many people feel "strange" or unlike themselves for varying periods after events of this kind, often from one to six weeks. The most common responses to traumatic events are:

- Anxiety about the possible recurrence of the event or a similar event.
- Emotional distress caused by events or objects that remind you of the traumatic event.
- Confusion, difficulty in concentration, memory problems, or an inability to estimate time accurately.
- Flashbacks of the event that may be visual or may take the form of reliving the event emotionally.
- Temporary mood swings, general changes in temperament, irritability.
- Sleep problems and/or nightmares.
- Feeling depressed or detached or estranged from others.
- A change of appetite or eating patterns.
- Shortness of temper, angry feelings, or a lack of patience with yourself or others.
- Diminished interest in significant activities (work, social, or family).

You may experience some or all of these symptoms. If you have a question about one of them or if it continues for more than six weeks, consult your doctor or one of the services listed below that provides counseling for people who have experienced trauma.

[A list of community agencies can be appended.]

---

and communication skills that a victim rarely possesses. Often, acutely traumatized people respond to questions of that kind with "It's okay" or "I'm all right"—not because they are, but rather in an attempt to convince themselves that they are. Another motive for answers such as these is an effort to get the questioner to leave them alone. They feel that the questions are, at best, too complicated to answer straightforwardly and, at worst, intrusive. The message is, "Please go away. You are asking too much of me."

Reality

The communication process between an acute trauma victim and a clinician should be focused on providing *information* about the person's reactions to the traumatic event, so that he or she can begin to feel more in control. It is the clinician's task to break down such information into portions that are sufficiently clear and simple enough for the victim to grasp. For example, phenomena such as flashbacks, sleep disturbances, startle responses, temporary problems with memory, mental confusion, and pho-bic reactions, as well as other trauma-related symptoms, should be ex-plained to the victim as being typical reactions. In addition, the person needs to know what to expect in the immediate future. The main purpose of explanations such as these is to help a victim realize that he or she is going through a *process* that has a structure and follows a sequence, so that the person feels less helpless and can think of himself or herself as being still within normal limits. Victims need to understand that most trauma-tized people experience these phenomena.

Practically all traumatized people question their sanity at one time or another after a traumatic event. They usually believe that they are the only ones who have experienced phenomena such as flashbacks or startle re-sponses, and see them as signs that they are going mad or are weak or incompetent. That is why the therapist should play an educational role, so that the victim is aware that such phenomena are expectable, understand-able, and run a predictable course.

In review, this process of trauma stabilization is a natural precursor to actual psychotherapy. The process is necessary for the trauma victim to reach an equilibrium in his or her perception of reality, before engaging in the more complex conceptual tasks of therapy. In guiding a victim in stabilization, the clinician becomes a sort of teacher or guide who provides realistic information about traumatic reactions such as flashbacks, startle responses, waves of panic, or being impatient with others, etc.

Because lack of sleep due to nightmares, night terrors, or anxiety about experiencing them can retard stabilization, the clinician should carefully monitor a victim's sleep patterns. If sleep is seriously disrupted, the client should be referred for medication, even though many victims resist taking medication for a trauma because of issues of control, as well as the stigma associated with taking psychiatric drugs.

A therapist will recognize that a victim has stabilized when he or she can begin to think in the abstract and can talk about the event, to some degree, without reliving it; further evidence of stabilization is when the trauma-tized person's defense mechanisms begin to function in a more integrated way as opposed to the survival mode, and he or she can begin to accept the reality of the experience.

The Medical Recovery Period

It is not uncommon for the emotional sequelae of trauma to lie dormant during the acute medical recovery period, such as when an injured person is convalescing in a hospital. There can be several reasons for this: (1) the trauma victim is in a sheltered environment, i.e., the hospital; (2) the person, in many cases, is totally focused upon his or her physical recovery and is reacting to medical procedures; (3) the victim does not have to cope with the demands of day-to-day life, nor is it likely that he or she will face events reminiscent of the traumatic event; (4) in cases in which the event was caused by another person, the victim may not have to encounter unfriendly strangers while being cared for either in the hospital or at home.

Another reason for delay in the trauma response may be that those who are close to a traumatized person are more attentive, sympathetic, and protective while the person is physically disabled. Because many people are not as comfortable with or aware of the invisible psychological wounds of trauma, their support may rapidly fade when the physical injuries heal. Often these people want to forget, to go on with their lives, and to put their own terrible memories of the event behind them. This can occur just when the traumatized person has begun to recover physically.

The clinician need not be concerned if a seriously traumatized victim is unable to acknowledge emotional, psychological issues during this physical recovery period. But, by no means should psychotherapy be postponed until after medical treatment is completed. It is important that the victim view therapy as a part of the fabric of trauma care, not as an indication of a secondary injury or weakness.

Even though it is quite logical to expect that psychological damage may not always become apparent until after medical treatment is completed, many trauma clients are profoundly startled by the onset of such symptoms. Many were so relieved to survive the event that during physical recovery they did not think about what returning to their day-to-day lives might entail. Hence, if the therapy process begins during the physical recovery period, the clinician will have an opportunity to prepare the client for the struggle that lies ahead.

People Who Resist Intervention

Many trauma victims are reluctant or resistant to therapy for a number of reasons. They may have been healthy, functional people before the traumatic event, and seeing a psychotherapist is yet another indignity. As Mollica aptly put it, many traumatized people associate psychotherapy with a "broken mind or spirit" (1988, p. 301). Because post-traumatic reactions are still linked with weakness, cowardice, malingering, or avarice, many victims do not wish to be identified with them. Others resist therapy because they simply don't want to talk about the traumatic event or its aftermath. For instance, people who do not understand what psychotherapy is may assume it to be some sort of endless reanalysis of the trauma experience. They fear losing control or being flooded by their emotions if they engage in such a process. In many cases, a victim will talk obsessively to a friend, a relative, a spouse, a priest (rabbi, minister), a lawyer, or a physician, but staunchly refuse to see a therapist because of not wanting to be labeled as "odd."

Many trauma victims frustrate or annoy medical practitioners with a sequence of complaints that have no medical basis; for these people, the only socially acceptable way to express emotional pain is through some sort of physical discomfort. (This is especially true in regard to ethnic groups such as Latins and Asians.) Other victims may be suffering from a conversion reaction of the classical clinical kind. In either case, what is needed is treatment for the emotional reaction instead of suspicion or annoyance.

There are some trauma victims who exaggerate their symptoms, but it has been our experience that the majority minimize or hide them. The popular stereotype of the histrionic weakling or mendacious malingerer serves as a societal rationalization that helps to protect the general public from facing its own vulnerability to trauma. The logic of this protective device is: If only the weak or avaricious suffer from symptoms such as these, I shall be spared because I am neither weak nor avaricious. We generally tend to blame traumatized people for their own symptoms as a form of emotional damage control against human frailty.

How does one deal with this kind of resistance and stigma? Above all, emergency service professionals as well as medical practitioners need to be trained about the realities of trauma response. Physicians and nurses need further training on how to cope with trauma victims who develop symptoms that have no medical basis. The sooner a traumatic reaction is identified and the person referred for psychological care, the less likely a victim is to develop maladaptive behavior or become socially isolated.

How does one get trauma victims to accept the care that they need? First, in addition to providing education for health care professionals, mental health agencies should reach out through channels such as the media, police, and churches. Moreover, we recommend that psychological services for traumatized people not be labeled as "mental health" services, because trauma victims, especially members of some ethnic groups, will not use them. (Two agencies that we founded, the Emergency Treatment Center and the Trauma Center, were so named to avoid any reference either to mental disorders or to psychological care.)

Secondly, attorneys should also be trained to identify and refer traumatized people. Despite the popular notion of the unscrupulous lawyer who represents a malingering litigant, most attorneys are opposed to referring their clients for psychotherapy because they fear it will complicate the case; above all, they wish to avoid the stigma that might be applied to a therapy client. Too often, traumatized people are referred by an attorney for treatment only after they have suffered a "breakdown" or have "fallen apart" during some part of a legal proceeding.

CHAPTER V
The Psychotherapy Phase

CLINICAL EVALUATION

At the outset of therapy with a trauma victim, it is wise to begin with a full clinical evaluation as the first step toward developing an appropriate treatment plan. In the event that the traumatized person is involved in some sort of legal proceedings, the clinician should clearly distinguish two forms of evaluation, namely, one that is intended to serve the legal process and one that serves psychotherapy. When possible, evaluation that is part of a legal procedure should be done by someone other than the victim's therapist (Everstine & Everstine, 1989, pp. 12–13). One good reason for this is that the rules of confidentiality pertaining to the results of an evaluation differ in the legal arena from the rules that pertain to therapy (see Chapter XII).

The primary duty of a therapist is to provide care for a client. In the ideal case, whether or not a victim's assailant is convicted, or whether or not a traumatized person's civil or Workers' Compensation case is won or lost, would not be permitted to interfere in the dialogues of treatment. Nonetheless, legal remedies are very important, and the success or failure of a legal proceeding can have a significant impact on the traumatized person. Legal developments are frequently discussed as a part of therapy. What is at issue here is the role that the clinician will play in these proceedings and its positive or negative impact upon the course of therapy. Many clients do not consider how exposed or vulnerable they would be if their therapist took the witness stand to testify about them in a courtroom. And even though we try to keep therapy separate from litigation as much as possible, in many proceedings, such as a civil suit or a Workers' Compensation case, the client, by claiming emotional injury, has placed his or her psychological condition at issue.

The solution is for the clinician to define his or her role at every stage of therapy and to discuss, with the client, any changes in that role as they arise. The subjects of the Independent Medical Evaluation and evaluation for the purpose of expert witness testimony will be discussed in Chapter XII. In the present chapter, the evaluation process to be described is solely a prologue to treatment.

Because many trauma victims have difficulty articulating their emotional responses, and because in some cases even the traumatic event may be lost to conscious thought due to head injury or dissociation, a clinician may need to get information about the event, as well as the person's response to it, from other sources. Even victims who talk freely, at times obsessively, about the event may not possess a full or accurate recollection. One may have to read police reports or medical records or interview witnesses to obtain significant facts about the traumatic event and how the person responded during and after. This information may be extremely useful during the later phases of therapy. For example, knowledge of how others perceived what the person did or did not do during the event may help a therapist to guide the direction of therapy; then, cautiously disclosing these perceptions to the victim may facilitate entry into the therapy process.

A case in point is that of the man whose car was struck by a truck. He was so stricken by the trauma and grief of the accident that all he could recall was that he had been the driver when his wife was crippled and his daughter was killed. His wife had been knocked unconscious by the force of the collision and thus had no memory of the accident. The fact that the accident was clearly not his fault and that he had struggled courageously to save the others, sustaining further injury while doing so, was simply unavailable to his conscious mind when he began therapy. If the therapist had not taken time to get the initial police report and talk to one of the police officers who had been at the scene, she would not have known this vital information about the accident.

After this man had been stabilized and could begin to participate in the therapy process, the clinician was able to induce him to "return" to the scene of the event and to recapture this significant information for himself, by utilizing a very structured form of hypnosis. As part of the hypnosis process, she incorporated data from the police report, as well as direct quotes from the police officer, to help the man formulate a more accurate perception of what took place on the night of the accident. This structured hypnotic experience helped the victim to let go of some of his guilt and begin directing his anger outward, chiefly toward the negligent truck driver who had struck his car.

Part of the rationale for having a victim's account of a traumatic incident verified by a secondary source is to determine whether or not the victim's reactions were appropriate and, if not, to look for reasons why. Is the traumatized person minimizing or blocking out a major facet of the event? Does the person's trauma response exceed what one would expect after an event such as this? Even when someone's response is of far greater magnitude than one would generally expect from the situation (and/or the accompanying injury), one should not jump to the conclusion that the person is malingering; one should examine the circumstances further. For instance, there may have been significant factors in the person's life, previously undisclosed, that predisposed an extreme reaction. Or, some hidden aspect of the traumatic event itself might hold a clue.

In a relevant example, two men were in an industrial accident. The event occurred without warning and with terrifying impact; both of these workers suffered injuries that caused them to bleed profusely but were only moderately serious. One man returned to work about a month after the accident and was relatively symptom-free. The other was plunged into a major depressive episode requiring medication; he was incapable of returning to work and became obsessed by the fear that members of his family or friends were going to die. Looking at this case superficially, one might say that the first worker responded appropriately to the event, while the other was dissembling for the sake of a Workers' Compensation stress claim. But an examination of the history of the latter reveals a justification for his severe trauma response.

When the man had been in therapy for a considerable period of time, the therapist began to suspect that he had experienced an "encapsulated" (blocked) war-related trauma. The man disclosed that he had been in Vietnam, but brushed the fact aside as being unpleasant but not painful. He was reluctant to talk about his war experiences, using the excuse that he had very few recollections of the war. His nonchalant dismissal of the war as less than traumatic indicated to the therapist that there was more to his experience than he had previously revealed. The therapist also knew, from working with veterans, that the client had been assigned to a battalion that had engaged in brutalizing jungle combat. After considerable careful exploration of the subject, and when the victim had grown to trust his therapist, the following story emerged. During an encounter with the Vietcong, this man's best friend had been fatally wounded; death came after excruciating pain, as the friend lay in his arms. Because of the battle situation, the man had not even been able to bury his friend. He had encapsulated this horrible event as something that had taken place in another world, a world far from home.

In the accident at work, the client's co-worker had sustained injuries that were strikingly similar to the mortal wounds of his friend in Vietnam;

superficially, they looked the same. Because the man had come home and hence had made himself safe from the horrors of war, he was caught without defenses. When the time capsule broke open, he lapsed into serious depression.

In summary, it is unwise to assume that malingering or deception is occurring merely because a person's symptoms appear to be out of proportion with the traumatic event. One must first review the person's history, as well as examine the circumstances of the traumatic event, before making even a preliminary judgment of this kind. For a more complete discussion of malingering, see Chapter XII.

It is certainly useful to learn what a victim's level of functioning was before the traumatic event. Sometimes this can be obtained from the client directly, but often a clinician will need to contact outside sources if he or she suspects that the client's perspective on the past was distorted or idealized. In particular, the therapist can make use of information about a traumatized person's history of coping with illness or injury or loss. First, had the person previously suffered from a significant loss or injury? If so, how did he or she deal with it? Is there evidence that secondary gain was derived from a prior illness or injury or, by contrast, does the person have a history of denying or minimizing pain? One may also wish to inquire about how issues such as these were perceived and dealt with by the client's family of origin.

Next, the clinician should attempt to learn what the victim's (and family of origin's) attitudes are toward health care. Is the person reasonable and responsible about health care in general, or does he or she take unnecessary risks? Is there a sign of possible hypochondriasis? Learned coping patterns such as these are extremely informative, both for clinical assessment and for treatment planning. They reveal the predetermined constructions that people bring with them concerning how one should respond to pain, to loss, and to injury.

In those instances in which a victim has no direct memory of the traumatic event, the clinician may try to find out how he or she processed the event emotionally, by indirect means. For example, a post-traumatic history of nightmares, or awakening from a nightmare the content of which the person is unable to recall, may be the only kind of symptom that a trauma victim will bring into therapy (Kramer, Schoen, & Kinney, 1984; Van der Kolk, Blitz et al., 1984; Mollica, 1988). A therapist may gain insight into the trauma through analysis of the dream content. The client may be asked to keep a journal of his or her dreams, from which recurring themes can be culled. Few trauma victims, even those who can recall the event, have repetitive dreams of the *actual* event. Instead, they tend to have dreams that symbolically represent salient issues or subjects related to the event. Some of these symbolic dreams can be repetitive.

For example, a woman who was orally raped dreamed repeatedly of being in an old house that was on fire. She ran desperately from room to room to find an exit, but could never find a way to escape. Meanwhile, in the dream, her teeth began to rot and fall out one by one. She could describe the horror and disgust that she experienced in the dream, long before she could talk openly about the assault itself.

Trauma victims who cannot recall the contents of their dreams can be given a structured format for writing down their associations upon awakening. The clinician can prepare a simple questionnaire that the client can fill out after having had a dream. The questionnaire method may provide an innocuous medium through which the person can disclose feelings. By contrast, merely asking a person to free-associate may be too open-ended and thus seem threatening. In many instances, writing about thoughts and feelings can make the person feel comfortable and enhance candor; some people can write more about themselves than they can say, perhaps because writing requires a shift from the emotional to the cognitive sphere.

Treatment Planning

When planning treatment for a severely traumatized person, the therapist should be prepared to make a commitment to continue working with the person through the entire process of recovery. Consider what an act of trust it is for some trauma victims to disclose aspects of their emotional lives to another person. For example, one client, a victim of war atrocities, was visibly relieved when his therapist said she believed that his treatment would probably take from five to seven years to complete, and that she would continue seeing him for that period of time. Many people would be horrified, rather than relieved, to learn that therapy might require seven years. But, to this client, it meant that he would not be abandoned, and he could feel empowered to control the pace of therapy. It is not surprising that eventually he was willing to disclose information about himself more freely, and thus moved ahead more rapidly than anticipated in the treatment process.

Some severely traumatized people, by contrast, just want to "get it over with." One young woman, the victim of a rape in which she was brutally beaten (her nose and jaw were broken), informed the clinician that she would give her one month to get this "trauma junk" over with, because she intended to "get on" with her life. The therapist, knowing that this was not possible, did not explicitly agree with her but reassured her that the goal of therapy was, indeed, to help her get on with her life as soon as possible; to that end, they would work at the pace with which the client felt most comfortable. This enabled the young woman to see the therapist as an ally and to participate in the therapy process, rather than getting sidetracked into a power struggle concerning the length of her treatment and recovery.

Many victims have a need to go over the traumatic experience in minute detail. Because the details can be horrifyingly graphic, clinicians should be prepared to stifle their own visceral reactions, lest they shock a victim into silence. These recapitulations, however vexing to the listener, are necessary ingredients of the recovery process for many traumatized people. Repeating what happened to them is an attempt to gain mastery over the experience by reinterpreting it again and again until it makes sense in some way. Moving on in treatment may be retarded by this process, but forcing it to stop carries a certain risk of losing the client. A therapist's patience may be sorely tested.

In the case of the avoidant victim, who copes with trauma by diminishing its importance, the moment of graphic recapitulation may occur much later in the course of therapy, and its arrival may catch the clinician by surprise. This late outpouring of emotion is not a form of regression but, in fact, a sign of progress in therapy. The avoidant client merely needed more time to regroup, during which the person's defenses have recovered sufficiently to permit this catharsis. When the therapist has gotten over the shock, he or she can gently encourage the process.

A Dynamic Systems Approach

Because, in many cases, trauma affects virtually every aspect of a person's life, we believe that treatment should concern both the internal, psychodynamic sphere and the key external systems with which the victim must interact. In effect, treatment can be focused both on the person's interactions with family, work, and other social systems, as well as on psychodynamic processes occurring within. Part of the rationale for this dual perspective is that many of the more significant injuries that a traumatized person suffers are systemic; i.e., they alter or damage the victim's family system, social system, and/or vocational system. A trenchant example is that of the victim of family violence, whose very definition of "family system" has been inexorably changed. The victim of an industrial accident may not only have to adjust to a changing role in his or her vocational system (or to the loss of this role entirely), but also has to cope with a loss or change of role in the family system.

A case in point is that of a man who was seriously injured in an automobile accident in which his femur and pelvis were broken and in which he sustained considerable back injury. Not only was this man traumatized by the shock, pain, and horror of the accident, but he also suffered several systemic losses: (1) He was unable to fulfill his role as breadwinner for his family; (2) while at home during his long period of recuperation, he felt helpless and inadequate, but when he attempted to assert himself with the children, his wife intervened because she felt he was intruding on her role; (3) driving, once a much-enjoyed activity, became something that he avoided; (4) if members of the family were a few minutes late, he exploded at them; (5) friends from work rarely visited him after the initial shock of the accident; (6) he often awoke late at night and felt the need to have a drink to relax and feel better.

Although a traumatic event is rooted in the "here and now," the victim's history is a factor in the trauma response because it was in the past that the person learned coping tactics for dealing with life's disasters. Another legacy of the past is a person's belief system concerning fate and his or her "destiny." These factors are added, by the dynamic systems approach, into the treatment equation. A diagram illustrating the process employed by *dynamic systems therapy* is shown by Figure 5.1. When trauma impinges upon someone, his or her personality structure is potentially pierced to the core. When therapy begins, its aim is to speed recovery at the deepest levels of personality organization, some of which are wholly beyond the consciousness of the victim. This early work proceeds through the medium of precise repair of the most primitive mechanisms of defense.

Even before this work has been completed, the effort to repair damage to the victim's personal systems (family, close friends) should begin. And while both efforts are underway, an attempt to reintegrate the victim into his or her primary social systems (work, community, etc.) will be started as well. By coordinating and timing these parallel activities, therapy can remove the invading traumatic element. In summary, treatment for trauma proceeds simultaneously at both internal and external levels, for the purpose of assisting the healing process to complete the tasks of recovery.

In another case that demonstrates this approach, a mother of four young children suffered a significant injury at her factory job. Prior to the accident she had been an active, outgoing person who was devoted to her family and had an excellent work record. Her main goal in life was to be a good wife to her husband and to raise healthy, successful children. There was no evidence of a preexisting condition. One afternoon, a piece of machinery at the factory malfunctioned and fell over. In an attempt to avoid the falling equipment, she fell and seriously injured her back. At first she thought herself lucky to be alive; she focused her attention on two co-workers who had actually been hit by the equipment and were obviously very seriously injured. After a while, she realized that something was very much wrong with her. She suddenly collapsed and was taken to the hospital, where it was discovered she had a significant back injury that would require at least two surgeries.

While the subsequent surgeries were essentially successful, she still had

DAMAGE CAUSED BY TRAUMA

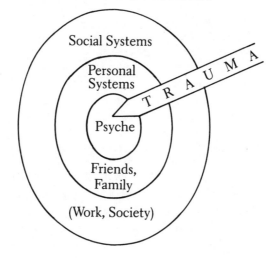

TREATMENT TO REPAIR DAMAGE

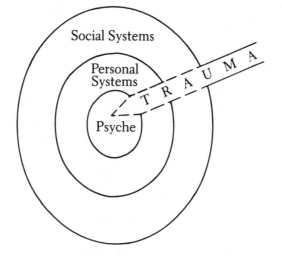

Figure 5.1
Dynamic Systems Approach to Trauma Recovery

some significant restrictions. After the second surgery, the surgeon became concerned about the woman's increasing symptoms of depression, and put her on antidepressant medication that he thought would help the situation; he expected the depressive symptoms to fade shortly after the woman returned home, because he knew how important her family was to her.

At home, her husband was supportive; he and the children did the best they could to shoulder the household tasks during her convalescence. Even though the woman made good physical progress, she continued to become more and more depressed. When she recovered physically, she still had significant problems such as limitations on bending and lifting, a limited range of movement, and she would periodically drop things. Although she was cleared to return to work in a part-time, sedentary job (away from heavy machinery), her symptoms of depression were such that she was unable to do it. The family physician referred her to a therapist when she broke down in his office and said that she was "worthless," "no good for anything," and did not "want to live."

When this trauma victim began therapy, her primary symptoms were periods of intense depression with periodic suicidal ideation, difficulty in sleeping, nightmares when she did sleep, loss of her sense of self-worth, withdrawal from friends and family, and intense fear that she would become reinjured or that a member of her family would be injured. Even though she had been medically cleared, she was not emotionally ready to return to work.

At first, the therapist thought that the primary issue in treatment would be the traumatic injury that the woman had suffered at work. As a part of the initial evaluation, the clinician met with the woman's husband and children. The husband said that he felt helpless and lost; no matter how hard he tried to be a good husband and help his wife, she seemed to withdraw from him more and more and to be getting worse. He went on to say that, even though he never complained, it was hard for him to do "women's work." He sadly shook his head as he reiterated that the more he tried to do things to help his wife at home, the worse she got. He said that she was even resentful of his mother when she would visit the home to help; now, his mother sent prepared food but would not come herself.

As the therapist continued meeting with the client, it became clear that she was exhibiting the internal dynamic processes of depression, but was also suffering from a systemic loss. To treat this woman successfully, both conditions would have to be treated. Because what she valued most in life was her role as wife and mother to her family, the woman took immense pride in performing these roles well. In her mind, her main reason for working was to help her family have a better life. Seeing her husband and children doing her routine tasks humiliated her and made her feel worthless. When the husband brought his mother to help with the housework and cooking, the situation got worse because it made her shame and failure manifest to the rest of the family. The final blow was when her doctor gave her the pills for "crazy people." She took the pills because he said so; she would not disobey her doctor. But the message she took from the prescription was that she was not only worthless — she was crazy. At one point, she sobbed that she would not mind going back to work if she knew that she would be killed in the next accident. That way, her husband could marry a woman who could take proper care of him and the children.

It was clear that the woman's industrial injury had caused her systemic as well as psychodynamic trauma because it had damaged her role in the family system; in turn, this had stimulated the symptoms of depression. And the members of her family system were, in a manner described by Watzlawick et al. (1967), making the problem worse in their attempts to make it better. The clinician continued seeing the victim individually to help her with trauma-specific anxiety and fear; for this purpose, desensitization, hypnosis, and relaxation techniques were utilized. The therapist also helped the woman to deal with the internal forces that caused her depression. She was taught to articulate her needs more clearly, in particular to feel less threatened by her negative, angry feelings and to express them more appropriately. She was also helped to develop a healthier self-image and to have more realistic expectations of herself as a wife and mother. Because her views on what the "good" wife and mother should be were so rigidly held, considerable working-through was required before she could see that even a good wife and mother might accept help from others.

Concurrent with these individual sessions, the therapist began meeting with the woman and her family. In the family sessions, the therapist was very careful not to discount the husband's efforts. Instead, an attempt was made to "reframe" the family situation in such a way as to credit the husband with having to make yet another noble sacrifice for his wife, namely to let her struggle with most of the household chores — especially the cooking — and only to help her if she asked for help. The clinician explained that she knew this would be difficult because the husband felt that it was his duty to take care of his injured wife; nevertheless, this sacrifice would be absolutely necessary for her recovery. It is worth noting that the therapist only made this intervention after checking with the woman's physician to make sure that it was medically safe for her to do household chores. The physician said it would be difficult, in fact more difficult than some of the activities required of her by her job, but that she could do it with some effort. The therapist also explained how the client perceived the antidepressants, and asked whether or not they could be discontinued; the physician said that if he saw sufficient improvement, he would discontinue them when he saw her next, in about six weeks.

After a series of meetings with the client and her family, the clinician began to notice improvement. Her self-esteem increased, she had more energy, and her sleep pattern improved. Even though the husband complained about how it caused him pain to see his wife struggle with housework, he could acknowledge that it was useful for her to try. At first, she asked for his help very rarely, but as she began to deal with her own identity issues in individual therapy, she was able to ask for help more often. The therapist continued to be supportive to the husband, reminding him that she knew how hard this sacrifice was for him, but that it was necessary for the good of his family. The wife continued to improve, and when she visited her physician he took her off the antidepressant medicine.

When the therapist was certain that the client had returned to her proper role in the family, the family was seen once a month for three months to reinforce and maintain changes within the family system. The victim continued her individual visits to discuss trauma-specific issues, as well as issues pertaining to identity, self-esteem, and depression. After about six months, she was able to return to work on a part-time basis. About four months after she had returned to work, she and the therapist agreed that she could discontinue weekly therapy and come back on an as-needed basis.

During the early stages of therapy, clinicians should be cautious about focusing too closely on getting the traumatized person to express anger — or other emotions, for that matter. Clearly, most trauma victims have considerable reason to be quite angry. Such anger, although obvious to the clinician, may be masked from others by primitive defenses such as denial, dissociation, or magical thinking, because it is too threatening. If this is the case, the therapist should not aggressively attempt to bring the anger to the surface. If a clinician persists in such a course, the victim may well feel forced to do something too dangerous, and may retreat from therapy. Or, in such a situation, the person might develop a masochistic transference with the therapist and, symbolically, repeat the traumatic experience in a therapy session. This may provide for emotional sessions but it rarely proves to be truly cathartic or even clinically constructive for the trauma victim. Instead, the clinician's efforts should be directed toward helping a client regain the ego-strength that will enable him or her, eventually, to express anger through normal channels of ventilation. Anger usually arrives spontaneously at one of the stages in treatment (see Chapter IV, Figure 4.1, Psychotherapy Phase), but well after other aspects of the trauma response have run their course.

Before anger can be ventilated in healthy ways, trauma victims must struggle with some shattered fantasies about life, i.e., that there is justice and that this is a rational world. Many people hold notions about being able to vanquish an attacker or how they would bravely cope with disaster, but often when a traumatic event strikes, its reality mocks these fantasies.

Therefore, it is the task of the clinician to help a trauma victim come to terms with, and to accept, what he or she did to survive during the event. Some clients need to obsess for considerable lengths of time over what they did or should have done. Throughout this process, the therapist tries to reorient them to the more self-accepting position that the event was horrible and that they did the best they could to cope with it.

SIGNIFICANT ISSUES IN THERAPY

Power, Trust, and Transference

Although a therapist may view the treatment relationship with a trauma victim as one of care and nurturance, he or she must always be aware that some traumatized people — particularly those who were the victims of violent crime, domestic violence, child abuse, war atrocities or those who have been held hostage or were political prisoners — may have experienced indescribable pain and torment at the hands of other people. Such experiences may not only change how the victim views human beings in general; they may also scar how the person functions in relationships, as well as how he or she interacts with the greater social system. Issues such as control, influence, and power within a relationship can send these people into a panic or into renewed cognitive survival state behavior. They may flee, adopt a rigid, hypervigilant attitude, assume a placating, dependent role, or attack angrily in a manner that is akin to identification with the aggressor.

The psychotherapy relationship is a very powerful one, and its power may be expressed both directly and in subtle ways. Hence, therapists must be observant of client reactions to issues of trust vis-à-vis control or influence, when treating those who were traumatized by other people, to ensure that the power inherent in transference does not evolve into a neurotic, dependent form of transference (described by Everstine & Everstine, 1983, pp. 169–170).

In masochistic transference, a trauma victim may turn the therapy relationship into yet another form of abuse. Some traumatized people literally act out or in other ways provoke their therapists to be angry or punitive toward them. Such behavior is usually a form of repetition compulsion and should be treated as such. The role of the therapist is to focus attention on why the person is acting out, as opposed to getting into a power struggle over sanctions for the acting-out itself.

For example, if a victim is engaging in some form of trauma-related, risk-taking behavior such as provoking fights, the clinician can either concentrate on issues such as rebuilding self-esteem so that the patient will take better care of himself or herself, or try to find out what message the client is attempting to communicate by such behavior. One way to do this is simply to feign being perplexed by such aggressive or provocative behavior on the part of a client who himself or herself has been the victim of violence. The therapist should attempt to help a victim work through this form of compulsive expression within the therapy process, until the person is able to bring the acting-out or risk-taking behavior to a stop. Unfortunately, in some cases of severe trauma, the acting-out may be so dangerous to the client or to others that the clinician may need to utilize external types of control, such as hospitalization or close observation by family or friends.

Clinicians should be alert to the possibility that risk-taking clients or those who repeatedly set themselves up to be victimized may be struggling with a heretofore undisclosed trauma or with some form of survivor guilt. Moreover, *because* of the new trauma, there may be aspects of the original trauma that the victim is unable or fearful to disclose. The person may be acting out feelings that cannot be described or that he or she believes to be "deserved." A fuller discussion of *hidden* traumas is presented in Chapter VI.

Flashbacks and Intrusive Memories

Flashbacks and intrusive feelings or images are common symptoms of the trauma response, often starting just after the traumatic event. In most cases, initial flashbacks are frequent and of overwhelming intensity. They usually represent a key moment or moments excerpted from the traumatic experience. The content often deals with the instant when the person realized being totally helpless to prevent the event (or protect someone from being harmed). In other instances, the flashbacks or intrusive feelings are symbolic of principal sequences in the person's traumatic experience.

Flashbacks and intrusive images or feelings can be so terrifying that they give the person the feeling of being about to lose his or her mind. Because of this, from the beginning of therapy, clinicians need to educate traumatized people about the nature and course of these symptoms, helping the victim to understand that the symptoms are a natural part of the recovery process: They *will* fade and there *are* things that can be done to diminish their intensity.

As a part of the trauma response, people can suffer flashbacks in any sensory mode—visual, auditory, tactile, olfactory, or gustatory. In cases of very severe trauma, the person may experience "flooding" in every mode, literally reliving the traumatic moment. The most common medium of the flashback is visual, and these sensations are often mingled with the auditory.

Because of the popular notion that only crazy people see or hear things that are "not there," many traumatized people are terrified when they first experience flashbacks. It is not uncommon for them to deny or attempt to conceal the fact that they are having a flashback, for fear that someone will think them crazy. Moreover, in some ethnic groups, seeing or hearing things is associated with being "touched" by the devil with the curse of madness.

Simply put, flashbacks seem to occur when one or more sensory modes are overloaded with sensations. As a consequence, these sensory channels become hypersensitive to strong stimuli from the environment. When something in the environment (even an event that is out of conscious awareness) that is somehow reminiscent of the traumatic incident stimulates this sensory mode, the already overloaded sensory channel "flashes back" the traumatic experience. These experiences can be vivid enough to terrify someone who may not comprehend what is happening; the typical reaction is that the person feels that his or her mind has gone out of control.

When treating a victim who is having flashbacks or other kinds of intrusive traumatic memories, one should first explain what causes flashbacks, so that the traumatized person understands that there is a rational basis for these phenomena. Next, the person should be aided in understanding that flashbacks and intrusive memories are stimulated by things that occur around him or her that are reminiscent of the traumatic event. It may be useful if, initially, a victim tries to avoid places or situations that might be stimulating in this way. That advice is not always realistic, of course, and all manner of things could happen that would catch the person by surprise and trigger a flashback. Even so, a therapist should encourage victims to be gentle with themselves about staying away from situations that could rekindle traumatic feelings. The concept of immediately getting back on the horse that threw you is an example of folk wisdom that can cause harm.

A trauma victim should not try to block or arrest flashbacks from occurring once they begin to occur. Trying to stop this process may only serve to intensify it. Instead, clients should be told to say to themselves, should they suddenly have a flashback, "I am having a flashback; it will pass." They should be told to say this until the sensation subsides.

Flashbacks and intrusive memories should be treated, in the context of psychotherapy, by means of a variation of the desensitization process. First, the victim is taught a relaxation procedure that stimulates endorphin and involves the dominant sense that is involved in the flashback. For example, a person who has visual flashbacks can be taught visual hypnotic exercises such as focusing the eyes on a spot, staring at a pendulum or crystal, or the Spiegel eye-roll (Spiegel, 1974). Those who experience tactile or kinesthetic flashbacks or intrusive feelings can be taught progressive relaxation or the pressure point technique. People who have olfactory or gustatory flashbacks can be taught focused breathing exercises or meditation using a spoken or silent word to focus on.

The client should be encouraged to practice these exercises at least three times a day for a minimum of ten minutes each. The exercises are soothing in themselves. People usually like them and they often provide victims with some relief quite soon. Learning these exercises can also give the traumatized person a corrective experience in that he or she knows how it feels to have some control over anxiety or other symptoms. Next, the client and therapist can work together to develop two or three simple, direct messages that will help him or her counter the negative feelings in the flashback, e.g., "The accident is in the past"; "I am safe now"; "I am a survivor." Of importance is that these messages be short and direct, that they place the trauma in the past, and that they give a victim key information that he or she can use to move beyond the trauma experience. The messages may be simple, but they need to be carefully crafted by the client in collaboration with the therapist.

At the next step, the person incorporates these positive messages into the relaxation process. Once a client can reach a state of relaxation while smoothly incorporating the positive messages, he or she should be encouraged to repeat the process at least three times a day. Then the clinician can ask the client to think about the flashback or intrusive memory while in the relaxed state *and* while saying the positive messages — which, by now, should feel quite natural to the client. The therapist may wish to have the client place some form of safe "container" around the flashback or feeling, such as fixing the memory on a video monitor or inside a picture frame or inside a tape recorder or radio. Once the relaxation process and the positive messages are paired with the flashback memory, the person should repeat this procedure with the therapist until he or she is able to experience the flashback in a relaxed state with the positive messages present. The last step is for the client to imagine that the memory will become less intense. For example, the client could imagine the image on a TV screen becoming smaller and smaller, or the volume of the radio being turned lower and lower until it is barely audible.

In summary, the primary focus of these procedures is to teach the victim a skill by which he or she can gain a sense of mastery over some of the more unpleasant symptoms of trauma. Because this process involves close analysis of key moments of the traumatic event itself, it is likely to bring up clinical issues at many levels. Hence, it should be done within the framework of an entire psychotherapy process.

Dream Dynamics

The range of emotions that is manifest during the traumatic event itself is often reflected in the dream processes and sleep patterns of traumatized people. Initially, many trauma victims are only able to sleep for very brief periods of time (15 minutes to an hour), sometimes awakening with a startle response or in a panic that they may be traumatized again. If, after about a week, a traumatized person is sleepless for increasingly longer periods of time, the clinician may wish to consider antidepressant medication at bedtime to help the client sleep enough to function. We have found that sleep deprivation, so common in victims, may seriously exacerbate other symptoms of trauma. Hence, trauma clients rarely begin to be clinically stable until some regularity is achieved in their sleeping patterns.

At first, the dreams of many traumatized people reflect the chaos, terror, and helplessness that were aroused by the traumatic event. Others may block the entire content of the dream because it is too threatening; many awaken with the feeling that they have dreamed something horrible but can't remember what it was. Still others relive the traumatic event in their dreams, often with details of the actual happenings changed: For example, a person who narrowly escaped death in a train accident is killed again and again in various types of crashes in his dreams. Soon, the actual dream content will probably take on symbolic forms that represent issues of survival, betrayal, loss, etc., that were raised by the event. Very rarely, in our experience, do people relive the event itself in their dreams for a long period of time. (In fact, one may begin to suspect that there could be a form of malingering or an exaggeration of symptoms in those who have exactly the same reenactment dream over and over.) Why most people only relive the event in dreams for fairly short periods of time, until the dreams evolve into permutations of the event and then on to more symbolic themes, is not fully understood. Perhaps the psyche simply cannot bear repeating the event while, at the same time, it seeks release for feelings that the event has produced. Therefore, by employing the defense mechanism of repression, it replaces the real with the symbolic.

Often there is a hiatus in the dream process, between the trauma-vulnerability-anxiety dreams and the angry dreams of a later stage. During this interval, a victim may have few or no dreams that relate directly to the event. Then, suddenly, the person starts having violent, sometimes horribly graphic dreams that may catch him or her very much by surprise. In other cases, there is a slower progression through the fear and anxiety dreams to the angrier ones. Frequently, traumatized people are ashamed or afraid of the grisly, gory content of their dreams. Because a victim may be shocked and horrified that such thoughts existed, he or she may hide them from the therapist, wishing to be viewed in a favorable light. Hence, it is wise for the clinician to prepare a client for the likelihood of trauma dreams — especially violent ones — well in advance. It is worth noting that angry, violent dreams, in many cases, begin *before* the victim enters the anger stage of recovery. For that reason, they may be incredibly confusing or frightening to a person who is still in the depressed phase of the cycle. Preparation by the therapist may make it easier for the client to disclose this frightening dream content when it arrives. Violent, angry dreams will probably continue for a considerable period of time. During this period, the client may reexperience difficulty in falling asleep because he or she simply dreads the dreams that are to come. The clinician should point out that such dreams are a natural part of catharsis and release.

Some severely traumatized people, such as hostages, victims of war atrocities, and veterans, may suffer from horrific dreams for years; some will have nightmares all their lives. Therapists should warn clients who were the victims of violence to screen, carefully, what they read or watch on popular media: i.e., they should try to avoid television shows or movies that have violent content as well as news stories about violent crime. These sensationalized accounts may prove to be extremely upsetting and result in the recurrence of nightmares. As one young woman, who was an assault victim, put it, "Violent movies are no longer entertaining because I know the true horror [of violence]."

As the client makes progress through the recovery cycle, violent dreams eventually turn to themes of mastery and resolution. When these latter themes emerge, a victim is usually approaching or has entered either the philosophical or the closure stage of recovery.

Repression and Distortion

The strategies described here pertain to repressed or distorted memories. (Techniques for working with adults are presented here, although they are equally applicable to treatment with children or adolescents.) Bringing repressed thoughts to the surface or changing severely distorted memories should be handled with extreme care and sensitivity. A clinician should bear in mind that the trauma victim has blocked an original thought because the psyche could not tolerate the memory. In extreme cases, he or she may have created a different personality to deal with the emotional pain.

Whenever possible, the repressed or distorted memory should be brought to light and worked through consciously. One way of doing this is to present the client with new information about the event, such as when the therapist gave additional facts about his accident to a distraught father (p. 63). If possible, it is best to do this through conscious process (i.e., not by hypnosis), because the client can be a sharing participant in the process and, therefore, will feel more in control. The experience can become one of mastery and thus more deeply corrective. Also, when the process is a conscious one, the therapist can judge whether or not a client's defenses have healed enough for the information to be assimilated fully.

In cases involving blocked or distorted memories in the more distant past, a therapist may wish to find a way to get photos or video and audiotapes that were made of the client at or around the time of the traumatic event. These can be used clinically as a kind of chronological probe to help retrieve lost or to revise distorted traumatic memories.

It cannot be emphasized too much that a clinician should make absolutely certain that a victim has recovered sufficiently from trauma to have developed functional defenses for coping with newly uncovered information, and that he or she is capable of being a willing participant in this process. Many acutely traumatized people do not know how to express to a therapist that they are not ready to deal with certain thoughts and feelings. Also, some traumatized people slip easily into a victim role or adopt a form of learned helplessness, in which they automatically tend to defer to those in authority—out of fear. If the person is not ready for the process of revealing traumatic memories, an experience of doing so will not be one of cathartic release; instead, it will amount to trauma at the hands of the therapist.

As noted earlier, one of the keys to helping people recover from trauma is the development of healthy, adaptive defense mechanisms. Once a clinician is certain that the client has developed flexible and functional defenses, so that the repressed thoughts and feelings can be safely brought to the surface, one or more of the following procedures may be employed. If the defenses are not fully functional, the procedures to follow are contraindicated.

The "structured form of hypnosis" that was described earlier in this chapter can be very useful in helping victims recall blocked traumatic memories. In this process, a therapist "takes" the person back to a specific time, to reexperience specific aspects of the traumatic event. In doing so, the therapist must be careful to bring forth only as much repressed material as the client is capable of comfortably processing. Often, counterphobic clients will push clinicians to delve into blocked memories prematurely, insisting that they want to "remember it all right now." Clinicians should *not* comply with such urgings, because the client's insistence is more rooted in maladaptive defense mechanisms such as the counterphobic wish to prove his or her prowess, as opposed to good sense.

Before beginning an hypnotic technique, a therapist should tell the client what information will be used, during the trance, to help him or her sort out the memories and deal with them appropriately. In this way, introducing the information during the trance state (which, by nature, involves concrete thinking) will not startle or confuse. Ideally, the new, higher-level information that is needed for understanding and resolution will be smoothly folded into the experience of retrieving the memories, with as little dissonance as possible. Later, when a therapist brings the person out of the trance, he or she can continue discussing the information on a conscious level until it has been fully integrated. In the case of the severely traumatized client, the therapist may have to break traumatic memories down into very small segments, so that the person will be able to cope with each one in turn.

An example of the use of hypnosis is that of an 11-year-old boy, Mark, who was referred for treatment three years after his mother was killed in a car accident. His father had been driving, his mother had been in the front passenger seat, and he had been playing in the backseat. The father first consulted a therapist because the boy's teacher had become concerned when she and other teachers noticed that his behavior had been "deteriorating" since the accident. At first, the teachers attributed his withdrawn, sullen behavior to grief, and thought that he would eventually "come out of it." Instead, it got progressively worse. Mark's personal hygiene became so neglected that the other children teased him and refused to play with him. His school work went from above-average to barely passing. Before the accident, Mark had lots of energy and a quick, bright sense of humor. Since the accident, his color had become poor and he had lost a significant amount of weight. When teachers tried to speak to him, he would look at them blankly and then look away or walk away.

The therapist first met with Mark's father alone to get a history. The father said he felt extremely guilty for not noticing that Mark was having emotional difficulties. He had been overwhelmed by the loss of his wife and his own physical recovery, as well as with being a single parent to two children (Mark had a younger sister who had not been in the car). He did not realize that Mark had such severe problems until the teacher spoke to him. He thought that, because it had been three years since the accident, Mark's behavior was just part of the difficult preteen period and would "pass."

When the clinician asked Mark's father to describe the accident, he said that it had happened after a fairly long drive. Mark, who had been playing in the backseat, was "getting a bit rambunctious" out of boredom; he had had to scold Mark several times to get him to be quiet. Suddenly, a truck swerved and hit the car on the passenger side. The car flipped and rolled several times, eventually coming to rest on the passenger side. As Mark's father spoke of the horror of this moment, the therapist could see that he was still traumatized because, as he described the event, he seemed to be reliving parts of the accident.

He had struggled to free himself and Mark from inside the car. His wife was pinned and unconscious. Although he and Mark were both badly hurt, they tried to free Mark's mother. Finally, he said, he lost consciousness and came to when the paramedics arrived. Mark was screaming and holding onto his dead mother; he had to be forcibly removed from her body. Mark's father lost consciousness again, and the next thing he remembered was being in a local hospital.

Mark had been an outgoing, pleasant child before the accident. He was a good student, was popular, and had never had any problems. As the therapist listened to the father's account of the traumatic event, it became clear that he had not recovered from the tragic loss of his wife, and probably wasn't able to be "present," emotionally, to help his child. The therapist also suspected that there was probably some unresolved issue (or issues) from the accident that was the cause of Mark's current problems.

When the therapist met with Mark, later that week, he appeared as his teachers had described him. He was clearly depressed and made little eye contact; he was thin and had dark circles under tired-looking eyes. He was quite uncommunicative, but the therapist was able to get a brief history from him, as well as his recollections of the event. He remembered nothing before or during the accident. He "sorta woke up" when the paramedics were pulling him off his mother. Then, he woke up again in the hospital. As he spoke, his voice was flat and emotionless; he looked at the floor.

The therapist took note of the boy's lack of memory of events before the accident; this was somewhat unusual. She recalled that his father had reprimanded him just before, and decided to look into this further. She felt, as well, that she should find out the exact details of the accident, because she was concerned that some misplaced sense of guilt or responsibility might be a clue to understanding the boy's trauma response. The source of this guilt probably had become repressed by the shock of the accident.

In the initial therapy sessions, she engaged the boy in interpretive play therapy. He was not directly communicative, but would obediently play card or board games with the therapist. As they played, she interspersed comments to the effect that some children experience grief and loss, but others mistakenly feel responsible when they have lost a parent. During this period, the father became involved in a survivor's support group, as well as a course of brief, focused individual therapy. The positive results of the father's therapy were quite readily evident, and he was able to be more responsive to Mark. When the therapist inquired into specific details of the accident, she learned that the driver of the truck had lost control of his vehicle, which slammed directly into the car in which Mark and his parents were riding. There was nothing anyone in the car could have done to avoid the accident. The driver of the truck had been prosecuted for driving under the influence of alcohol.

As the clinician continued to meet with Mark, she had parent meetings with his father. During these meetings, she worked on persuading the father to be more helpful and attentive with Mark's dress, hygiene, and homework. She also asked the father to talk with the boy about the accident periodically; he was to convey the idea that he was open to talking about the accident, or to answering any questions Mark might have. She told the father how important it was that he speak of the accident as a terrible external event that happened to the family, that nothing any of them did could have caused it or prevented it. The accident was the truck driver's fault and the court had convicted him for it.

Mark continued to improve over the next few weeks. He was much more communicative with the therapist. He began to comment on some aspects of the accident, as well as his mother's death, at an age-appropriate level. He shared some of his dreams with the therapist; most involved themes of his doing something to cause or his being responsible for some awful, catastrophic event. Mark continued to have no memory of the accident. When he engaged in projective play activities (sand tray, drawing) that might have drawn unconscious thoughts and feelings to the surface, his affect was flat and robot-like. The therapist felt that the key to eventual resolution lay in his repressed memory of the traumatic event and what immediately preceded it.

Because Mark had made good progress in the first three months of therapy, he now had more functional defenses available to him. In addition, his father was now much more helpful to him as a source of emotional support, and was working in conjunction with the therapist to help Mark resolve his conflicts. When the clinician broached the possibility of helping Mark to remember events before and during the accident that he had been unable to recall, his attitude toward the suggestion was markedly different than before. In earlier discussions, he would reiterate that he couldn't, and then give a clear message that the subject was closed. If anyone pressed the point, he would refuse to talk and look away. This time, when the therapist brought up the subject, he replied that he was "sorta scared" but wanted to know what happened, because, "It's weird, not knowing."

Mark's shift in attitude told the therapist that he was ready to deal with the repressed content. She described the procedure, including the type of hypnotic induction to be used and exactly how much of the accident he would review during it, namely, just up to the point of impact. Then, because the traumatic memory would involve so much pain and feelings of loss for Mark, the therapist provided some added distance and protection for Mark: She told him that visual images would be seen on a video monitor; if Mark wished, he could make his memories larger, smaller, or turn them off. She added that, when the accident happened, Mark was a little boy playing in the backseat of a car; he could not have caused or prevented the accident. She repeated this theme until she was sure that he understood it—at least intellectually.

At the next session, Mark said again that he was willing to go ahead with the hypnotic process. The therapist used an Ericksonian story-telling injunction that took Mark into a light trance. As hypnosis progressed, she interspersed the same information that she had given Mark in the previous session, i.e., that as a little boy playing in the backseat of the car, nothing he could have done before or during the accident could have prevented it from occurring or changed its outcome.

While he was in a light trance, the therapist took Mark back to the time, well before the accident, when he had begun playing in the backseat. She asked Mark to tell her what happened to him in words; as he did so, she continued to reassure him and to intersperse information. What surfaced during this first hypnotic session was that Mark had been playing noisily. His father scolded him and told him he was being so noisy that he could not concentrate on his driving. Within a few moments, the horrible event occurred. Mark believed that his loud play had distracted his father and caused the accident. This belief was so impossible to accept that it and the rest of the accident had become encapsulated and repressed. When Mark remembered this, the therapist was able to refocus his attention to the true facts of the traumatic event. At this point, she brought him out of the trance and helped him to reflect on what he had recalled.

After the session in which the repressed memory was retrieved, Mark's therapy became even more productive. He was able to participate more intensively, and soon it was clear that he was beginning to move toward resolution. Mark's repetitive nightmares began to subside and he reported spontaneous recollections of the day of the accident. After three more hypnotic sessions, he was able to recall it completely. Subsequently, he continued in play therapy as well as some family systems work, before gaining final resolution of the trauma. He was in therapy for about ten months altogether, but he may need to return briefly when he is an adolescent and begins driving a car himself.

In some more complicated cases of the trauma response, clinicians may need to spend considerable time with the person to reveal and resolve unconscious memories through this hypnotic process. In other cases, one or two hypnotic sessions may be sufficient to unlock the memory bank, so that many of the repressed thoughts and feelings can come to the surface in an ordinary course of therapy.

It should be emphasized that these kinds of interventions are *not* to be used with victims who are "flooded" with traumatic memories or are experiencing intense flashbacks. Using hypnosis or inducing "abreaction" with people in this condition can actually worsen their suffering. It has been our experience that the cognitive/behavioral approaches that are described in Chapter IV are more appropriate for symptoms such as "flooding" and flashbacks of overwhelming proportions.

Guilt and Shame

In addition to agonizing about their inability to prevent the traumatic event or feeling that they are somehow being punished for past misdeeds, many traumatized people feel immense emotional pain because others suffered more than they did, or died during the event while they were spared. Therapists need to be extremely sensitive to this kind of issue. For example, one should be careful not to comment on how fortunate the person is to be alive or to have been spared more serious injury, lest by doing so the person is silenced or further shamed. Here is another instance in which one must use the traumatized person's view of the event and its reasons for occurring as a starting point. A therapist should be especially mindful of the possibility of survivor guilt in trauma victims who cannot move beyond the depressed stage (see Chapter IV, Figure 4.1). Further, this form of guilt may lurk beneath the surface when traumatized people engage in risk-taking or self-destructive behavior.

Issues of guilt, shame, and responsibility will surface many times and in many ways during the recovery process. Each time they do, the clinician will be called upon to help the victim cope with them. It has been our experience that traumatized people are rarely able to lay these issues to rest until they are past the anger stage of the recovery process and well into the philosophical stage.

Mood Swings

The mood swings stage of the recovery cycle is a confusing and turbulent time for trauma victims. Although the clinician, who is aware of the changes that occur in recovery, views this stage in a more positive light because it is one in which the client's depression is breaking apart, the person who experiences it finds little solace because it often feels as though he or she is on an emotional roller coaster. The victim catches a glimpse of psychological stability, feels good for a while, thinks, "I'm finally through the horror." Then, something happens, and the person is slammed back down into the grey pit of depression. Many fear that, once back in the depressed state, they will never be able to climb out again. During this stage, clients require a lot of reassurance because they often have the sensation that they are about to lose their minds. A therapist should look upon the turbulence of this period as an early warning sign of the arrival of the anger stage.

Anger

The anger stage often arrives quite suddenly, much like an eruption, catching family, friends, and lovers quite by surprise if they are unprepared, because this period usually begins long after the traumatic event ended. So, when the victim's anger finally surfaces, the significant others in the victim's life have probably worked through much of the trauma themselves and often want the "horrible thing" to be "over and done with." This lack of synchronicity between the arrival of the traumatized person's anger and the state of mind of significant others can frequently lead to painful conflict and misunderstanding. For this reason it is wise, as noted earlier, for clinicians to meet with significant others very early on, to educate them about the various stages as well as the probable length of the recovery process. Certainly, the therapist should meet with them before the anger stage if possible, because they will need considerable guidance and support through this difficult but necessary time.

The therapist's role during this crucial period is to help the trauma victim to articulate and vent his or her anger in an appropriate manner. In this way, the client will avoid the experience of further pain caused by damaging important personal, social, and professional relationships through hostile outbursts. As one victim put it, "Sometimes I want to say and do horrible things, but I don't want to hurt anybody." Many trauma clients are sufficiently aware of their angry impulses, having had preparation for them in therapy, to be able to redirect these impulses into the therapy process and, thus, deflect them away from key people in their lives. Nevertheless, some clients need to be monitored *very* carefully, because they could lose control and harm someone, or previously unresolved identification with the aggressor could surface and lead to violent acting-out.[1] One should never underestimate the amount of rage and pain in need of expression that is characteristic of this period. It is the task of the therapist to utilize his or her clinical skills to see to it that this anger is channeled in such a way that, when released, it leads to healing and recovery rather than to further calamity.

Traumatic anger is a form of free-floating rage that seeks out objects to attach itself to. There is often a logic to the choice of an object as the target of this emotion; in other instances, it can be a pure, amorphous wish for vengeance. Some victims may fear their own aggressive impulses and utilize obsessive-compulsive rituals as a defense against them. Others withdraw socially, because they fear that they may lose control in a social situation. An example of this is a rape victim, normally a quiet, soft-spoken young woman, who became nearly agoraphobic as a result of the following incident: She was leaving a store with two friends, when a male passerby whistled at her and made some suggestive, inappropriate remarks about her figure. Suddenly, she ran after the man, screaming obscenities and shouting that he had no right to assault her. She had to be physically

[1]It is a serious clinical error to assume that, because a person has been the victim of a violent traumatic event, he or she would not act out to harm others. This is simply not the case, especially if the victim of violence leaves treatment suddenly, is self-medicating with drugs or alcohol, or has suffered an injury that bears a stigma or doesn't evoke sympathy.

restrained by her friends to keep her from attacking the man. When she
had calmed down sufficiently, she was so horrified by this loss of control
that she refused to leave her house except to go to work.

The anger of some trauma clients is more predictable when it is focused
on the cause (or symbol of the cause) of the traumatic event. An example is
that of a woman who was held hostage on a plane when she was on her way
to visit her native country. She had once taken great pleasure in traveling,
and particularly enjoyed going home. After the hijacking, she developed a
vehement dislike for anything associated with the native country—people,
food, customs, and clothing. She broke off all relationships with people she
had known there, even relatives. She also developed an almost paranoid
hatred of big businesses, which she associated with the airline. Her belief
was that the hijackers were able to gain entry to the plane because the
airline, "a big business," had been too cheap to provide adequate security.

Many victims express intense rage at those persons or institutions who,
they perceive, were "failed protectors": e.g., an airline that did not keep
hijackers off its plane, the police who could not catch a perpetrator, the
district attorney who failed to convict a criminal, manufacturers of the
auto that malfunctioned, the flood control system that failed, the spouse or
lover who was not there to protect the person at a crucial moment. The
failed protector category can incorporate almost anyone. Even if the protectors did, in reality, all they possibly could have done, this logic is rarely
appreciated by a trauma victim at the outset of the anger stage. It will be
the task of the clinician to help the client, eventually, to adopt this logic.

Of course, certain victims did, in fact, suffer because of the negligence
or inattention of others. In cases in which there was an actual failure to
protect, the client's anger may follow a much longer course. Sometimes it
can be helpful if this anger is directed toward a legal resolution. Even so, a
therapist should be quite careful about how this is done, because if the
traumatized persons' anger is unleashed inappropriately in the legal system, that strategy can bring even more pain and humiliation. In our experience, clinicians who are unschooled in the realities of the legal system may
unintentionally encourage a victim to have unrealistic expectations about
legal retaliation; they may, in the short run, enable their clients to vent
some anger, but do harm in the long run. For a complete discussion of a
therapist's role in this process, see Chapter XII.

If legal redress is not available to the trauma victim, a clinician may wish
to direct the person toward symbolic forms of release within the therapeutic process itself. For example, a therapist may use the guided fantasy
technique or a structured hypnotic process, in which those who were negligent or directly responsible for the trauma are "brought to justice." A
client may also be invited to utilize the empty chair technique to say what
needs to be said to those who have wronged him or her. If a version of

psychodrama involving other people is used, the clinician should be sure that the victim is in sufficient control of his or her impulses so that no one gets hurt in the process. The client's need for revenge and meting out punishment is most powerful during this angry period and its expression should be carefully monitored.

Acts of nature such as tornadoes, floods, and earthquakes also raise complicated questions regarding guilt, blame, and punishment. Sometimes, victims of natural disasters are able to bond together in a support system that may permit them to see the disaster as the tragic whim of fate. But, more often, the anger is displaced onto builders, planners, and other public officials who, they believe, could have or should have done more than they did.

Traumatized people have a powerful need to see those who were responsible for the traumatic event punished. If the retaliation of "an eye for an eye" is not possible, a victim may displace these angry feelings onto safe objects such as friends, relatives, spouses, or lovers. This is another situation in which a therapist may need to involve people who were not victims in the treatment process, because in many cases they may not understand why, a long time after the traumatic event, the victim is suddenly "turning" on them. Often, and rightly so, significant others feel that they are being unfairly treated by the traumatized person, when this rage or need to punish reaches them. In such instances, the support and guidance of a therapist can help these people to realize that even anger is a part of the process of recovery; it will pass, and they needn't take the attacks personally.

Displaced anger may take a form in which the victim has very limited tolerance for being told what to do or for allowing another person to have any control over him or her. One of the reasons for this intolerance is a core element of the trauma experience, namely the sensation of total helplessness and loss of control. Hence, if the victim believes that someone is attempting to control him or her in some way during the anger stage, there is a possibility that he or she will lash out at the other person. This may even be the case in situations in which the person has made a request of the victim in very reasonable, polite terms. For example, one evening a young man who had been the victim of a brutal armed robbery was leaving his house to do some shopping. As he left, his wife said, "Dear, while you are at the store, could you pick up some laundry soap and bleach? We're almost out." At once, he angrily turned on his wife and yelled, "You are so thoughtless and inconsiderate. How dare you take advantage of me. You are always taking advantage of me with your thoughtlessness," slamming the door on his way out. As the man recounted the incident during therapy, he said that he had not heard the request as polite. What he experienced was that someone was again trying to control him and he had to fight back. He added that, when it happened, he was convinced he was right: trying to reason with him at the moment would have been useless. Not until several hours after the incident did he realize that his reaction had been totally inappropriate. Such outbursts of displaced rage are very common with trauma clients and, if significant relationships are to survive intact, they usually require the significant other to participate in the client's treatment, so that such behavior can be put into perspective.

Some other forms of trauma-induced rage may appear even more irrational but are, nonetheless, very logical to the victim during the anger stage. Some people will be quite ashamed of such irrational eruptions, while others feel justified in their rage. For example, a victim may feel anger toward those who died during the traumatic event because they "abandoned" him or her. Conversely, clients may feel an unacknowledged resentment toward those who were not injured or traumatized to the degree that they were.

This angry period, naturally difficult or even painful for the traumatized person as well as the significant people in his or her life, will pass in time. Eventually, the person will move toward the philosophizing stage that precedes closure.

Philosophizing and Closure

Most victims need to pass the anniversary date of the traumatic event, especially if their trauma was severe, before they can begin to bring the trauma response to closure. Often it is only after this anniversary (or subsequent anniversaries) that a victim can begin to move outside of the experience and see it as something that *happened to* him or her, but that fell short of being an overwhelming or engulfing experience. In order to achieve closure, a victim's defenses must be rebuilt. Further, the person's cognitive processes must be sufficiently restored so that he or she can think abstractly enough to observe himself or herself as an object. In that way, one can see oneself in relation to the event and to the others who were involved in it. This process of externalizing the traumatic event as something that happened to (past tense, passive voice) the person is the talisman that permits entrance to the last stages of recovery. As the trauma client approaches closure, the therapist can help him or her to form a newly realistic and adaptive self-image. The therapy process is vital in shaping the eventual contours of such a self-image, preferably one on which the client can build a healthy future.

In these final stages, it will be useful to reevaluate the victim's own role in the traumatic event — not in a way that will bring up feelings of guilt and shame, but "framed" in a question such as this: What should the person reasonably do to protect himself or herself from future trauma? This is part of the work of rebuilding feelings of self-worth, because one component of a healthy self-concept is self-care and valuing oneself enough to avoid taking unnecessary risks.

Not only do traumatized people come to view themselves differently if they move appropriately through the sequences of the recovery process, they will come to view life differently — as many people do when faced with their own mortality. If handled well clinically, this can be a positive time, when the client looks over his or her values and reassesses what he or she truly wants from life and what life should mean. Through the stage of closure, the person can find new meaning as a survivor, and go on to choose a future path. Some trauma survivors are able to make positive life or career changes out of a renewed sense of value in life. Tragically, not all trauma victims are able to achieve this successful completion of the ordeal. Many struggle with the emotional ravages of trauma for the rest of their lives.

PART THREE
The Different Faces of Trauma

CHAPTER VI
Hidden Trauma

MANY PEOPLE WHO suffer from a past trauma do not disclose this fact to a therapist when they commence therapy. There may be several reasons for this reticence. The client may be ashamed of the event, or may have been urged by family members to forget about it or not talk about it. The memory of trauma may have been diminished in intensity by the defense mechanisms of rationalization or dissociation. Or, the traumatic event may not be consciously available to the person due to the powerful, primitive mechanism of denial.

In another scenario, the person may be displacing anger about a traumatic event onto a "safe" object who is quite dissimilar to the person who inflicted the trauma. Making the issue more complex, there are people who have had prior trauma who may not have defined the events as traumatic. The person may have rationalized it as "a part of life" or accepted it as some form of magical punishment for an imaginary misdeed. For these reasons, a clinician cannot assume that people whose lives may have been horribly scarred by a past trauma will (a) know that they were traumatized or (b) be able to tell a therapist about their experience.

We have found that people tell a therapist much simply by their behavior during the initial stages of therapy. Hence, it is vitally important to be attuned to the panoply of symptoms that a client may display shortly after entering therapy. Therapists should also be sensitive to the fact that many people who have an undisclosed past trauma may have been in therapy, or may even have been hospitalized, in the past. These people may have ambivalent or negative feelings about the value of past treatment. Others who have experienced trauma in the past may be reluctant or involuntary clients who have been forced into treatment by employers, spouses, or courts.

Symptoms That Reveal Hidden Trauma

Discovery of undisclosed past trauma may become possible only after considerable inquiry and analysis. The following are some of the symptoms that are commonly found in cases of this kind. People who have suffered traumatic events in childhood and adolescence frequently display significant memory gaps. It is not uncommon for a person to begin an account of his or her life history at an age considerably older than most people do — for example at eight or nine; or, the person may begin by describing the history in reasonable detail and then skip a significant period of time, as though nothing had taken place during that period. People who have had an undisclosed trauma may also omit an entire sphere of their lives: for example, home life, or work experience during a critical period.

Many clients of the type described here are unaware of these sizable gaps in their histories and may even be surprised or bemused at a clinician who finds such errors of omission significant. An example is that of a woman who was referred to therapy because she began to have severe panic attacks after she was married. Although she could describe her early childhood and entire school history, she had no memory of her home life between the ages of nine and fourteen. When the therapist inquired about this obvious gap, she seemed surprised and said that she simply couldn't remember anything. Then, after pondering for a few moments, she said that it was probably because school was so important to her. But, in the next breath, she said that she had saved enough babysitting money to move to the United States (from another country, thousands of miles away), and that she had been "on my own ever since." When the therapist noted that her parents were both successful professionals and that, in a family such as hers, it would be considered very unusual for a young girl of 14 to be permitted to leave home, she replied that she was very mature for her age. It was only after a considerable time in therapy that the woman could begin to remember the severe abuse that she had suffered at the hands of her parents.

Some people whose childhood or adolescent traumas were not previously disclosed may have had a long-standing history of suicidal, self-destructive, or self-injurious behavior. As noted above, these people may have been in treatment, but the trauma did not come to light. Clinicians should also view those clients who are described as "cutters" with suspicion, because their self-inflicted pain and mutilation may be a means to break out of dissociative states that originated long ago in trauma; or, it may be their means to drive away uncontrollable thoughts or impulses connected with the traumatic event.

Those who have an undisclosed past trauma may repeatedly choose abusive mates or abusive employers. These people do not make these choices because they enjoy the abuse in some masochistic fashion. They do so because their earlier traumatic experiences (usually within the family context) have caused them to create an internal construction of reality which, for them, means that to be in a relationship entails being abused. In effect, a past trauma may cause the person to misdefine relationships. Or, he or she may be engaging in a form of repetition compulsion that was initiated by the original trauma.

Ironically, people who suffered past trauma may place themselves in situations similar to the original traumatic one, with the unconscious fantasy that, this time, things will magically work out for the good. This time, they will be protected from trauma; someone will right the original wrong. Such a corrective reenactment seldom occurs. Instead, the person is usually retraumatized and, in addition, labeled as someone who "takes risks," "sets up" himself or herself to be punished, or is masochistic.

Somewhat like the person described above is the person who lives the life-style of the perpetual victim. This person is repeatedly taken advantage of and makes self-defeating life decisions. In many cases, the person was cast in the role of victim of trauma so early in life that his or her fundamental definition of "self" is solely that of victim. When such a self-identity or persona is created at an early stage of development, at a time when the young person has limited linguistic and cognitive capabilities, redefining the self can become a lengthy, complicated process.

In sharp contrast to clients who have the life history of the eternal victim are those who are perfectionistic and driven to succeed. It is a common misconception that those who suffer from trauma become failures in life. On the contrary, many who suffer in this way are driven toward success in an attempt to compensate for their feelings of worthlessness or of being damaged by the traumatic event. It would be a lapse of clinical judgment to be deluded by the client's professional or social success into thinking that he or she could not possibly have been traumatized.

Many people whose trauma has remained hidden have histories of drug and/or alcohol abuse. Some are attempting to self-medicate their anxiety and depression, while others are engaging in a form of self-destructive or risk-taking behavior. When found, substance abuse of this origin must be brought under control before the underlying issues of trauma can be resolved. In addition, we have observed that a large number of anorexics and bulimics have been sexually abused or otherwise maltreated as children. It is a common misconception that eating disorders of this kind are uniquely women's problems. While many men suffer from anorexia or bulimia, such conditions are often masked by involvement in extreme forms of athletic activity, fitness regimens, or faddish diets. Hence, what is seen as a cause for concern in a woman may be dismissed as an overzealous commitment to sports or mere eccentricity in a man.

Many people who have suffered hidden trauma express their emotional pain in psychosomatic ailments. A clinician should be aware that, in many cultures (for example, Hispanic, Middle-eastern, and Asian) it is not acceptable to have emotional problems or to seek psychological treatment; this results from the shadows of stigma cast upon people who are mentally ill (i.e., psychotic). Because there is less stigma associated with having medical problems, one is more likely to see emotional trauma expressed in an array of aches and pains. Clinicians should also be wary that, in some professions that are associated with male prowess, e.g., police work, firefighting, the military, it is also not socially acceptable to express emotional pain or fearfulness. Because some physical injuries that naturally occur to people in these professions are themselves traumatic in nature, one needs to take note that a client who fits in this category may deny the emotional trauma of the injury and express it through an unrelated psychosomatic complaint. A fuller discussion of this subject is presented in Chapter XI, "Trauma in the Workplace."

Some people whose hidden traumas were severe will be found to utilize either the defense of dissociation or of depersonalization. Such primitive defense mechanisms are not under the conscious control of the victim, and they may suddenly surface if the person experiences something reminiscent of, or symbolically akin to, the traumatic event. When this happens, the person may do things for which he or she has little or no memory later. For example, the person may wander or drive around aimlessly or may engage in anti-social behavior.

Antisocial behavior of this origin is often done in such an obvious manner that the person is sure to be caught. By means of the behavior, a traumatized person is acting out infantile rage at parental or other figures who abused, or did not protect him or her; The behavior is patently self-defeating, in that the person will be "punished" for forbidden rage. Self-punishment serves to replicate the abuse.

Reckless driving and shoplifting are common forms of this kind of acting-out. An example would be that of a woman who had been the victim of physical abuse by her parents, and rape by a nonfamily member, when she was a very young girl. She left home at a young age because of the parents' physical abuse of her and her younger sister. She was extremely hardworking and determined to make a success of her life; she worked at two jobs and got her high school diploma. As soon as she had saved enough money, she brought her sister to live with her and put her through high school. She had little conscious memory of the most severe instances of physical abuse, and described the rape as being like "a dream that happened to someone else"; she was 11 when it occurred.

After she left home, the woman pretended that the rape and the abuse had not happened. She was determined to succeed and attempted to be "perfect" in everything she did. Because she avoided conflict at all costs and did everything that she could to accommodate superiors, she was often seen as "the perfect employee." She became very successful professionally and eventually put herself through college.

To all appearances, this woman embodied the true success story of the poor girl who became a successful, respected professional woman. Although everybody liked her, few were close to her, so no one was aware that, outside of work, she had no personal life. Her entire existence consisted of being liked and respected in her profession. But when her industry experienced an economic downturn, she was given the difficult task of "laying off" a number of employees. She accepted the task without complaint and proceeded with the onerous task of dismissing people whom she liked and had worked with closely. Unwittingly, her boss had placed her in the symbolic role of a rejecting and (in light of her own experience) abusive parent. Shortly after starting the dismissal process, she began to spend entire weekends trying to rationalize, to herself, that the task was necessary to cope with the company's current economic difficulties. She began to eat less and less, and found it more and more difficult to sleep. One Saturday afternoon when she had gone to the office, she simply got up from her desk, left the building, and began to drive with no destination in mind.

Eventually, she arrived at a shopping center and found herself walking from shop to shop. When she entered a department store, she began randomly to pick up certain things and put them into her purse and her pockets. She made no attempt to conceal her actions, and was eventually stopped by the store detective. She had taken a strange assortment of small items, most of which she could have no use for; their value was about $400. When the detective stopped and questioned her, she seemed to be in a daze. She said that she did not remember taking anything, but when she was confronted with the things in her possession, she said, "I must have taken them." She was arrested and charged. Later, when she retained an attorney and told him the details of the theft, he suggested that she undergo a psychological examination. At first, she strongly resisted the idea, but the attorney was eventually able to persuade her to accept being evaluated. It was during the evaluation that her past abuse came to light.

It is significant that not all victims who go into dissociative states of this sort are aware of the fact that they do so; it may require an observant clinician to discover them. For example, one of the person's significant others may be puzzled about how he or she obtained certain objects; in some cases, the person may even say, in a perplexed or nonchalant way, that he or she does not know where they came from. There may be blocks of time that the person cannot account for; there may be people who recognize the person whom he or she does not know. Other victims may be frightened or anxious because there are periods of time that they cannot account for or during which they had been only partially conscious. The woman who was described above spoke of her shoplifting incident in this way: "It was as though I was in a cloud. I could hardly see people. I was only vaguely aware that there were people around me. It was almost euphoric, while at the same time deeply frightening." Some clients, like this woman, may have no idea what triggered a dissociative episode.

The most extreme form of "splitting-off" is the development of a multiple personality. Once believed to be a rare disorder, multiple personality is now considered to be more common than previously thought. In such cases, some of the original trauma response may be known to the person, but much of it is hidden within the other personalities. Here the traumatic event may have been so horrifying that the person has survived by creating another personality; if the event occurs in the "other" person's life, the primary personality is protected. Because these people have, in many cases, been repeatedly and brutally traumatized, there can be several hidden sub-personalities.

Although cases of multiple personality are fascinating, they should only be treated by experienced clinicians who have specific training in working with this disorder. There are times when people who suffer from multiple personality disorder can be dangerous to themselves or others. They may require medication or hospitalization and very skilled treatment.

The case described above is typical of those in which traumatized people develop a style of personality that is extremely accommodating to other people. Sometimes they do this because they cannot tolerate any form of conflict. In other instances, they automatically assume the victim role in a wide variety of situations. Some develop passive-aggressive tactics that can be extremely self-defeating and annoying, as a highly nonfunctional means of fighting back.

Clinicians should also view with suspicion those who are only able to have brief, promiscuous liaisons, but are unable to form healthy, lasting attachments. They may speak of healthy, responsive people who are interested in them as "boring" or "uninteresting." This is another instance in which behavior suggestive of trauma may draw clinical attention more rapidly in the case of a woman than that of a man. It is our experience that many men hide the scars of a traumatic childhood under behavior such as this; because of sex-role stereotyping, the behavior is often dismissed rather than viewed as a response to trauma.

People like the woman described above may present quite a puzzle because, although they appear to possess all the qualities necessary to form close, lasting friendships and love relationships, they live socially isolated lives that are devoid of both friends and love. They will rationalize that close relationships are not possible because their careers are so important; or, they may have a list of vague, disconnected reasons about why their lives are so empty. Others are dismayed that, just when a relationship becomes serious, they become disinterested or "panic" and have an inexplicable desire to be free. When they enter therapy, they may be genuinely perplexed about why these "serious" relationships simply never work out. Because of their past traumatic experiences at the hands of a loved or trusted person, these people do not realize that, on an unconscious level, they equate love and/or trust with trauma.

Similarly, many people who were abused by family members may enter into couples therapy because they do not want children and their spouses do. In some cases, they thought that they wanted children when courting, but once married they become quite anxious about the subject and seem to change their minds for no apparent reason. Others may exhibit signs of panic, anxiety, or depression when they learn that they are to become a parent, or when their child approaches the age when they, themselves, were abused.

Sudden personality changes, changes in life-style or values can also be telltale signs of a hidden trauma when they surface in adult life. Emergence of these symptoms can plunge the person into a sort of existential crisis that, if not understood by those around him or her (as is frequently the case), can create a ripple effect that may compound the original trauma. For example, a man in his late 40s had a long, stable marriage and four children. Most people who knew him would describe him as a quiet, conservative person who earned a good living, was cautious with money, and put the needs of his children before his own.

One day, this man was injured on the job. Although his physical injuries were not serious, they required a fairly lengthy recovery period involving protracted immobilization. By nature, this man did not talk a great deal about his emotions and tended to minimize or to dismiss problems. No one thought much of it when he responded to his accident in a rather stoic manner. After he returned to work, his wife noticed that, although he was normally a very moderate drinker, he was beginning to drink more and more. He began to come home late, preferring to stay with friends in bars. Shortly thereafter, without consulting his wife, he purchased a flashy new car. As his behavior became more and more erratic, the wife attempted to talk to him and was summarily dismissed by statements such as, "I'll do what I like for once" or "It's none of your business." Such angry statements from a husband who was usually even-tempered and logical both frightened and saddened her.

Eventually, fearing that her husband was having an affair and their 20-

year marriage was in jeopardy, she consulted a therapist. At first, her husband refused to see the clinician with her, but eventually he agreed to attend a few meetings. As the therapist was taking a history of the couple's married life, she became suspicious that the husband's injury on the job had been a catalyst for the couple's current marital problems. She announced that she would like to see the husband for a few sessions alone, so that she could, as she put it, "more fully appreciate your side and your concerns."

During these initial individual sessions, the therapist was very careful about how she approached the suspected traumatic event. As she and the husband spoke, it became clear that his accident on the job, although not that serious physically, had been terrifying. When it happened, he believed that he and a co-worker were going to die. Even though he survived, the accident caused him to face his own mortality and to accept the fact that he was in a dangerous profession. By nature, he was a person who repressed or rationalized away emotions, and because he was in a profession in which it was not acceptable to admit fear, he tried to put it out of his mind. Even so, underneath it all, every day that he went to work he was terrified. The fear that he experienced at work became transferred to his family life and resurfaced in the form of free-floating dissatisfaction and a compulsive desire to "have fun now." This case exemplifies how a trauma response can "migrate" beneath the surface and express itself as behavioral change in another sphere of the person's life.

People may hide past traumas not only because of their being horrific and painful, but also because they are ashamed of what they had to do to survive. This is frequently the case with survivors of war atrocities, people who have been taken hostage, and some victims of sex crimes or domestic violence. As noted above, it is essential for a clinician to be in touch with countertransference issues, so that he or she can assume a nonjudgmental position that clearly conveys to the victim that the clinician accepts what the person had to do to survive. Even if a clinician takes such a position, the whole story may take a very long time to be told, and the therapist should be prepared to be "tested" from time to time by the victim.

Many people whose traumas were hidden are misdiagnosed as having borderline or histrionic personality disorders, or even as being psychotic. On the surface, the person's behavior may appear to be the acting-out of a character disorder, when, in reality, it may be the person's attempt to show what was done to him or her. In cases of those who were traumatized as very young children, such behavior may be a response to trauma that was internalized as part of a definition of "self," rather than true antisocial or self-destructive impulses. We believe it essential that careful differentiation be made in diagnosing a personality disorder as opposed to the response to past unresolved trauma. Treatment for trauma differs markedly from treatment for a personality disorder. Treatment of the latter requires structure, containment, and, at times, confrontation. In a sense, to employ these tactics with people who suffer from undisclosed trauma could be considered a form of psychotherapeutic abuse. By this, we do not imply that a therapist should never impose structure upon a traumatized person; sometimes it is necessary or essential, but it needs to be done in quite a different manner.

Our experience is that psychotic reactions to trauma are rare. When they do appear after a traumatic event, the person may have suffered from a serious psychological condition for a long time before the event, in which case trauma has exacerbated this condition. There may be a history of psychotic breaks that went untreated. A third possibility is that there was a past hidden trauma for which the present traumatic event became the last straw. When a psychosis develops for the latter reason, the past trauma usually was felt during childhood and was severe.

The following is an example of a psychotic reaction. A woman was in a fairly serious automobile accident with her two children. Their injuries were serious and painful but not life-threatening. The mother suffered numerous broken bones and skeletal injuries that caused her to be fitted with several uncomfortable casts, as well as being placed in traction. Her children were also hospitalized, but they soon were released and recovered as well as could be expected. As the mother remained in the hospital, she became more and more despondent. She ate less and less and eventually refused to eat at all, claiming that she wanted to die. At first, the hospital staff believed that she was responding to the effects of the accident and to being separated from her injured children. When repeated visits by the children did not have a positive impact on her depression, the hospital staff became deeply concerned. By the time the victim recovered from her injuries sufficiently to be released from the hospital, her despondency had become so severe that she was transferred to the psychiatric ward of the hospital. She still was not eating; she claimed that she wanted to die by her own hand, so that she could at least be in control of how she died. She repeatedly had horrific nightmares of being trapped in various situations, usually encased in metal, and dying an excruciating death. At other times, she had dreams of her death by various forms of suffocation.

When the woman was admitted to the psychiatric ward, a detailed history was taken. She had no record of depression or suicidal behavior. She had good work and academic records, as confirmed by her family. She was a popular person who got along well with her family and friends, and had been thought of as the ideal single parent. Her first marriage had been a disappointment, but she and her husband had had a relatively amicable divorce. She was a healthy person who had not suffered any prior traumatic injuries. Her only other serious medical experience was being hospitalized for polio when she was very young. She noted that she had been so young that she could hardly remember it.

This client remained somewhat of a clinical puzzle. After about two weeks, she still refused to eat and claimed that she wanted to die by her own hand. Only with coaxing and pleading by her sons would she consent to eat anything. The inpatient staff asked that an evaluation of the woman be done by a therapist who specialized in trauma cases. When the specialist reviewed the woman's history, she decided to interview her in more depth about her early hospitalization for polio. The woman again described this hospitalization in a fairly matter-of-fact way, saying that it wasn't terribly bad, and, besides, she hardly remembered much of it because she was so young. She added that the specialist could ask her older sister and mother about this hospitalization, because they would remember the details better than she.

When the specialist interviewed the woman's sister and mother, a very different picture of her earlier hospitalization emerged. Both the sister and mother described her struggle with polio as a horrible time when, on several occasions, she almost died. They said that the reason the family moved to America was so that they could obtain the medical care necessary to save her life. Her mother described, with considerable emotion, how the young child at times had to be restrained; eventually, she was confined to an iron lung. The mother said that her daughter was a good child who tried to cooperate with the doctors; but, because she was so young, she could not understand why the doctors and nurses did so many painful and frightening things to her. As the specialist listened to the details of this early hospitalization, the client's dreams of suffocation and dying in a metal container began to make sense. The specialist then engaged the woman in a course of treatment that was aimed at bringing the original trauma to light by means of hypnosis, education, and supportive therapy. Once the original trauma had been brought to light, the woman was able to work it through and to achieve closure.

WHY SILENCE?

People hide past traumas for both conscious and unconscious reasons. If a therapist is to uncover these hidden traumas, he or she must be prepared to accept that the traumatized person's reason for hiding the trauma was a valid one. If the therapist does not grasp this initial premise and start with the victim's reality, it is unlikely that the person will go on to reveal much about the hidden trauma. Some people hide past traumas because they feel ashamed or guilty. Others hide trauma because of a sort of defensive logic that goes this way: "If I pretend it didn't happen or don't tell anyone, it will go away." Still others are able to lock the past trauma away in a time capsule of denial, repression, or dissociation. Some hide past traumas because speaking about them brings back the pain and horror. Others fall prey to certain commonsense myths that serve to silence trauma victims and to protect people close to them. The themes of such myths are: "If [he or she] does not talk about it [he or she] will forget it" or "[He or She] is so young that [he or she] will forget about it." In effect, the victim's family and friends may be able to put it out of their minds. But if the traumatized person is not able to, he or she will be left in silence, struggling with a hidden wound.

A further complication is that many people who are traumatized at a very early age may not possess the cognitive ability or verbal skills necessary to express their response to trauma at the time; hence, an erroneous or distorted meaning of the event may emerge. For a more complete discussion of this issue, see Chapter VII on the traumatized child or adolescent.

The work of Lister (1982, p. 875) revealed that many therapists perpetuate the silence of victims whose trauma was hidden, writing of:

> ... technical errors or countertransference phenomena [including] 1) a focus on intrapsychic processes at the expense of attention to external realities, 2) subtle insinuations that 'if something happened, perhaps you set it up,' 3) frankly overlooking material that relates to violence, threats, or fear of violence and 4) refusal to entertain the possibility that what we are being told may literally have happened. The frequency of these and similar phenomena reflect how painful it can be for us to confront and empathetically experience the extremities of man's capacity for sadism or helpless suffering.

As noted in Chapter V, transference issues must be handled with extreme sensitivity with trauma victims in general; but, in a case in which the person suffers from a hidden trauma, the transference relationship takes on even greater vitality and complexity. The therapist may be cast into myriad roles, impersonating people totally unknown to him or her. The victim may engage in a game characterized by various maneuvers and acting-out episodes, in an attempt to manipulate the therapist into abandoning, disappointing, or in some other symbolic way abusing him or her once more. This behavior may take the form of overt sexual advances or other provocations intended to draw the therapist out of the professional role and into some form of personal relationship.

Suffice it to say that therapists need to keep professional boundaries extremely clear, while at the same time nurturing and supporting the trauma victim. The client's testing and acting-out may take the form of the risk-taking behavior that was described previously in Chapter V. Frequently, just when the therapist is beginning to make progress toward bringing a suspected hidden trauma to light, the client may act out. Frustrating as such behavior may be, this acting-out will best be handled clinically as described in Chapter V.

In review, the therapist may be called upon to solve a riddle, to dispel a myth. And, as vexing as acting-out behavior and transference issues are, they must be worked through patiently and resolved. The therapist may be asked to play the parts of all the failed protectors, those who did not understand, or even those who may have caused the traumatic event. And, until the clinician has been cast into roles of this kind, and has created a corrective experience within the therapy process, the victim of past trauma may not be able to confront it.

When the Pact of Silence Is Made

Because, in many cases, trauma responses that are hidden were reactions to events that occurred when the victims were young children, an event is registered according to the cognition and affect of the child at the age when it occurred. A victim may be unaware of this and believe that he or she is dealing with the situation solely by means of the rational processes of an adult. Others, in approaching the issue of hidden trauma, become shivering, terrified children in facing the specter of an abuser. As the trauma emerges, the room may be filled with the shadow-figures of past tormentors. At the moment of remembering, these people become very real and menacing once more. For example, recollections of war atrocities can suddenly become alive again in all their horror.

Before a victim will be strong enough to confront past trauma, he or she must be secure within the supportive matrix of a healthy therapeutic process; the person must have built a stronger internal core and developed more functional defense mechanisms than were present at the critical time. The person will likely have tested the therapist to insure, at the moment when the god of silence is to be defied, that the therapist will be a faithful guide through the ensuing storm. Not only does the victim need to know that the clinician will stand by and not be shocked or disgusted by what happened, he or she needs to be assured that the clinician can control this process of breaking silence should the need arise.

WHEN THE MEMORIES COME

In cases of severe trauma such as that caused by sexual abuse, physical abuse, or torture, a therapist should consider the fact that when memories come they may not have a visual component: The memory may be of smells or sounds. Even so, these media of memory can be powerfully stimulating and, in fact, may appear to be hallucinations to the untrained observer. At the first encounter with buried pain, the person may exhibit other false signs of psychosis because of the intensity of this catharsis.

An example of how the recollection of trauma can give the appearance of a psychotic process is that of a woman who was kidnapped and held prisoner for almost a year when she was young. During her imprisonment, she was physically and sexually tortured in the most sadistic ways imaginable. She was able to escape, but even the escape was horrific because it occurred during a period of civil war in her country, and it took her almost eight months to be reunited with her family. Because her health was fragile, the family arranged for her and her brother to come to live with relatives in the United States. Here, she went through a period of adjustment, but her health improved rapidly.

Because it was extremely important to the family that she and her brother continue their educations, the woman focused all her energies on learning the new language. She had very few friends outside of the relatives who lived in this country, who had no idea about her having been tortured. They simply thought that she was a good girl who was dedicated to her studies. The only thing that was strange in her behavior was that she ate practically nothing, even though she was already very thin and despite the fact that they constantly encouraged her to eat. Moreover, she rarely slept more than two hours at a time. She was frequently found wandering around the family home or sitting alone, staring off into space. Although she was a kindly, polite girl, she always kept a distance from people, even family members, and was clearly uncomfortable about being touched in any way. Another oddity was that she frequently needed to consult the family's doctor about one gastrointestinal complaint after another.

The family was understanding about the woman's unusual behavior, because they knew that she and her brother had experienced hard times during the war, and because of the separation from their parents and others in the home country. Eventually, the woman's parents were able to come to America—the family was overjoyed. They thought that, with the parents' arrival, some of her strange behavior would stop. It did not: in some aspects, it became worse. She became obsessed that there was something wrong with her stomach.

The woman was sent to a series of specialists, whose results were invariably negative. At one point, the family physician, who was aware of the war conditions in her home country, asked the parents if anything had happened to her there. They sadly replied that they did not know: She had been mysteriously separated from them for almost two years, and she would not talk about it except to say that "bad men" took her. They added, with evident pain, that things were so bad they were afraid to ask, and that all they thought about was that, at last, they had their daughter back. They had tried to put the terrible time behind them and start a new life.

As a result of his inquiries, the family doctor suggested that the daughter be seen by a clinician who specialized in treating trauma. The parents were reluctant; they said that they were sure things would improve, now that the family was reunited. As time passed, the daughter's symptoms became worse and worse. The physician consulted the therapist, who agreed to come to the physician's office to meet the woman, on the chance that she and the family would be more accepting of psychotherapy if it was clearly associated with her medical care.

On first meeting the woman, the therapist found her to be a fragile-looking person of 19; she had poor coloring and dark circles under her eyes. Although she made virtually no eye contact with the therapist, she was hypervigilant about the therapist's every move. When the clinician asked the woman to give her life history, she complied in a vague, defensive manner that was full of gaps and inconsistencies. When the therapist made a comment about a gap or inconsistency, she did it very cautiously, in an indirect way; this let the woman know that the therapist knew there was more to the story, but also conveyed that the woman would be free to tell more when she was ready. The clinician remarked that she needed to know what had happened in order to help her, but, she would not push her to tell anything that she did not feel safe or ready to tell. The therapist also gave the client control over the length of the sessions by stating that they could meet for the full hour if she was comfortable with that, or for a shorter period of time if she wished. (This technique of shifting control of the length of the therapy session to the client is especially useful with a victim who was held captive and had no control over time.) After a few therapy sessions in the family doctor's office, the woman agreed to meet with the therapist at her office.

In the office visits, the client utilized the full hour on most occasions, but sometimes a painful memory would stir within her and she would ask to stop. When that happened, the therapist would make one or two gentle inquires, but would always respect the woman's wishes for safety and control. With time, the client would begin the session by asking for advice about present-day issues, and little by little reveal facts about her past experiences. Along with these fragments of memories were mixed feelings about her family's inability to find her when she had been held captive, as well as some misconceptions about why she had been sent to America with her brother. Although at this point she had not told the clinician any details concerning the captivity, she mentioned that she believed that her parents had sent her here because they were ashamed of her "because of what happened." When the clinician inquired about what had happened, she stared away blankly and changed the subject. On several occasions, the therapist asked about her dreams and was told, "I do not have dreams."

From time to time, the client would complain of strange smells in the therapist's office. The therapist noted that these comments often were made during or shortly following her talking about events in her home country. She would say, for example, that the office smelled "dirty" or ask if the therapist had left any filthy rags in the office. These comments were voiced in a strange whispering monotone; as she made them, she appeared to be only "half present." When this occurred, the clinician suspected that memories of what happened to her when she was kidnapped were beginning to surface. At first, each time the client complained of the strange smells, the therapist would say, in a gentle, hypnotic tone of voice, that she was with her there in the office; she would stay with her and protect her if the memories came.

As therapy proceeded, the young woman began to complain more and more about the smells. Now the clinician would ask her, using a hypnotic tone, how she felt when she would smell these bad smells. At times she would curl up in a fetal position in the chair and say that the smells made her sick to her stomach; then she would silently rock back and forth. As these incidents of recalling the smells became more frequent, the therapist offered to meet with her more often, giving her the option of going to the hospital if she felt the need to be in a protected environment.

The client declined both offers at first, but soon after agreed to see the therapist more frequently. When the therapist asked for permission to talk with her parents, she replied that she was willing, but she did not wish to be present as well because she was afraid. While the clinician respected her feelings in this matter, she knew that the woman would eventually have to work through her feelings about why her parents did not rescue her, as well as her belief that she was sent to the States because her family was ashamed of her—not for medical care, as they had said. At that point, though, the girl had to work through her own past trauma experiences, become significantly less depressed, and develop healthier, more resilient defense mechanisms before she could deal with issues concerning her family. The therapist also felt that, if the client were ultimately capable of dealing with these family issues, it would provide her and the others with a corrective experience; this experience could help them rebuild their traumatized family system as well as restore her to full family membership.

When the clinician met with the young woman's parents, she discussed the complaint about smells with them and told them what she suspected its meaning might be. The parents said that their daughter had never talked about smelling filthy rags at home. The therapist then asked about the painful subject of their daughter's confused feelings and repressed anger at their not rescuing her, as well as her insecurities about their reason for sending her to America for medical care. She explained that the daughter viewed their not inquiring about what had happened, nor wanting to talk about her disappearance, as being another indication of their not caring.

At first, the parents were defensive about their past behavior. But as the therapist continued to reassure them that she did not perceive them as unloving or uncaring, they began to realize how their daughter could have misunderstood their actions. Once the parents were able to make this cognitive shift and understand their daughter's current struggles, the clinician was able to work with them to facilitate the process by which she could bring the trauma fully to light in therapy. By way of example, the therapist suggested that if the parents suspected that the woman was having a sleepless night, one of them should go in and reassure her that her parents were there to protect her and that they loved her. This would be preferable to leaving her alone because they didn't know what to do and were afraid they would make matters worse.

As therapy continued, the woman began to act out and test the therapist. Clearly, she was projecting consciously unacceptable feelings about her parents and others who failed to rescue her onto the therapist. Self-defeating behavior appeared, such as doing risky things in which she could be, and often was, physically injured: She missed appointments and went to bars in dangerous neighborhoods; she picked up strange men. This behavior was not at all characteristic of this client. Instead of confronting her in a way that she might misinterpret as punitive, the clinician commented on how uncharacteristic it was. She explained that she believed the young woman was trying to tell her something about experiences from her past. She affirmed that the woman was a worthwhile person who was deserving of better self-care. The young woman reacted to these statements in a manner that on the surface was nonchalant, but beneath this veneer it was clear that she was calculating whether or not the therapist's words were genuine. When the therapist next met with the client's parents, she warned them of the angry storm that was about to come. They reported that it had already begun at home. They then discussed how best to respond to this storm.

For the next few, angry sessions, the woman's complaints about smells were absent. One day, when she did not appear for her appointment, the therapist waited for about 15 minutes and then drove to the client's house. At first, the woman said, with indifference, that she had simply forgotten the appointment; the therapist reminded her that this had been their regular time for more than six months. When she became sarcastic and defensive, the clinician remained calm and caring, but made it clear that these therapy appointments were important and that she expected the woman to accompany her back to the office for their session.

When they arrived at the office, the client spent the next hour curled up in the chair, crying and repeating that she didn't like the therapist: She was unfair, and nothing good could come out of their meetings. The clinician remained nurturing but firm: She felt that the treatment was worthwhile, and she would stand by her even if she was angry, because she thought the woman was worth it. At the end of the session, the therapist told her that she would telephone her that night to see how she was doing; she added that she was going to call the woman's father to give her a ride home from the office, because she did not want her going home alone as upset as she was. After a brief protest, the client agreed to permit the clinician to call her father to come and get her.

At the next therapy appointment, later that week, the client acted as though nothing had happened and commented that she had a puzzling dream; she took no note of the fact that this was the first dream she had ever admitted to having since she began therapy. She explained that the dream was odd because in it her therapist had moved to San Francisco (about 40 miles away), and she had to walk all the way there to see her. The therapist commented that possibly the woman was afraid that she would abandon her, just as the other significant people in her life had done at one time or another. The woman curled up in the fetal position in the chair and quietly sobbed, as the clinician slowly repeated that neither she nor her family would abandon her. For the rest of the hour, the woman said very little except to mumble that she was frightened while the therapist tried to reassure her. Once more, the therapist called her father to come and get her, explaining to him what had happened in therapy and that his daughter should not be left alone. She added that the parents should not "hover," but instead should reiterate to their daughter that they loved her and would not abandon her.

The two sessions described above were turning points in the woman's treatment. During the next session, the reference to smells returned. By this time, the therapist was sure that the smells represented olfactory trauma memories. If she interpreted them slowly and gently, she could unlock the reservoir of trauma that had been previously hidden.

As the story unfolded, the puzzle of the traumatic event took shape. The woman had been kept prisoner in a small, filthy room; her bed was a pile of dirty rags in a corner. When she heard one of her captors coming toward the room, knowing that some form of torturous abuse was soon to follow, she would wrap one of the rags around her hand, bury her face in it, and bite into the rag. As she did this, she would, in effect, begin to dissociate her mind from her body. She would imagine that she would leave her body and go into the gray or brown darkness of the rag until the men had finished with her.

The actual "bringing back" of the entire period of her captivity and her means of survival took more than a year. During this period, the therapist utilized a combination of techniques to help her gain access to and process these recollections. There were times when she would free-associate to words representing various sounds and smells. At other times, the clinician would use a structured hypnotic technique to help her reconceptualize the past traumatic events in order to regain a sense of mastery over them. In tandem with this process, the therapist treated the client's depression while helping her to develop the defenses necessary to express her emotions without feeling guilty for expressing them. Eventually, she was able to participate in family therapy with her brother and parents, resolving the misconceptions that she had about their actions during and after her captivity.

WORKING THROUGH

As epitomized by the preceding case, a clinician should be prepared for some difficult periods during which the trauma client can be extremely resistive. The acting-out that is displayed toward the therapist may be an attempt to get him or her to replicate the repressed traumatic event. Further, the client may engage in risk-taking behavior, or actually reenact the trauma, while in therapy. In fact, when hidden trauma emerges, it rarely comes forth all at once or along a smooth path. It appears in fragmented form, and often takes a nonvisual aspect in the initial presentation. These delayed responses to trauma eventually need to be resolved on both the intrapsychic and the systemic levels.

To begin the healing process, a clinician must provide a safe milieu in the therapeutic relationship with the victim. Safety and structure are necessary to protect the client from the fear that memories will be overwhelming, causing him or her to lose control. There must be, as well, a sense of commitment from the therapist that he or she will not be frightened or disgusted by the description of past events. Above all, the clinician must clearly communicate that he or she will not abandon the victim.

Once trust is solidly established, we utilize a therapy process that weaves back and forth between remembered traumatic events and present therapy concerns. In this way, the client is permitted to return to the event and provide the therapist with information about how it was experienced. The client will also work in the present, in an interactive psychotherapy process, to change his or her perception of himself or herself in relation to the past event. After the working through of the trauma has been accomplished in the present, the clinician can help a victim to return, symbolically, to the traumatic event with a new perspective that may contribute to an experience of closure.

A guided fantasy or structured hypnosis process is often useful in transporting a victim back to the traumatic event. "Structured hypnosis" refers to the way that the therapist puts clear boundaries around the event to be recalled under hypnosis. There is a specific goal for the hypnotic recall, with a specific time-period established in advance. There is also a clear strategy for ending the hypnotic process should it become too painful for the victim. Initially, the therapist can utilize this kind of process to obtain information, later returning to the traumatic event with new information. The client is encouraged to weave back and forth between present and past, restructuring the trauma response until mastery of the trauma is achieved.

At the same time that recall is being induced, the clinician will need to treat trauma-reactive pathological behavior and/or preexisting pathology such as depression, anxiety, hypervigilance, or paranoia. It is not uncommon for some clients to require medication and, in extreme cases, hospitalization during the recall period. In this context, it is useful to strive for an understanding of the person's pre-trauma level of psychological functioning, and to incorporate this knowledge into the treatment plan.

Once past trauma has been revealed and resolved, a clinician should develop a strategy for systemic intervention with the victim. In many cases, uncovering past trauma can mean major changes in the person's family or social systems, affecting how he or she will interact with these systems in the future. It may be that the actions or inactions of significant others can be worked through and resolved in a way that will serve to strengthen the family system—as in the case described above. By contrast, when the person who inflicted the trauma is a family member or trusted member of the community, disclosure of the trauma may cause significant changes, realignments, and/or severe conflicts within the person's family or social systems. Sadly, not all family and social systems are supportive or protective of the victims of trauma. If such is the case, the clinician will be called upon to help a client cope with such systemic losses, as well as to resolve the trauma and go on with life. As referred to above, trauma is an emotional injury that cuts across the victim's social system and family system to penetrate the psyche. Successful therapy for such an injury must strive to reach all three elements of this constellation.

CHAPTER VII

Trauma in Children and Adolescents

F ROM A DYNAMIC systems point of view, a child's personality is in a continual state of evolution and change. Both psychodynamically and systemically, the developmental process flows on without ceasing. The internal growth of the psyche, with its twin elements of thought and emotion, is paralleled by changes in the child's role in the family system. The latter involves intensely powerful interactions within the family that will largely determine the child's ultimate construction of reality.

A child's formulation of a framework for reality occurs well before the child has acquired words to describe the environment that he or she observes; nor does the child possess, in this early stage, a sense of self or self in relation to others. In effect, the foundation for a child's perception of what is true or what is real has been laid in advance of the development of a critical faculty — the capacity to weigh or to doubt. The influence exerted upon a very young child's psyche by the family system flows along a one-way passage. What is learned are answers to questions of significance: is the world one of chaos or order, rapid change or stability, violence or tenderness, deprivation or nurturance?

The child, through observation, experiences the unfolding of these facts of existence: Does he or she inhabit an environment that is caring, supportive, comfortable, stimulating, tranquil? Or, is it one in which, literally and figuratively, the sound of sirens is often heard? Is there a place for the child at the core of this world, or is he or she an appendage, a burden, an afterthought, or an "alien" being who can only thwart the desires of those who are responsible for the child's welfare? These and other orientations to reality are established with little awareness on the part of most parents that they are being taught. And while it has been said that a child's values have been learned by the age of nine, it is equally certain that the child's world view has been implanted by the age of four or five. As the child grows older, his or her systems interactions expand and become more complex. They push beyond the borders of the nuclear family, on to the extended family and family friends, and further to the social system that the child first encounters at school.

ORIGINS OF THE TRAUMA RESPONSE

When trauma strikes a child, the developing connection between internal process and external systems is disrupted; the result can be change of catastrophic proportions. At the very least, it will probably divert energy away from healthy development, into modes of survival and self-protection. Specific qualities of the child's or adolescent's response to trauma will be discussed below in this chapter.

The Developing Psyche

At first, children exist in a primitive, magical realm that is filled daily with glorious surprise; for example, the child watches in amazement as liquid falls from a container, shiny stuff flying through the air and splashing to the ground in a puddle. Without words to categorize or evaluate what he or she has seen, the child is suspended in a limbo of awe and wonder. This helpless state may soon be invaded by commotion or rage, if an annoyed parent discovers that another cup of milk has been thrown to the floor. If the child is fortunate, he or she will be scolded appropriately by a parent who is aware that the child was indulging a need for discovery and was making a misguided attempt to manipulate the environment. If the child is not fortunate, the parent will project adult anger onto him or her, accusing the child of throwing the milk in defiance of authority. If the child is terribly unlucky, the parent will use the incident as an excuse to act abusively.

During childhood, an atmosphere of primitive and magical forces prevails. A cast of powerful fantasy figures create glorious mental pleasures or threaten terrible physical punishments. At the vortex of this imagined realm is the child himself or herself. Because of the child's omnipotence, he or she feels capable of loving unreservedly, without questioning, and of wreaking horrible vengeance on those who do wrong. With time, the forces of reason will take over and these fantasies will recede before the chill winds of logic.

Prevalence

Traumatic experiences in childhood are much more prevalent than is accepted by the mainstream of public opinion. Our view in this matter is confirmed by a number of sources: Elmer, 1977; Lister, 1982; Lyons, 1978;

Eth & Pynoos, 1985; and Terr, 1990. Perhaps one reason for this apparent insensitivity to a basic truth lies in the tendency of adults to dismiss a child's account of distress as the product of imagination, or to diminish its seriousness because of the child's poor judgment. An adult is seldom capable, after all, of seeing things from a child's perspective. One example of this sort of clouded insight is the case of a three-year-old boy who was riding in the front seat of a car that was involved in a violent accident. Although no one was seriously injured, the car's severe damage included a shattered windshield. The boy's mother bled profusely because her nose struck the steering wheel; more importantly, both the boy and his mother were profoundly shaken by the impact.

After the accident, the boy's parents felt much relieved that there had been no serious injuries, and focused their energy on being angry at the negligence of the other driver. They noticed that their son had become reluctant to eat, but they attributed this to a "stage" in his development. When, after three days, he still refused food, they became concerned. They had also observed the child playing "ambulance" and "going to the hospital" games with his toy trucks and cars. When the puzzled mother called their pediatrician, he helped her comprehend how frightening and traumatic such an event might have been from a three-year-old's perspective. The pediatrician pointed out how terrified the child must have been on seeing his mother covered with blood and acting disoriented, and how small and helpless he must have felt at the moment of the crash, with glass falling all around him. To the child, it must have seemed that the world was coming to an end.

The pediatrician suggested to the mother that psychotherapy oriented to desensitization and mastery of the traumatic experience might be of help to the child in recovering from the accident and in preventing future anxiety-related problems. This shows the value, in situations that involve children, of attempting to consider what may have happened from the child's viewpoint, with his or her more limited cognitive resources. One must literally contemplate what it means to be a child's size and to see with a child's eyes.

The Child Witness

When intervening after a traumatic event and trying to figure out which of the persons involved needs help, a clinician should not overlook the child witness to the event. The vulnerability of a child is composed of elements of gullibility and magical thinking, and children, in an effort to make sense of life and being overdetermined to learn by experience, try to find hidden meaning in every event that occurs before them. When required to bear witness to a traumatic event, a child may be more acutely traumatized than the actual victim.

Pioneering research by Pynoos and Eth (1985) especially focused on children who had been present when a parent was murdered or committed suicide or when the mother was raped. Their work has raised consciousness about this phenomenon among mental health professionals, and has greatly broadened the scope of case-finding. In Caplan's classic schema (Caplan, 1964) this contribution leads the way to "secondary prevention" at its most fruitful — i.e., the discovery of incipient mental illness. By intervening in the child's response to trauma, potential pathology may be averted.

In this context, it is worth emphasizing that many children who have been traumatized do not possess the linguistic skills to communicate their experiences directly to a clinician. For example, some will have become enmeshed in family systems that are, and have been, the actual source of their trauma (e.g., a home in which father beats mother). These children may define their suffering as "the way life is," while others live in such a state of perpetual terror that they will tell no one for fear of making matters worse. For this reason, the therapist may have to rely solely on inference from symptoms, as well as the heightened sensitivity to the child's viewpoint that we have advocated above.

In general, the reactions of a child witness fit within four categories (Pynoos & Eth, 1985):

1. persistence of memories of the event; many children describe it as so upsetting that they will never forget it
2. reliving the event — principally in the form of dreams or traumatic play
3. psychic numbing in the form of subdued behavior or muteness; some children adopt a third-person, almost journalistic, way of talking about the event
4. symptoms such as avoidant behavior and sleep disturbances

It is nearly impossible to prevent these traumatic reactions in children, when we live in such violent times. For instance, as noted by Pynoos and Eth (1985, p. 41), children are at risk because nearly 40% of murders are the result of domestic violence; a majority of the victims of these murders are in the primary child-rearing group of 20- to 39-year-olds. In Los Angeles, it is estimated that between 10% and 20% of homicides are witnessed by children. (The same potentiality may apply to rape, because 40% of rapes occur in the victim's home.) And since young married women are a high-risk population for attempted or completed suicide, it is estimated that many thousands of children each year are exposed to a parent's suicidal behavior.

Child witnesses who are *not* directly injured themselves by the traumatic event are affected differently from those who *are* injured along with another person. They experience no physical pain and thus may not go into shock; nor do they rely on the defense of denial. To the contrary, they have no doubt about the reality of what they have seen. They focus directly on what has happened to the victim, and they dwell on their actual or threatened loss. One child said it well: "I hear everything at school, and then it's gone because what I saw happen to my Mommy comes right back to me." These children suffer guilt for not having prevented the victim's ordeal, but the worst possible outcome occurs when there is identification with an aggressor, or an obsessional impulse for revenge. For example, one 11-year-old girl whose mother had been killed by a boyfriend, dreamed that her extended family lined up before the killer as a firing squad. In the dream, she and her sister knife him as he had done to their mother; then, his blindfold is removed, the girl shoots him, and stands back while the other relatives fire their rifles. On another note, a study of homicidally aggressive young children showed that the most significant contributing factor is a father who behaves violently, often homicidally.

The worst *possible* impact on a child witness is engendered by watching a parent commit suicide. The conflict fluctuates between blaming the parent for abandonment and blaming oneself for letting it happen. Here, the trauma response often takes the form of repetitive, unconscious reenactments. In one case, the father of a seven-year-old boy took an overdose of pills that caused serious neurological damage. Within a week, the boy began to ask his mother what would happen if he were to take ten pills — or eight, or six. Then, he asked how many he would need to kill himself.

In short, we see that a traumatic event can have a devastating spread of effect. Our case-finding efforts with children should reach out to these blameless bystanders, who are awash in a sea of helplessness and recrimination.

THE DYNAMIC SYSTEMS APPROACH

When he first wrote of the stimulus barrier, Freud thought that external crises could cause pathological symptoms. Later, of course, he became absorbed by the then unappreciated concept of the unconscious mind; one can only imagine how transfixed the great genius was by this complicated, dark web. Eventually, he came to doubt that a traumatic event alone could cause neurotic symptoms, instead believing that the symptoms were caused by an unconscious, preexisting conflict that the external crisis only brought to the surface. It follows that this underlying, historical condition or flaw was the ultimate source of post-traumatic distress. This point of view became readily adopted and probably has been so tenaciously held because it serves to protect clinicians from reflecting on their own vulnerability.

By contrast, the authors believe that there is a constant dynamic interchange between the person's external systems and his or her unconscious process. Hence, trauma can penetrate the core of the psyche. A child, for instance, may develop trauma-reactive symptoms that can persist and become ingrained, chronic pathology if left untreated. Moreover, as Terr noted in her research on children who were involved in the Chowchilla kidnapping case (1983), a traumatic event can negatively affect the development of previously normal children's personalities. To complicate matters further, the presenting symptoms of a child who has been traumatized may contain aspects of prior abnormalities that have become exaggerated or confabulated by the effects of the recent event. In cases such as the latter, both clinical assessment and treatment planning may present a complex puzzle indeed.

A traumatic event may cause children to regress to a pretraumatic developmental level at which they had come to feel safe. A child's mechanisms of defense may be so exhausted by his or her attempts to cope with the trauma that the child has difficulty in learning new things or simply in coping with the ordinary demands of life. The child may adopt trauma-engendered defensive maneuvers that are functional enough in a trauma state but manifest themselves as dysfunctional behavior in everyday situations. If trauma is undisclosed or not understood, other unfortunate consequences may follow. The adults around the child or adolescent may misdiagnose him or her as difficult, dull, or pathological, thus retarding further the child's dynamic and systemic development. These child or adolescent victims may find themselves in programs and institutions that were designed to treat problems that they, in fact, do not have.

A traumatic event may suddenly alter a child's family and larger environment in ways that can deprive the child of sources of support that he or she vitally needs for recovery. For example, immediate family members may be lost to the child at least temporarily, because of their own injuries. Children might suddenly face moving to a new home or encountering new caretakers, some of whom may be strangers to them. Patterns of life that were well-known and comforting or attitudes that were signposts to reality may have vanished or been altered in surreal ways. A child might be plunged into doubt about what is actually true or reliably safe, asking internal questions such as, "What kind of a life is this?" or "Who am I now?"

It is sad to reflect that a child or adolescent might be neglected in the aftermath of a traumatic incident — even by his or her parents. An example of this is the case of a man whose wife and children were involved in a car accident in which the mother was killed and one child crippled. The father, struggling to restore some stability to the family's finances and to care for the nine-year-old son's medical needs, could scarcely be blamed for not being able to see the situation from the perspective of his four-year-old daughter who was also in the car when the accident occurred.

This four-year-old was trying to cope with the fact that her mommy had left her, perhaps because of some misdeed on her (the child's) part or because of a wish-fulfillment fantasy in which she sought to take the mother's place. She recalled the horror of the accident itself and remembered her mother and brother being taken away by ambulance. She suffered as a result of her father's inattention to her, and also felt jealous about the father's preoccupation with her brother's needs. Then she was sent to live with an aunt, because her father felt that the aunt could provide her with better care.

By sending her away, the father succeeded in complicating the already acute dynamic and systemic aspects of his daughter's trauma. At first, the child had been faced with issues concerning the loss of her mother and accompanying oedipal conflicts (not to mention the injury to her brother), but now she had to come to terms with expulsion from her family. The tragic denouement of this story is that the family was not referred for treatment (until much later) because it had been functioning normally before the accident occurred. The attorney who represented the father and the children did not want to complicate the case with psychological "side issues" and saw no necessity to recommend therapy.

It wasn't until this little girl developed obvious counterphobic symptoms that her aunt and uncle consulted a therapist. Unfortunately, many children in similar situations may not display obvious symptoms that will bring to light their attempts to cope with injury. In such cases, their future personalities may be unnecessarily shaped by guilt, shame, or anger emanating from the trauma. Without intervention, these issues can reshape a developing personality and its world view.

GUIDELINES FOR DIAGNOSIS

There is no "right" or standardized response that a child or adolescent will make to a traumatic event. People differ in their experiences and perceptions of similar situations. Even so, one aspect of the child's response to trauma tends to be different from that of adults: Children are less likely to be able to express the nature of their feelings verbally. Frequently, a child or adolescent's response is behavioral. In some situations, it is obvious that the child or adolescent's behavior is trauma-related; in others, the connection may not be so clear. Here, we present an overview of the traumatic reactions that are commonly found in children and adolescents, organized by developmental stages.

Ages One to Five: The Preschool Child

Preschool children may exhibit regressive behavior such as loss of toilet training and/or thumb-sucking. They may cease to be adventuresome or inquisitive about their surroundings, and become newly (or more) fearful of "monsters," strangers, or even things that were once familiar to them. Terr (1991, p. 13) has pointed out that the onset of a fear of the dark or of other mundane places and situations can be indicative of trauma. A child may show increased separation anxiety and react to new experiences with anxiety and trepidation as opposed to his or her normal level of curiosity.

The preschool child may express anxiety about a traumatic experience by behaving in an uncharacteristically irritable, disobedient, or angry manner; by contrast, a normally outgoing, "rambunctious" child may become docile, timid, or unusually dependent. Speech and language acquisition may be delayed or show regressive signs. The child may acquire a nervous tic, a stammer, or revert to baby talk.

Traumatized preschool children may develop a somatic reaction to trauma. Clinicians should also be sensitive to the fact that some children come from cultures that are intolerant of the expression of emotional pain or that stigmatize people who have psychological problems. As mentioned earlier, in Asian, Middle-eastern, and Latin cultures, many people customarily somatize their emotional pain. These somatic reactions can take the form of diffuse "aches and pains" or pain that is directly or symbolically linked to the trauma. Some somatic problems can be linked to issues of control, such as chronic vomiting or loss of control of the bowel or bladder. Trauma may also be reflected by a child's eating behavior, and can result in either loss of appetite or overeating.

A traumatized child may also engage in self-injurious behavior such as head-banging, biting himself or herself, hair-pulling, or intentional falling to the ground. Although suicidal behavior is rare at this age, when it occurs it is usually quite lethal. A child's fears may also be reflected in sleep patterns. The child may resist going to sleep or suffer from night terrors. A more detailed description of trauma-related sleep problems and dreams will appear in a later section of this chapter.

Finally, the traumatized preschool child may talk obsessively about the traumatic event, but he or she is more likely to engage in obsessional play or behavior that reenacts (attempts to master or undo) the traumatic event. The authors, as well as Terr (1991), have noted that the reenacting play of traumatized children is in sharp contrast to the carefree joy of normal children's play. Even though a child victim may describe it as "fun" or "a game," this play usually has a grim or driven quality to it, as the child acts out elements of the traumatic event again and again. Such repetitive play is also present in preverbal or in very young children whose linguistic abilities are limited. Disturbances of play of this kind warrant serious clinical attention, because a child so young may lack the cognitive resources to express what he or she is doing. In the worst possible case, this obsessional behavior could develop into a form of repetition compulsion that, if untreated, would become self-perpetuating and cause future problems.

Ages Six to Eleven: The Elementary-school Child

Children in this age group can also regress. Their regressive behavior may take the form of clinging and crying, in general, or separation anxiety in particular. The child may wish to play with things that he or she had once dismissed as being "for babies." The child may suddenly become jealous or competitive with younger siblings and demand the extra care of being fed, dressed, or in other ways treated like a baby. A school-age child may become hypervigilant or hyperactive, scanning the environment for clues confirming his or her safety or the absence of impending new traumatic events. He or she may anxiously talk of being afraid of death or having a future that is somehow foreshortened or blunted. This is also in considerable contrast to the normal child's exuberance in talking about the endless possibilities that the future holds.

A child who is characteristically friendly and compliant may become irritable, aggressive, or oppositional following a traumatic event. The child may develop uncharacteristic fears of people, places, or objects. He or she may also engage in primitive self-injurious or potentially self-destructive behavior such as head-banging, falling for no reason, or cutting himself or herself. A trauma victim may also engage in risk-taking behavior such as riding a bicycle dangerously, starting fights with bigger children, or crossing the street in a careless, provocative manner.

The traumatized child's school performance may drop because of anxiety or a trauma-produced attention deficit. Even so, many severely traumatized children continue to perform well in school. Often the structure and consistency of the school setting is a source of relief and shelter in an otherwise chaotic, frightening world. In fact, in some cases the school performance of the traumatized child actually improves.

Ages 12 to 18: The Preadolescent and Adolescent

The traumatized preteen or adolescent, although moving toward individuation and independence, is equally capable of regressive behavior. This may take the form of loss of interest in previously all-important peer activities, exemplified by preferring to stay closer to the parents or younger siblings, or putting a lot of energy into competing with younger siblings for parental attention. These youngsters may suddenly become oppositional, resist doing chores or homework, and generally defy authority. Others, by contrast, may compulsively try to do things "perfectly," as a magical means to ward off future harm.

Some traumatized preteens and adolescents engage in antisocial behavior such as vandalism, stealing, being promiscuous, or using drugs and alcohol. Others become depressed, dependent, and socially withdrawn.

Sleep disorders are common: Some youthful trauma victims are so anxious that they cannot go to sleep at night; others awaken in the middle of the night, unable to go back to sleep. Unfortunately, most preteen and early teenagers are reluctant to seek the comfort and reassurance from their parents that they need at night, because it would be too babyish or immature. Hence, the sleepy teenager who can't wake up in the morning, or who wants to sleep all day, may be misperceived as lazy or manipulative instead of as traumatized. And while the school performance of the preadolescent or adolescent may be either positively or negatively affected by trauma, a drop in school performance is the more common outcome.

The youthful victim may express a response to trauma by changes in grooming habits or in dress. For example, a sexually traumatized preadolescent may dress in a slovenly, unattractive way or, conversely, in an overly seductive, provocative way. Dressing in this bizarre or outrageous fashion goes much further than normal adolescent experimentation. In addition, the victim may exhibit self-injurious or risk-taking behavior as well as suicidal behavior. Clinicians are aware that adolescence is, in general, a high-risk period for suicidal behavior; suicide is the second-highest cause of death in this age group (after death by accident). Their vigilance should be even more acute in cases of preteens or teenagers who have been traumatized.

A young trauma victim may express his or her suffering in psychosomatic ailments such as chronic aches and pains, or those that prevent the person from engaging in activities that might be threatening in some way. Another effect that trauma may have on physical functioning is that sexual development may be delayed or accelerated, especially when the traumatic event was sexual in nature. Reactive skin conditions are also common in youthful victims of trauma.

Because adolescence is, of itself, a turbulent developmental stage, the acting-out or antisocial young person is more likely to arouse suspicion that a traumatic event has occurred. But a quiet or withdrawn reaction to a traumatic event can be equally serious from a clinical standpoint. Unfortunately, the latter reaction is often perceived as a positive sign and viewed with a sigh of relief by the adults in the young person's life. Moreover, because the symptoms described in these pages may also be symptoms of other problems in childhood and adolescence, the traumatized youth's current difficulties are often ascribed to conditions other than trauma. Clinical assessment can also be complicated when a young person is still suffering from a condition that preceded the traumatic event, or is enmeshed in a dysfunctional family system. Consequently, one should always bear in mind that there is always a reason for a child's behavior, no matter how bizarre. By their behavior, children attempt to communicate something to adults around them. It has been our experience (as well as that of other clinicians who work in this field, e.g., Lyons, 1978; Eth & Pynoos, 1985; Terr, 1990, 1991) that many children who are traumatized are misdiagnosed or their suffering goes unrecognized. A clinician should always err on the side of caution, taking care not to rule out the possibility of some heretofore undisclosed childhood trauma.

When Trauma Is Deeply Hidden

In cases of pronounced avoidant reactions to trauma, the child or adolescent may totally block the traumatic event from conscious memory. In the most extreme situations, usually situations involving repetitive physical and/or emotional abuse, a child may develop a separate personality or even multiple personalities as a means of protection from the terror of the events that he or she is attempting to survive. Cases like this can pose a considerable clinical challenge, because frequently the true circumstances may be unknown to the clinician. In some cases the adults in the child's abusive family system may be actively colluding to keep the events a secret.

The following are vital symptoms that may indicate that a child or adolescent is suffering from a blocked or hidden trauma:

1. Gaps in time for which the child or adolescent has no conscious recollection. Often, a young person will skip over such time periods and be unaware that weeks, months, or even years have been "lost." Another might be puzzled or anxious about this same lack of recollection.
2. Sudden changes in personality, attitude, or behavior.
3. Regressive behavior or loss of developmental progress.
4. Sudden avoidant or aggressive behavior.
5. Repetitive or compulsive behavior, often with a ritualistic quality to it.
6. Difficulty in concentrating and/or in retaining information.
7. A sudden, inexplicable drop in school performance.
8. Flagrant promiscuous behavior. Clinicians should be aware that such behavior in either boys or girls may indicate a hidden trauma.
9. Sudden withdrawal from school or social activities and/or sudden phobic behavior.
10. Thrill-seeking, risk-taking, or self-destructive behavior. Related to this is the case in which a child or adolescent suddenly becomes accident-prone.
11. Drug or alcohol abuse. Frequently, traumatized young people attempt to self-medicate with drugs or alcohol.

12. Eating disorders such as bulimia and anorexia, as well as food-hoarding, can be symptoms of hidden trauma.

13. Sudden or unexplained alienation from peers or family and/or repetitive runaway behavior can often indicate trauma. It has been our experience that among the population of street adolescents — a group that was once viewed as acting-out, antisocial, or delinquent — a large percentage are fleeing from traumatic situations.

14. In the older age category, traumatized adolescents are especially vulnerable to recruitment by cults, or to being proselytized by extreme religious sects. Those whom clinicians encounter who are dropouts from groups of this kind should be carefully evaluated for the possibility of hidden trauma.

FURTHER CLINICAL ISSUES

Adolescents and younger children share many characteristics that are irrespective of age. For example, they tend to utilize similar mechanisms of defense, albeit at different levels of effectiveness. Their dreams tend to be similar, though with differing sophistication of content. When a person of any age is traumatized, flashbacks and distortions of reality can occur.

Defenses

Trauma occurs when the defenses are overwhelmed; hence, the rebuilding of adaptive defense mechanisms is pivotal to the process of recovery from trauma. Generally, the more functional and resilient the defense mechanisms were before the trauma, the better the prognosis and the more rapid the recovery Yet, here lies the problem in the treatment process for traumatized children: Young children do not possess the full complement of adaptable defenses that adults do. Child trauma victims are, for that reason, in double jeopardy, because they have fewer necessary resources. One only has to read Terr's moving accounts of traumatized children (1990) to realize how quickly a child's cognitive and emotional capacities can break down in traumatic situations. Very rapidly, they become concrete and primitive, often reacting with trance-like rigidity as they try to marshall whatever defenses are available to them. Treatment that only alleviates symptoms and does not address the task of helping the child or adolescent build functional defenses may slow the processes of the trauma response and leave him or her unprepared for the next developmental stage.

Young children may have to return for brief courses of therapy as they mature, to supplement the process of developing appropriate defenses. One must be able to rationalize and one must be capable of self-reflection before one can truly lay a trauma to rest. In that sense, treatment of the traumatized child is an incremental process. But there are many cases in which, after the initial course of therapy, a therapist can prepare the parents to carry on this building-block process.

Dreams

Many children and adolescents convert trauma-related thoughts and feelings into the stuff of dreams; even very young children dream. Therapists should make a point of asking child and adolescent victims about their dreams, looking for information that may be significant for resolution of the trauma. We, as well as Terr (1990, p. 210), have observed that children's and adolescents' traumatic dreams fall into one of the following categories:

1. *Exact repetition of the traumatic experience.* This is fairly unusual in the authors' experience, and may be an indication that the child is exaggerating symptoms for one reason or another. Most traumatized people cannot endure the emotional pain of exact repetitions of the event for protracted periods.

2. *Modified repetitions.* These are more common dream patterns, in which the basic theme of the trauma remains the same but the setting of the event or the persons involved are somehow modified.

3. *Symbolic repetition.* This is also a common form of trauma-related dream in which the event takes on a more symbolic form (e.g., the person who abused the victim becomes a monster, or something that injured the child or adolescent becomes a frightening animal who attacks).

4. *Repressed terror dreams.* These are dreams whose content is so fearful that the young person represses it upon awakening. He or she may feel anxious or afraid on awakening, but doesn't know why.

Because the dreams of traumatized young people often migrate rapidly from themes of the event to modified or symbolic versions of it, neither the victim nor the parents may recognize a dream as part of the trauma response. For that reason, the therapist should inquire not only about trauma-specific dreams, but about dreams in general.

Because of the anxiety that is generated by the frightening content of trauma-related dreams, many children and adolescents become anxious about, or fearful of sleep; young children may want to sleep with their parents because they are too afraid to sleep alone.[1] Nevertheless, trauma-

---

[1] Although unusual, cases in which adolescents want to sleep with a parent or parents are not unknown. The rationale for prohibiting this practice applies doubly to these cases.

tized children should not be permitted to sleep in the same bed with parents, because of the confused generational boundaries that it creates. Instead, if a child is too fearful to be alone, the parents should make up a separate bed in their room and encourage the child to return to his or her room as soon as possible.

The following are some of the techniques that we have found effective in assisting fearful children to return to their rooms and resume more normal sleep habits. For children who are afraid of the dark, a night-light might help, or a light that illuminates a path of escape or access to the parent; the child may want to select a night-light that represents a favorite cartoon character or reassuring object. He or she might be given a bell or whistle to summon the parents when becoming fearful; the procedure should be practiced a few times before bedtime to reassure the child that it really works. The child can also be given a toy to sleep with that has positive and reassuring associations.

In the treatment of a child victim, it is ideal if he or she can work through the dream material as a natural process, but, unfortunately, some victims are too anxious and fearful to do so. If this is the case, a clinician may choose to meet with the parents to develop therapeutic bedtime stories that contain similar content to their dreams about the traumatic event, but with positive outcomes. These therapeutic stories can also be interspersed with messages that will help the child move through the stages of the recovery cycle. When telling these stories to their child, parents should have already prepared him or her for sleep and have the room lit in the way that is usual for sleeping. A parent should continue telling the story or at least stay with the child until he or she has drifted off to sleep. This is especially meaningful for traumatized children, because the story content does filter down into unconscious dream content. This process also has a positive systemic impact because it creates a parent-child interaction that is "trauma corrective." It puts the parent in the role of healer, not only for waking life but also for sleep. This can only strengthen the family system.

Some young children who have night terrors may require more intensive clinical interventions. Breathing or relaxation exercises that were described above can be helpful. A therapist may choose either to teach the parent direct or indirect (Ericksonian) hypnotic techniques or to work directly with the child. Once children become familiar with the hypnotic process, hypnotic sleep tapes that include positive suggestions about sleep and/or dream content can be very useful.

Many adolescent trauma victims who suffer from night terrors or sleep disorders may hide these problems because they are ashamed that such fears will be considered babyish. They may also be too alienated from their parents to be able to admit fears that reveal their dependency needs. An adolescent may also be using such pervasive denial or repression that he or she is not aware of what the source of the anxiety actually is. Consequent-

ly, the clinician should be aware that adolescent behavior that, superficially, appears to be acting-out, may instead be a sign that the adolescent is
suffering from a trauma-related sleep disorder. Examples:

1. Adolescents who stay up all night, often watching TV, and then
   sleep during the day.
2. Adolescents who sneak out of the house and roam all night.
3. Adolescents who self-medicate with drugs or alcohol, especially
   those who do this alone at night.

Most child and adolescent trauma victims will need to come to terms
with the content of their dreams during the course of their therapy. In fact,
dreams and other sleep-related issues can be predominant during the initial
stages of treatment — they will then subside for awhile only to reemerge
later. During the closing stages, dream work will blend and intertwine with
the ordinary processes of therapy. In addition, when working on dreams,
sand tray and art therapy can be extremely useful media for children and
adolescents, while the therapist reflects on and interprets the reproduction
of the dream content.

CHAPTER VIII

Treatment of Children and Adolescents

T RAUMA OF RECENT origin may be more amenable to clinical intervention than traumas of the past, chiefly because the young victim and
the adults in his or her environment are less likely to have adopted nonfunctional methods of coping. In such cases, there is a shorter history of
misunderstanding and unbridled magical thinking about subjects such as
guilt and blame than there are with traumas of earlier origin. Pathology has
had less time to incubate, and family myths about what happened have not
yet become family history.

Aspects of the Trauma Analysis Protocol that was presented in Chapter
III provide a structure for the strategies of therapy that are presented here.

AGES TWO TO SEVEN:
THE YOUNG CHILD

Origin and Responsibility

Young children analyze much of their brief experience of life according to
terms of obedience to the adults who have authority over them. Their
energies are largely devoted to gaining approval or avoiding punishment.
For this reason, issues of blame for a traumatic event, and who is to "pay"
for it, are clouded by this power-based relationship of unequals. To the
child, the traumatic event itself may have been a punishment for past
derelictions of filial duty. How the child feels about matters such as these
may be accessible to the therapist only by inference from, for instance,
themes expressed in the child's play or through the medium of figure
drawings. Some children may be able to verbalize their feelings, but many
will not.

Questions of the meaning and cause of a traumatic event become even more complex when one considers the child's egocentric orientation to his or her world. Even when an event was clearly caused by someone (or something) else, a child's fantasies can contradict the evidence of the senses. The young child believes that, by wish alone, he or she can wreak vengeance on an enemy or manipulate nature. Children's optimism is boundless — as epitomized by fairy tales of wizards and elves who magically save, or the frog who becomes a prince; simultaneously, their pessimism is boundless — as shown by a closet-full of superstitions such as "Step on a crack, break your mamma's back."

One reason that play therapy using dolls, puppets, and toys that resemble people is so effective with young children is that they can help the child externalize the event by ascribing its occurrence to other causes. The clinician can guide a child to play out a traumatic event again and again, until the child begins to reframe it as something that "happened to" him or her. In some cases, in which a child has been "struck dumb" by what happened, and has not even been able to tell the therapist the extent of his or her magical thinking, this projective play may serve as an unlocking mechanism.

Because a child's logic may attribute a correlation to events that occur concurrently in time, it is a good idea to explore what else was going on when the traumatic event happened. An example is that of a little girl who was traumatized two days after her fourth birthday. She thought that being four was the cause, and resolved to become three again. She reverted to behavior that had been typical of her in the past, and told everyone that she was three years old. A complicating factor was that her parents did not believe she had been traumatized. They thought that she was going through a stubborn stage that called for firm discipline. The child's response to this treatment was to draw the conclusion that she was a "bad" and "lazy" person. Her self-concept received a scar in the process.

Beginning in infancy, the child seeks to control his or her body through experiences such as toilet training, and strives to manipulate the environment to obtain food and warmth. These techniques of influencing others are as primitive as "I want" and "give me" at first, and are eventually supplanted by more complex forms of interaction. Based upon qualities of these interactions, the child arrives at a set of beliefs concerning the extent to which the environment will meet his or her needs, as well as his or her role in this system.

When a traumatic event disrupts this formative process, the child may face issues such as, "Is this what people do to you?" "Do people do this on purpose?" "What does 'accident' mean?" "Is my family safe?" "Am I safe in this family?" "Are some people never safe?" Doubts about reasons for what happened may remain, no matter how often the child is told that it was an accident and that the other person involved "didn't mean it." The genuine attempts of adults to dispel a child's doubt may go unheard or misunderstood, for reasons as different as bravado and deference. In an attempt to please, a child may only pretend to understand, thus permitting the adults to close the issue.

The clinician who enters this system can play a major part in explaining the traumatic event in terms that a child can grasp at his or her current developmental stage. In this work, the child's own interpretation can be sorted out from what the child has been told by adults. It can first be validated for the child by the therapist, and then gently revised to conform with the reality of the situation.

When love and trust relationships are tarnished by trauma, young children often engage in repetitive play into which they project themes of good people (animals, objects) that become bad. Here the child is trying to resolve the complex moral question of how a person who was loved— hence, was good—could have done a bad thing. A clinician can help by interpreting these issues for the child, breaking them down into cognitive "bits" that he or she can comprehend and digest. One way to do this is to create plays or stories that clarify the issues, guiding the child to a resolution that allows for shades of gray or the concept of duality.

Many children who have suffered trauma at the hands of a trusted grown-up wrestle with feelings of wanting to punish the adult while fearing the loss of the relationship. Again, through projective play, these impulses toward retribution can be refocused and diffused. The therapist may wish to use an Ericksonian interspersal technique (Erickson, 1980a,b,c,d) to aid in leading the child to redefine and redirect anger. Another effective device is mutual story-telling in which the clinician and the child alternate in creating parts of the story, each contributing equally to the direction it will take. Some children will want the same story to be told over and over, and the patience of the therapist may be well and truly challenged. The severity of a child's need will vary by the degree to which he or she was traumatized, as well as the strength of the trust relationship that trauma has called into question.

Parents of a traumatized child should be prepared for the possibility that the child may raise the same issues of origin and responsibility at later stages of development. This does not imply failure on the part of parents to lead their children to a resolution of trauma. It may be a positive sign, in that the child has now progressed to the point at which newly-acquired cognitive skills can be used to analyze the issues, or newly-acquired emotional strengths can be used to heal some of the remaining traumatic damage.

Acceptance or Stigma

A young child views the world in the concrete terms of good versus bad. The feeling of shame dwells at a primitive level that is normally based upon the fact that he or she *has done something* bad or forbidden. Since a child of this age cannot grasp the notion of a stigma in the adult sense, he or she is likely to conceptualize it as a direct result of something that he or she has done. A therapist, for this reason, had best use very clear, concrete terms in working with a young child, until it is certain that the child has a healthy understanding of issues pertaining to stigma. To do this, a clinician may utilize play situations and themes to inculcate the concept that the child has done nothing wrong and need bear no shame.

Because of the dependence of young children on their parents, and because their ego boundaries are enmeshed with those of their parents, learning about a child's true perception of a traumatic event may be quite difficult in some cases. The primitive nature of children's mechanisms of defense, not to mention what they have been told to feel by their parents, may compound the problem. They may have assimilated any or all of the parents' unresolved issues about the event, i.e., feelings about guilt or being stigmatized in their roles as parents, or on behalf of the "family name." Influences of this kind may color each of a child's references to his or her trauma response, in ways that could lead a therapist to misread the child's reactions. Adults, for their part, may also lack the sensitivity to follow the child's clues, partly because they are looking inward at this time of crisis, and partly because they may have little prior experience in coping with traumatic situations. Further, communication can become even more garbled if the child concludes that the adults, who by definition are "all knowing," must surely know how he or she feels. And, if a child's parents maintain an eerie silence about the traumatic event when speaking to friends or acquaintances or neighbors, the child can sense that there must be some sort of social disapproval of what has happened.

Warning and Duration

In working with a traumatized child, it will be useful if the clinician finds out whether or not the child received any warning about the traumatic event. When there was no discernible warning, a child may become convinced that life is dangerous and wild, and that random forces defy logic and prediction. Typical symptoms of the response to totally unpredictable calamities include hypervigilance, sleep disorders, and emotional blocking or "numbness." As a means to alleviate symptoms of this type, cognitive/behavioral methods may be of value. Even very young children can be taught relaxation techniques to relieve anxiety and help them sleep. Both direct and Ericksonian hypnotic induction have been successful with children as young as two years of age. In most cases, Ericksonian techniques of hypnosis are indicated because, with them, the child is enlisted as an active participant and, as a result, can achieve a greater feeling of mastery over a symptom. In addition, this approach is more likely to be "fun" for the child. Treatment by this medium may turn out to be a positive experience in at least three ways:

1. pleasant thoughts and feelings are paired with traumatic ones, thus diluting their impact
2. in the same way that acquisition of a skill raises confidence, so does mastery of a symptom
3. a beneficial interaction with an adult may make up for interactions that have become strained since the traumatic event

The authors also recommend the use of audio tapes that contain Ericksonian story-telling inductions. These can impart therapeutic messages, interspersed throughout, and have proven generally effective with children who are anxious or phobic or have difficulty sleeping.

Children who may be too frightened to cope with hypnotic procedures may relate well to progressive relaxation. The child is asked to tighten a muscle group, hold the breath, and count to five. The child may feel relief from tension after repeating this exercise two or three times. If so, a therapist can build on the experience of relief by leading the child toward other mastery experiences.

Desensitization, although a generally useful therapeutic procedure, should be employed cautiously with young children. They can easily be overwhelmed—even traumatized again—in the process of being reexposed to traumatic experiences and sensations. The child who becomes a victim again, if only in fantasy, may revert to psychic numbing as a defense against this new assault, in which case the therapeutic benefits of the intervention would be lost. Moreover, the clinician might mistakenly assume that the child's newfound emotional control is a genuine step toward recovery, when it is really no more than blunted affect. In summary, desensitization must be used with restraint, and should be limited to children who have been carefully assessed as being appropriate for it.

Severely traumatized children, especially those who suffered through repeated traumatic events, may need to give vent to some of the primitive rage that is part of their trauma response. This might have to happen before they can be treated by some of the methods described above. They may find release in engaging in aggressive play, or even by pounding on pillows, beating on stuffed animals or inflatable dolls, or smearing paint.

But, at the same time that a clinician serves as a guide to this activity, he or she should note that the child may have a magical fear of the consequences of these displays. It will be part of the therapist's task to establish a setting, and carefully choose the occasion for this kind of catharsis to occur. The child must feel safe to act out, even in this symbolic form.

Emotional release and mastery of symptoms represent only a first step toward achieving the goals of therapy with a traumatized child. Treatment needs to follow for the unresolved dynamic systems issues that originated in the traumatic event.

In review, cognitive/behavioral methods can be utilized to help a child gain control and mastery of some symptoms. Often these are chosen and exclusively used by therapists who find the suffering of a child too powerful to bear. A therapist's countertransference may also lead to the selection of a treatment technique that holds promise of quick recovery, even though it is capable of no more than symptom alleviation. In fact, techniques of this kind do not work with every case of anxiety or phobia in a *general* clinical population; they should only be used within the larger framework of psychotherapy.

When it comes to trauma, most clinicians who have never suffered through a traumatic experience can scarcely intuit what horrors a child victim may have endured. For that reason, it can be hard for a therapist to realize that he or she may be inflicting some measure of "therapy trauma" on the child client; further, a therapist may have no idea what the child's limits of tolerance are, and may press on blindly until forced to stop. No one doubts that this clinician "means well," and it is very likely the misplaced motive of wanting to "make things better" that leads to making things worse.

In our view (Terr, 1990, pp. 307–8), therapists who work with severely traumatized children should consult frequently with senior clinicians. In addition, a team approach with frequent case discussions can be valuable, especially to prevent the kinds of transference issues identified above.

Closure

The play therapy scenarios of some young children will naturally evolve and migrate toward themes of mastery. These children will create new play that involves helpers, caretakers, or situations in which injured or needy persons are rescued. When this occurs, a therapist can help a child by interpreting these new themes to the child in a way that will assist him or her in relegating the traumatic event to the past. The authors agree with Terr (1990), who observed that traumatized children do not experience such interpretations as intrusive or anxiety-provoking. Instead, most children find interpretation of this kind to be reassuring, to confirm their sense of reality, to place their feelings in context, and to help them to move on from the painful event. As Terr so aptly put it: "The child hopefully learns that although he was helpless in one particular situation, he will have other options in the future to avoid helplessness" (Terr, 1990, p. 301).

During the interpretive phase of therapy, the clinician should work closely with the child's parents to ensure that they are in harmony with the therapist's plan, and do not inadvertently interfere with this part of the process. As noted earlier, inappropriate information from anxious adults may not be viewed skeptically by the child, because he or she has not developed the capacity to weigh and criticize these data. The child simply attempts to cope with and defend against what the environment has inexplicably cast his or her way.

Through play, a therapist can help the child dramatize imagined situations that are similar to the traumatic event, in which he or she is not helpless. In this way the child can be taught appropriate ways of obtaining help and protection in dangerous situations that may arise in future. For example, one can lead the child into scenarios that involve locking doors, using the telephone, and staying out of dangerous places.

When the child's thoughts drifts into the realm of fantasy and away from real-life concerns, he or she can be guided to such themes as vanquishing demons, monsters, and dragons. This kind of mythical, magical exploration should be kept separate from the more realistic plots of play therapy. In other words, the clinician acts as a sort of gatekeeper to the child's creative process, in which one role is to remind the child that even though there is no dragon in the house, he or she may have to dial 911. In time, the child's wounded ego will have become strong enough to know the difference between the bad person and the symbol.

AGES EIGHT TO TWELVE: THE SCHOOL-AGE CHILD

The school-age child who has been traumatized presents a unique array of clinical issues. Even though a child may need to regress to a previous developmental stage to feel safe enough to begin the recovery process, the core issues that must be confronted reside within his or her true stage of development. A school-age child reaches out for the first time toward independence, as expressed by the declaration, "I can do it myself." Social norms and rules are first questioned by "Why?" and "That's not fair." The child of this age reaches out toward the hands of peers as he or she lets go of the parents' hands.

With a very young child, the sex of the therapist is not an issue as long as the therapist is sensitive to issues of boy-girl differences. This factor will change significantly with the onset of the latency period. Because of the

gender identification issues that arise at this time of life, same-sex therapists are usually advisable for this age group, unless the specifics of the
traumatic situation indicate otherwise. For example, if a boy was subjected
to physical or sexual abuse by a man, having a male therapist could be too
threatening to the child. Yet even in a situation of that kind, boys of this
age group might eventually need to work with a male therapist as a step
toward complete recovery from the abuse. In general, a same-sex therapist
can help a child to develop a healthier gender identity. A same-sex therapist can more easily "mirror back" to the child appropriate responses in the
therapeutic interactions. In this way, the child will not develop an inappropriate, trauma-reactive personality style, such as counterphobic, aggressive
risk-taking or, conversely, becoming placating or obsequious or seductive.

Origin and Responsibility

The school-age child leaves behind the black or white, good or bad world of
the younger one who usually measures traumatic responsibility concrete-
ly—in terms of punishment, or by how much he or she has personally
suffered. This older child finds a less ego-centered world that is governed
by rules, social conventions, and social consequences. Because of the perceptual growth and the shifting of focus and interest that take place during
this stage, clinical issues pertaining to traumatic origin and responsibility
are significantly different for the school-age child.

A school-age child interacts with numerous social systems beyond the
family system; above all, he or she has a broader experience of how families
differ. Moreover, because the child has a longer past, he or she may be able
to conceptualize that an event taking place at one time might be different
at another and, in fact, might never recur. For these reasons, a therapist has
more rational thought to work with and can help the child approach a
higher level of trauma resolution. On the other hand, because the psyche
of the school-age child is more complex and utilizes more complicated
defense mechanisms, trauma that becomes hidden at this age may be more
difficult to uncover and resolve later on.

The school-age child is usually capable of sorting out some of the issues
that pertain to traumatic cause or origin. For instance, he or she can learn
to differentiate accidental from intentional acts, as well as comprehend
"acts of nature" that cause disasters. Even so, a therapist will be well-
advised to check into the possibility of magical thinking, especially on the
subject of causality. A child of this age often hides magical thinking because he or she fears being shamed for being "babyish." At this age, the
child is struggling to be a "little man" or a "little woman," and can be quite
convincing in his or her pseudomature behavior. This is especially true if
children perceive that their parents want them to appear "grown-up."

Even though the school-age child is developing new understanding of social interactions and how systems work, a therapist should proceed cautiously. This aspect of cognitive growth may be rudimentary and ill-formed. A child of this age can try to understand another's feelings and point of view, but this understanding is mostly based upon social rules and expectations, plus whatever genuine empathy the child has managed to acquire over so few years. The clinician may utilize dolls or puppets and play out complex traumatic situations for the child to confront some of the more complicated social and relationship issues that a traumatic event brings to the surface. A therapist can show the child, in concrete, observable terms, what he or she may not be able to process internally. This kind of play empowers a child to experiment with various roles, make various decisions, and achieve satisfying outcomes in a safe environment. While this is in progress, the therapist can comment, interpret, and offer useful information for the child to analyze the traumatic event and/or relevant other events.

The school-age child will, like a younger child, experience considerable emotional pain and confusion if the traumatic event was caused by a loved and trusted adult. A therapist can help resolve this conflict by "framing" the adult's behavior in terms of broken rules and doing bad things. The clinician may later need to reframe the behavior along the lines of, "Sometimes good people do bad things." "Grown-ups are responsible for obeying the rules about children, and if they break these rules they will have to be taught to obey the rules." "Some grown-ups have problems or are sick, so they need help to learn to obey the rules about how to behave with children." Statements such as these, worked into a play context, can help the child to gain perspective on a relationship that has been bent or broken by traumatic responsibility.

In some traumatic situations, a child will totally lose the relationship of someone trusted or loved, who has inflicted trauma on him or her. Many are sad, vulnerable children who have had to make tragic compromises (without much awareness of doing so) for adult love and attention. In such instances, a therapist can work with the child on two levels: first, on the dynamic level, building the child's ego so that the child will see himself or herself as being worthy of (healthy) adult attention and care; secondly, on the systemic, interactional level, so that the child will be able eventually to redefine the abusive relationship as abusive. It is not unusual for such a victim initially to view the therapist as some sort of abuser ("the enemy") who has taken away the love or attention of a person who loved or was good to him or her. Hence, a clinician may need to be prepared to "work through" a considerable period of anger, provocative behavior, and "testing" before there is a shift in the child's perception of things. The therapist will have to help the child come to terms with the harsh reality that what he or she thought was love, in fact, was abuse. Further, the child may have to deal with the possibility that the abusive adult will not change and that the relationship has been lost to the child forever.

With trauma cases of this complexity, a therapist should be very cognizant of countertransference issues, especially those of anger felt toward the
child's abuser. One way to do this is to accept the child's perception of the
abuser as a loved and trusted person. Having entered this frame of reference, a therapist can begin to help the child to view things differently. This
therapeutic work begins with the rebuilding of the child's fragile or damaged self-image. Until the child's ego is restructured, the abuse will remain
ego-syntonic and the child may even seek out other abusive situations and
relationships. When the child's ego has recovered sufficiently, he or she will
perceive the abusive relationship as it truly was, grieve its loss, express the
pent-up anger, and move toward a mastery experience. If a therapist leads
the child toward that expression of anger prematurely, there is a risk of
frightening the child away, silencing the child, or getting stuck in a "blind
alley."

Often the school-age child's viewpoint on traumatic responsibility is
limited to a variant of "It's not fair." The child may state this directly or
transfer the feeling attached to it into oppositional behavior such as refus-
ing to eat vegetables at dinner. A clinician can help the child's parents
understand which among oppositional behaviors are trauma-related, as
opposed to general acting-out or a "stage." This is not to suggest that
parents should ignore or dismiss this trauma-related form of acting-out.
Instead, the therapist can point out that, when they take some action
against the acting-out behavior, they are also confronting the child's displaced reaction to the traumatic event. So, when a child exclaims that
going to bed at 8:30 is "unfair," it may actually express a feeling that comes
from another source.

The school-age child sees issues of traumatic origin and responsibility
more in the social context of rule-breaking, as opposed to the magical
forces of evil and good that preoccupy a younger child. For this reason, the
school-age child looks to parents and other rule-givers for logical answers
that can be integrated into his or her world view. Nevertheless, because
their psyches cannot sustain the intensity of a traumatic process for extended periods of time, many children will dwell on concerns such as
"Why?" and "It's not fair" for brief periods. Then, after a period of concentrating on other issues, those of cause and blame will suddenly resurface
with characteristic intensity. In fact, the child may need to return to this
subject many times, with many variations on the theme, before gaining
closure.

Acceptance or Stigma

Matters such as these hold far deeper meaning for the school-age child.
Because the child has moved from the egocentric realm of infancy to an

environment dominated by parents, teachers, and peers, the values and conventions of this larger world play a part in one's sense of self: now, whether the child is accepted or seen as an outcast is of vital importance. If the school-age child feels that he or she is somehow socially unacceptable or "different," it can have a profound impact. Hence, a clinician and the significant adults in a child's life should do all they can to prevent the child from feeling stigmatized. Adults need to realize that some things may be perceived as stigma by a school-age child that may not be seen in that way by an adult; for example, the child may feel stigmatized because a parent was disabled in an accident; another child might feel stigmatized because his or her mother died ("All the other children have mothers."). Other traumatic events such as incest, child abuse, or becoming an immigrant in a strange land are more obvious injuries and can be dealt with on a more direct basis. Even so, at the age of nine it is "awful" to feel different.

With respect to resolving the contradictions of stigma versus social acceptance, teamwork between therapist and parent(s) is vital. The clinician's role is to ensure that what parents do about this is, in fact, helping the child. Many misguided parents rationalize that trying to *hide* a stigmatizing traumatic event is "best" for the child; in reality, they are protecting themselves and abandoning their child in the process.

Children who are victims of socially misunderstood or stigmatizing traumatic events ought to feel that they are not alone; first and foremost, they need to know that their parents still accept and love them. Some children need to talk about graphic details of the event with their parents over and over, merely to be reassured that the parents do not see them as "damaged goods" or "marked" somehow. Many parents cannot cope with this without considerable support. Of course, not all children of this age have to repeat the details to their parents, but most need to go over them at least once to confirm that the parents feel the same way about them as before the event. One can advise parents to encourage their child to talk about what happened, because how the child feels is important; nevertheless, a child should not be forced to talk about the traumatic event.

When adults take the position that the child will "forget about it," a secondary emotional injury is often created. Because of the school-age child's new focus upon peers and his or her emergence into new social systems, a child may interpret this parental attitude as not caring or acknowledging the stigma ("I'm different" or "I'm the only person in the world that this has happened to").

Most traumatized children of this age group need peer validation. This will be a vital ingredient in their ability to move forward, beyond the trauma. Peer validation can come in many forms: the best and most meaningful are the spontaneous acts of support from friends and relatives of similar age that are offered in the wake of the traumatic event. Also effective is information about the fact that many other children have gone through traumatic experiences; this medium can be most helpful if it includes photos or videos of other children who have been injured by similar events, so that the child can have direct confirmation of not being alone. Meeting with other children who are victims is often helpful. This can be done by means of a therapy group of no more than six children who were traumatized by similar events, and who are in the same or a comparable stage of the trauma response. In our experience, large groups of traumatized children (ten or more), who may not have been carefully screened and could be in very different trauma phases, may not be clinically productive; in some instances, they could be harmful. Small groups of properly selected children, led by an experienced clinician, can provide the children with a highly positive validation experience.

A Case Study

Eleven-year-old Victoria was horrified that she had to attend "that class": a class on child sexual abuse prevention. When she expressed her discomfort concerning the class, her therapist tried to reassure her that it might be helpful. The therapist believed that the class would be a positive experience for Victoria, who had been a victim of incest that lasted for three years. The therapist was familiar with this particular abuse prevention program, and knew the person who was going to be teaching it.

Victoria agreed to go to the first class, and afterward told the therapist, with wide-eyed excitement, that many other kids had been abused in the same way—even though her therapist had said that often. It was the experience of actually seeing other children in a film that made it real to her. She went on to tell her therapist about a therapist in the film who told a child, "Just like you did," that it wasn't her fault. After the second class, Victoria said, with great emotion, that one of the other girls in the class had told the teacher that her father and her uncles were "doing it" to her. The other girl had told her mother, but her mother did not believe her. Then Victoria proudly reported that she told the other girl that her mother had not believed her at first and that this "hurt" almost as much as what her father had done to her. She also told the girl that some adults do understand, and it would help her if she would talk to them. As Victoria spoke, it was clear that in "that class" her sense of being "different" and "the only child in the world it happened to" was nullified when she was able to help the other girl.

The educational group experience provided Victoria with real-life validation of several kinds: (a) she was not alone, strange, or different; (b) her difficult decision to tell another adult when her mother did not believe her was the right one; and (c) by seeing another child in the same situation as she once had been, she was able to realize how far she had come after eight months of therapy. Finally, helping the other child served to give Victoria a sense of mastery and competence.

This case illustrates how group experiences can be extremely helpful in treating traumatized children. But, it cannot be emphasized too strongly that a child needs to be clinically ready for the experience; if not ready, he or she might be confused or even overwhelmed by it. Further, if a child has assumed a pseudomature or "little parent" role as a way of coping with trauma, one must be careful that the child does not act the same in the group as a defense. Being in the appropriate, child role is very threatening and anxiety-producing for these children, because it implies dependence and vulnerability. This, to them, means risking repetition of the traumatic event. Even though these children like groups because they often can play a dominant role, it will very likely not be possible to work on the issues that they need to address in a group setting. They should work with an individual therapist until they can tolerate resuming the role of a child.

Warning and Duration

As with younger children, symptoms pertaining to lack of warning of a traumatic event are best treated with cognitive/behavioral techniques, within the broader context of dynamic psychotherapy. School-age children enjoy techniques such as progressive relaxation and breathing exercises to reduce anxiety. Learning relaxation and anxiety-reducing techniques can help a child reduce his or her symptoms — when that happens the child will have more emotional energy to devote to the work of therapy. Merely the acquisition of some of these behavioral methods can enhance the child's mastery and competence. The pleasure derived from achievement can be a cornerstone of the school-age child's recovery.

Startle responses and other anxiety-related symptoms may be more firmly fixed in cases when a child:

1. missed the warning signals of an impending traumatic event;
2. ignored the signals and, as a result, now doubts his or her judgment;
3. was traumatized in a well-known situation that was assumed to be safe, and to which the child must return frequently in future;
4. was repeatedly victimized in a variety of situations.

Circumstances such as these require more than just symptom-reduction methods of treatment, because they also involve deeper questions of a child's ability to think, judge, and analyze. Each of these faculties is a vital part of development at this age, and a setback of this type can have considerable consequences.

Protracted traumatic events may have the effect of stunting the child's social development as well. The long-term effect of this kind of recurring nightmare is that the child's world view becomes distorted and contaminated by rage and doubt. By the child's logic, if no one could have saved him or her from this series of assaults, then who is worth associating with, let alone forming a social bond with?

Methods in General

When a traumatized school-age child regresses, it is to reestablish a pre-trauma emotional base from which to find a new path. If the clinician receives an indication that the child has regressed, some toys that are for slightly younger children should be included among the selection of toys in the playroom. The initial therapy session should be a neutral, getting-acquainted time during which the therapist introduces himself or herself and defines the rules and procedures of the therapy meeting for the child, clarifying what is and what is not confidential. As a part of the initial process, the therapist should take a history from the child. Sometimes, the child's historical narrative, when contrasted with the parents' history of the child, can yield revealing information. The clinician can analyze a child's narrative to see what his or her levels of emotional and cognitive functions are. One can also look for gaps in the narrative sequence, inconsistent information, and other data that reveal the types of defenses used by the child. Does the child block or dissociate, or rationalize away emotional pain as "not so bad"? Is the child emotionally bland and constricted, venturing no opinion on any subject? Is the child counterphobic in the sense of risk-taking? Has he or she formed an identification with an aggressor? During this early period in therapy, projective drawings may be useful to assess a child's level of functioning. Some child victims who present a complex clinical picture may need to be given a complete battery of tests, because they are simply not capable of communicating directly about their traumatic experience.

In time, a therapist will sense the appropriate moment to ask the child about the traumatic event itself. Children who have trouble talking about this subject candidly may find it easier to draw a picture of the event or play it out with dolls or puppets. The clinician should convey that what is important is that the child tells how he or she felt about what happened. The child who does not want to talk about what happened should not be pushed or coerced in any way: A therapist can usually find out details from other sources. In any case, if the therapist forms a positive therapeutic relationship with the child, and therapy is eventually perceived as safe, details of the event will surface at some point.

Once the therapist has obtained sufficient information about the child and the event, he or she can utilize the Trauma Analysis Protocol to formulate a treatment plan that focuses on dynamic systems issues. Based upon specific issues identified in the protocol, a clinician can select toys and games for play therapy that will guide the child in the direction of the issues.

With the school-age child, we generally prefer noncompetitive games that tend to focus on interactive process. Even so, children of this age can be extremely creative in adapting such games as checkers, chess, cards, and Monopoly to suit their symbolic needs. The rules, as well as the roles of the players and objects of the game can be altered in myriad ways to represent trauma-related issues on which the child is working. As the game progresses, the therapist can help interpret or reflect on themes of the child's play, commenting and interspersing information as needed.

Some children may be too terrified to express anger during the early stages of therapy. One may have to spend considerable time to make the expression of this forbidden emotion possible. Some children are so critically angry that therapy must wait until some of this primitive rage has been vented. Clinicians should approach this subject with sensitivity, never pushing the child, because the anger will surface on its own when the child is ready to express it.

Parents and significant others such as teachers frequently need additional support during this "angry period," because the child's expression of anger usually extends beyond the therapy room. It may occur some time after the traumatic event, and thus a parent or teacher may not connect the sudden eruption of acting-out with trauma.

Mastery and Resolution

The school-age child needs to go through a mastery phase in therapy. The therapy themes of this period often involve the child's influencing people and situations to be better, as well as reenactments of the traumatic event that lead to a positive outcome. He or she may become fascinated by games and stories in which heroes vanquish evil forces. During this period, the child will usually have to act out, or discuss and then play out, past and future potentially dangerous situations, with the scenario of preventing a traumatic event or of avoiding being affected by it.

In the mastery phase, the school-age child begins the process of closure and resolution. As this process continues, the therapist will begin to observe that the activities of school, sports, and friends take a preeminent position, as the child returns to the task of growth and maturation at the appropriate stage.

AGES 13 TO 18: ADOLESCENCE

Adolescence is both a turbulent and painful time, as well as a richly complex stage of development. The young person is suddenly caught up in a
swirl of forces cognitive, emotional, and biochemical. This unfortunate
puppet reaches up for adulthood and falls back, drawn by the gravitational
pull of childhood. An adolescent's therapist is presented with the not-so-
simple task of developing a therapeutic strategy that will reach the "injured
child," while not challenging the pride of the would-be adult.

In adolescence, a young person is capable of sufficient abstraction to
brood about many of the central social and philosophical questions that
pertain to trauma. The young person feels acutely the pangs of joy, love,
and sorrow, but lacks the adult logical capacities and observing ego to
temper them. Even though an adolescent "speaks adult" and may genuinely believe that he or she thinks like an adult, judgments are made experien-
tially. Here, the primary driving force is emotional energy as opposed to
logic. Often, when adults find themselves engaged in a vexing, circular
confrontation with an adolescent, the miscommunication arises out of this
discrepancy in logical process. While an adult can arrive at understanding
of a concept through analysis and synthesis, an adolescent may need to
experience the meaning of the concept in real-life terms to do so. A traumatic event can seriously disrupt this learning-by-doing aspect of adolescent development, thereby derailing the young person's journey toward
maturity.

Origin and Responsibility

Because of the narcissistic, risk-taking propensities of adolescents, issues of
traumatic origin and responsibility may be a focal point of both intrapsychic and systemic clinical interventions. In fact, it may have been the
adolescent's own natural inquisitiveness, tendency to push limits, or mere
foolhardiness, that led to a traumatic event. The authors have observed
that, when a young person's own peurile foibles have contributed to factors
of traumatic origin, there can be severe dynamic consequences if this
subject is not addressed and worked-through in therapy. The ironic part is
that the adolescent, who was simply doing his or her "thing," has become
traumatized in the bargain.

Unresolved conflicts of traumatic origin can cause the future adult personality to become arrested in either a "trauma-repetitive" or "trauma-
defensive" mode. The former usually results in a counterphobic type of
behavioral tendency; the latter usually results in an avoidant or phobic
behavioral tendency. Clinicians should be wary that some parents and
teachers may view trauma-defensive, avoidant behavior as a positive sign,

when it is, in fact, a symptom in its own right. Adolescents often hide traumatized feelings, especially when the event was caused by their own poor judgment, by a friend, or by a known and trusted adult.

Parents who are struggling with an adolescent's acting-out and risk-taking may get so preoccupied with the struggle that they can miss their child's dilemmas with issues of traumatic origin. The adolescent may be trying to make sense of an event, in which he or she could have died or been disfigured, that arose out of a situation that was judged to be safe, or one that he or she could "handle." If a parent is obsessed by "obedience" or with reenforcing safety rules, the young person will very likely feel added guilt for what has happened.

When the traumatic event was a recent one, it may be relatively easy for a clinician to sort out systemic issues such as these with the adolescent and the family. But if the trauma is one of older origin that is now being brought to the surface because of the adolescent's newly-acquired powers of reflection and abstraction (or recent sexual development), the situation is more complex. For instance, the parents may find differentiating between the young person's "normal" mischief and this trauma-related behavior a mind-boggling task. Besides, they may prefer that the entire affair rest conveniently in the past.

Clinicians should proceed with extreme caution when the traumatic event was the death of a loved or idealized person that is not yet resolved. In many of these cases, an adolescent should be considered to be at considerable risk of suicidal behavior. This may pertain even if the death occurred in the past, because unresolved issues may emerge, in adolescence, in the form of grief so profound that the young person cannot cope. To resolve these feelings, the adolescent will probably have to reexperience the grieving process. Ideally, this would occur in the context of therapy, with family support. Adults may have difficulty understanding that the young person is struggling with loss revisited. If they cannot understand because they have resolved their own grief, a family-systems crisis may arise. The distraught adolescent may retaliate with a suicidal gesture or attempt, in an effort to "punish" the adults who are so insensitive, or to "join" an idealized loved one. Even when these gestures are intended as punishment or as a "cry for help," they may prove fatal.

Stigma and Acceptance

Adolescents dwell in an idealized world in which people and the values they profess are viewed in a harsh light. In addition to their unending quest for an individual identity, fueled by the narcissism that comes with their growing physical prowess, they are imbued with a set of values quite unlike that of adults. Their principles are guided by shame, by contrast with guilt.

In this regard, adolescent values are closer to that of most Eastern and some Middle-eastern cultures, as opposed to the Judeo-Christian beliefs that govern ideas of right and wrong in most Western and Nordic cultures.

Because shame is such a controlling force during adolescence, factors pertaining to traumatic stigma or acceptance are extremely important variables in the treatment of traumatized adolescents. A younger trauma victim may suffer feelings of alienation from his or her peers, but for the adolescent this kind of feeling can cut much deeper and pervade more aspects of functioning. When an adolescent is the victim of a stigmatizing traumatic event such as sexual abuse or being responsible for another's injury, both dynamic and systemic complications multiply. The adolescent now asks, "Who am I?" "What do they think of me?" "How am I like them [my peers] and how am I different from them?" "What good is my life?" For the adolescent, being the victim of a traumatic event is one thing, but being shamed by peers may be the end of the world, and the adolescent may act out accordingly — even resorting to self-destructiveness.

Warning and Duration

Symptoms of traumatic onset such as hypervigilance, startle responses and sleep disorders in the adolescent may also be treated by utilizing the cognitive/behavioral procedures for the school-age child that were described above. Techniques such as sleep tapes and relaxation tapes will, of course, require more mature themes for adolescent listeners. Also, because adolescents have more complex cognitive abilities and better attention spans then do school-age children, some may respond very well to meditation exercises as a means to control anxiety. Biofeedback can also be utilized effectively with the adolescent victim.

Issues of independence and competence, as well as self-image, are of paramount importance to the adolescent. When the traumatic event resulted from an adolescent's ignoring or misreading warning signs of impending danger, or was the direct result of his or her poor judgment, this subject must be addressed with considerable sensitivity. If the clinician is not careful about how these discussions are framed, the subject may be fended off by wounded adolescent pride. Hence, the adolescent may spend useless energy in defending mistakes of omission or commission, as opposed to working on strategies for a safer, wiser future. One way to approach this kind of discussion is to reframe the desired problem-solving as a mutual task. The issue of safety and taking care of oneself is one that both therapist and adolescent must deal with in their lives. By adjusting the frame of reference and making it a mutual problem, a therapist can avoid being perceived by the adolescent as giving a lecture or, in some way, "putting me down."

The question of traumatic duration is a more complex one with adolescents, because many traumatized adolescents were also the victims of past traumatic events. Past trauma reaction may not be consciously available to the adolescent, or the issues that he or she left behind may have become blended or blurred with the current reaction. Moreover, unresolved trauma may have led to an adolescent crisis of acting-out that was a causal factor in the current traumatization. Hence, clinicians should inquire carefully about past traumatic events when working with adolescent victims. They should also be wary that many adolescents who have suffered traumatic reactions may, at first, deny that they occurred. This is particularly likely if the adolescent was traumatized by a family member or trusted adult, or somehow feels a misguided sense of blame or responsibility for the event.

CHAPTER IX

Family Trauma of External Origin

W HEN A FAMILY experiences a traumatic event, the family system is assaulted at many levels. Individual members of the family may have suffered intrapsychic injuries that, in turn, could alter relationships between and among other members of the system. Roles may temporarily shift; some may be permanently destroyed. Figley (1988b) has pointed out that while trauma can solidify a family system and cause family members to pull together, it can also break a family apart, setting its stunned members adrift. Even in the case of a family system that has been flexible enough to stand firm against tragedy and loss, certain traumatic events may wreck its homeostatic balance and render it nonfunctional or pathogenic. Most families have a vast reserve of stabilizing mechanisms on which they draw during times of crisis. But every system—like every diamond—has its cleavage point: If properly struck, a system may sustain damage from which it will not be able to recover without help.

As with individuals, some traumatized families will have had problematic psychological conditions or pathology prior to a traumatic event; some will not, functioning quite normally until the fateful occasion. For a clinician, the difficulty lies in the fact that much of the literature and research on family therapy is based upon the treatment of family pathology, in which the aim has been to identify maladaptive behavior and interactions. Hence, one must use caution when applying such concepts to traumatized families (Figley, 1988a, pp. 137–8). Many family systems that show trauma symptoms give no evidence of underlying pathology. If approached with the assumption that "there must have been something wrong with these people," some families will leave or avoid therapy. If pathology exists within the system, it will surface and can be addressed at that time by the therapist.

146

Because a potentially traumatic event, by definition, transcends the normal range of human experience, it can propel one or more members of the family system into situations for which they have no readily available defenses (Rosenthal et al., 1987, pp. 88-90). The first recourse of the family system may be to draw upon religious beliefs and/or family myths for support (Ollendick & Hoffman, 1982, p. 162). If these resources, bolstered by faith, are sound, the trauma response may soon approximate stabilization. As Figley has aptly noted (1988a, pp. 135-6), when family mythology is largely affirmative it can be central to a family's recovery from trauma. But when the belief system is not a healthy one (e.g., the finding by Ollendick & Hoffman, 1982 that some victims viewed disaster as God's punishment), it will be the task of the therapist to offer the family a new frame of reference. In our experience, as well as that of Figley (1988b), this kind of reframing is essential to recovery in cases in which the belief system contains extra-punitive elements or is maladaptive in some other way. In fact, traumatized families—especially those that have survived a disaster—can be helped in this regard by sympathetic religious practitioners.

Trauma can cast a family into emotional experiences that its members never dreamed possible. Thoughts and impulses that once rested safely behind variously well-constructed defense mechanisms can come crashing into the light of day, reverberating through the system. Some families possess resilient defenses and have contact with external resources that will help them cope with the emotions brought forth by trauma. Others will need help in coming to terms with these emotions.

Therapy with traumatized families will ideally be conducted on several levels. Psychodynamically, each family member will be trying to sort out his or her emotions and repair overworked defense mechanisms. The family system will confront questions concerning how members interacted during the event; it may need to deal with shifting or changing roles within the family that are the result of trauma, and it may have to adjust to changes in living conditions as well. Further, the members may see a need to develop new or strengthened family coping mechanisms to prepare for future traumatic events.

Relations with the larger social system may have to be addressed in the course of family therapy. The effects of trauma may have altered the family's status within the social system, or the family may incorrectly perceive that its status has changed (i.e., real or imagined stigmatization). A clinician can help family members to perceive the situation accurately and adjust accordingly. Finally, because many traumatized families have faced real danger, as for example in a natural disaster that could occur again, the therapist may wish to provide educational counseling that will supply practical coping strategies for situations that potentially threaten survival in the future.

THE FAMILY AND ADVERSITY

Myths and Beliefs

Each family holds to beliefs and shelters myths about injury, adversity, and loss. These certitudes are, in many cases, an amalgam of religious teachings, cultural attitudes, and family history, unified by magical thinking, random reinforcement, and the logic of superstition. Some families are strongly influenced by religion, while others profess popular cultural mores such as those promulgated by television. Yet another type of family may look to family tradition as a primary source of values. In treating a traumatized family, one must comprehend and be sensitive to this belief structure. Families in traumatic pain often shut out those who, they perceive, do not share or respect their beliefs. This is a fundamental self-protective, homeostatic mechanism that the family can rely upon to create a sense of safety and stability in the face of potential chaos. Unfortunately, this facade can be quite maladaptive.

Most severely traumatized families lack the emotional flexibility to change their views rapidly in the wake of a traumatic event. Hence, the clinician's intervention must reflect appreciation of the belief system of the family. The problem is that the nature of their beliefs are not always made clear by family members at the beginning of the intervention. And, because of the tendency of a family in crisis to draw together and exclude outsiders, a therapist may have to expend considerable effort in learning about the belief system and gaining trust. This trust is a touchstone in the treatment of family trauma (Figley, 1988b; Rosenthal et al., 1987).

Friends and relatives often form a sort of "membrane" or shield around traumatized families or their members (Green, Wilson, & Lindy, 1985, p. 61). Although this protective action is intended to prevent further trauma, it can also serve to keep those who would help outside of the circle. Our experience has shown that understanding and respecting a family's beliefs will help in penetrating this barrier, at the same time that it engenders requisite trust.

DISASTER AND
CATASTROPHIC TRAUMA

The unique dimensions of trauma produced by catastrophic events have been measured and catalogued by much research in recent years. It is well known that disaster survivors are affected by one or more of the following trauma-producing elements (adapted from Figley, 1983, pp. 13–18; Wilson et al., 1985, pp. 149–153).

1. Rapid onset: Few disasters wait until potential victims are warned; exceptions include the flood that builds slowly to a critical stage, or the hurricane that marches steadily up the coast. The more sudden the event, the more devastating to survivors.

2. No history of dealing with a similar event: Because disasters are fortunately rare, people often have to learn how to cope on the spur of the moment; even in the wake of disaster, advice or guidance may be ill-informed or too late in coming.

3. Duration: This factor varies from case to case. For example, a flood that develops slowly may be slow to recede, but an earthquake can be as brief as a few seconds and cause more damage to people than a flood. Nevertheless, for some victims of prolonged terror—e.g., a plane hijacking—the traumatic effects can multiply with each passing day.

4. Lack of control: By definition, one has no control over a natural disaster; it may be a long time after the event before a person can regain control over even the most mundane aspect of his or her daily routine. If this loss of control is felt for a protracted period, even a competent, independent person may show signs of learned helplessness.

5. Grief and loss: A disaster survivor may have become separated from a loved one or have lost the person by death; the worst part is probably waiting to find out how much one has lost. Moreover, a victim may lose a role or social position because of disaster. During an event that persists in time, there may be no opportunity whatever to grieve what has been lost.

6. Permanent change: The destruction caused by a catastrophic event may be irreparable; a survivor may be faced with an entirely new and hostile environment.

7. Exposure to death: Even brief exposure to life-threatening circumstances may alter a person's personality structure and "cognitive map." Repeated brushes with death can create profound changes in adjustment level. At the very least, coming close to death may bring about an extreme existential crisis.

8. Moral uncertainty: A survivor of disaster may be called upon to make value-laden decisions that could change his or her life—for example, whom to save, how much to risk, or whom to blame.

9. Behavior during the event: Each person would like to display "grace under pressure," but only a few can manage this. What the person did or did not do while a disastrous event was occurring may haunt him or her long after all other wounds have healed.

10. Scope of the destruction: After the catastrophe has ended, the survivor will likely be affected in some way by the impact that an event has had upon the community and its social structure. To the extent that new cultural rules or normative behavior is required by what has happened, the person may be forced to adapt or become alienated; in the latter case, emotional injury may be compounded by societal insult.

Each of the foregoing components of the trauma response in cases of disaster can be clarified, modified, or alleviated by treatment. In preparing to treat a disaster survivor, the therapist should take these elements into consideration when formulating a treatment plan.

FAMILIAL VERSUS EXTRAFAMILIAL ORIGIN

A traumatic event is familial in origin if it occurs without outside agency or influence. Vivid examples are incest and domestic violence. Extrafamilial traumatic events are the environmentally produced accidents of life, from car crashes to natural disasters. The major difference between these two kinds of events, in the context of this book, is that familial origin implies preexisting family pathology. Of course, pathology may exist in the family traumatized by an external event, but it was neither necessary nor sufficient for the event to occur.

The treatment of trauma caused by these two types of events will differ significantly when the dynamic systems approach is employed. We agree with Terr (1990, p. 297) that many cases of familial trauma are not amenable to the traditional methods of family therapy. In the category of extrafamilial trauma, family therapy may be the treatment mode of choice; at the very least, it can be a useful adjunct to individual therapy. Further, when more than one family has suffered trauma of extrafamilial origin (e.g., in cases of disaster affecting a community), groups of families brought together for therapy, education, or support can be effectively utilized.

DISASTER PROCESS

Not unlike the stages of grief described by Kubler-Ross (1969), the reaction to a natural disaster follows a sequential pattern. We identify six distinct stages of this form of trauma response, namely:

- shock and disbelief (seconds to several days)
- facing the reality of the event (hours to days)
- cognitive survival (days to weeks)

- adding up the losses (days to a year)
- acceptance (months to years)
- rebuilding (months to years)

Those who provide therapy to disaster victims will certainly observe this process unfolding, but appropriate treatment can assuredly compress the time frames noted above.

One key to successful intervention with disaster survivors is to facilitate their "joining" others who have survived as well, so that they have a sense of having shared the terrible experience. Conceptually, this will help the person overcome the isolated feeling that he or she was, somehow, "singled out" for punishment by the event. A second key to therapy is to encourage, as soon as possible in the treatment process, a proactive or future-oriented outlook on the part of the survivor. We have observed that the sooner a victim is able to look ahead—resuming or revising plans made before the disaster, devising a set of precautions in readiness for a similar event in future—the earlier he or she will begin the process of healing and rebuilding.

A natural disaster most often affects groups of people and, in most instances, there is more than one survivor. Apart from the individual person's terror, injury, and loss, there is inherent to the experience a group dynamic that cannot be evaded. What a survivor did or did not do in the event may well be judged according to group values, as opposed to a private standard. Did the person "freeze"? Did the person become fixated on trivial matters? Did he or she give voice to futile anger, in such a way as to increase the anxiety of others? Did the person behave with rigid, robot-like calm, giving an insensitive or uncaring impression? The clinician who works with a traumatized group would do well to be curious about how each group member is perceived by the others in this respect. What needs to be prevented, of course, is scapegoating of persons who did not react as nobly or appropriately as the others would have wished.

It is true that, in most catastrophes for which retrospective data are available, the majority of survivors have "rallied 'round," and there are many documented instances of prodigiously high functioning in the aftermath of disaster (e.g., Quarantelli, 1985). In effect, the cognitive survival state (p. 17) into which the person has been thrust, permits him or her to do "what needs to be done." This is a highly defended state of consciousness that keeps the person going in the face of deadly peril.

The cognitive survival state is not without its negative effects. There is the danger that normal channels of rational thought may temporarily become blocked or shut down. For example, a survivor who is capable of tolerating excruciating pain may adopt a single-mindedness that reaches the level of obsession. This may motivate heroic feats, but if it persists after the event has ended it may impede recovery. A clinician who works with such a survivor may encounter impairment in judgment, as well as retardation in the capacity for abstract thought. In fact, successful therapy may have to move at a slower pace until these faculties are regained.

As the defenses that had been mobilized to cope with the initial stages of the trauma response are relaxed or have become exhausted, a period begins in which the survivors assess what damage has been done. In this time of counting losses, symptoms can be expected to appear in those survivors who will experience symptoms. Those who have lost loved ones will begin to grieve — excepting those who are caught up in a new crisis, such as having to find a new place to live after losing their homes.

Some students of disaster responses have taken a skeptical view of the amount of trauma involved; for example, Quarantelli cites sociological data that show considerable group cohesion and rapid recovery from myriad catastrophic occurrences (1985, pp. 191-6). After the San Francisco earthquake of 1989, people attempted to resume their normal activity as soon as possible and a professional football game was played the Sunday just after the quake; despite aftershocks, many people attended this game. Nevertheless, group functioning is not a valid indication of individual functioning, and even the latter can mask much anguish.

It is often remarked that new cases of mental illness were relatively rare in London during the "Battle of Britain" in World War II. But, while schizophrenia may have taken a holiday, the effects of the almost daily bombing certainly took their toll. In fact, many people were severely traumatized. They did not seek treatment out of stoicism or because of the lack of its availability, and many carry emotional scars to this day. Holocaust survivors tell how they had encapsulated feelings about their torture for 30 or 40 years, only to relive them when visiting the site of their ordeal or when meeting a fellow survivor.

It cannot be overemphasized that people may receive an emotional injury and bravely hide it for years. The very symptoms of trauma can be denied, even as they occur, or can be attributed to some other cause. This phenomenon, discussed previously in Chapter VI on hidden trauma, operates by the same process that permits people to perform admirably when disaster strikes. On a mass level, it is the same process that enables group members to collaborate smoothly in the work of disaster relief. Even so, as Chapter VI makes clear, the consequences of this suppression of feelings about a traumatic event can be pernicious.[1]

---

[1]This is an example of mechanisms of defense that have done their work too well in protecting the person from having trauma symptoms; in effect, the mechanism has functioned out of control, as does the fibrillating heart. What is not obvious is that the person may have endured added emotional hardships throughout the years of repression, such as when problems along the way were not as easily solved because of the "unfinished business."

The best part of working therapeutically with disaster victims is their encouraging prognosis for recovery. After all, the vast majority were functioning well enough before the catastrophe. With time and with help, most can attain their former levels of adjustment. The only counterweight to this optimistic assessment of outcome is the problem of case-finding. Some disaster victims may never have given a thought to emotional difficulties before the event and may, therefore, tend to avoid defining their new-found concerns as psychological issues. They seek advice from religious counselors, colleagues, teachers, and medical practitioners, rather than mental health professionals.[2]

Among the most promising solutions to this dilemma are these:

1. Public education to alert people to the possibility of having emotional reactions to catastrophic events, as a part of "disaster preparedness" training.

2. Education for community helpers (clergy, teachers, etc.) in strategies for short-term intervention with disaster survivors.

3. Widespread dissemination of information about treatment resources that are available for trauma victims.

Ideally, a prevention program for minimizing the impact of a disaster would incorporate elements of each of the approaches listed. A community structure built on this foundation would be ready for almost any possible calamity.

For our private practice, we have written a brief brochure that can be given out to survivors shortly after a natural disaster has ended. It is adaptable for use by any agency, clinic, or practice that has an emergency response service. The text of this brochure is presented in Table 9.1.

TREATING A FAMILY AFTER DISASTER

The treatment methods described here are based upon a model advanced by Figley (1988b), and are intended as steps in an intervention process for fundamentally normal families that have survived a natural disaster.

---

[2]A deterrent to recovery happens in the case of people who seek help in the wrong place, for the wrong reason. A common sequel to natural disasters is that survivors present themselves at hospital emergency rooms for a variety of psychosomatic complaints, chiefly because they do not recognize or acknowledge that they are suffering trauma. This is a source of concern to medical personnel who are trying to care for the dying and wounded. Clinicians can perform a service for hospitals by training doctors and nurses to be sensitive to the needs of these people and to refer them to mental health resources.

TABLE 9.1

We have experienced a profoundly traumatic event together. The staff of _____ would like to let you know that we are here to help in any way we can. We are available 24 hours a day to answer questions or to meet with you; our services are confidential.

Effects on Adults:

An emotional reaction to a traumatic event is very natural. The most common responses to traumatic events are:

1. Anxiety about the possible recurrence of the event.
2. Confusion, difficulty in concentration, memory problems, or an inability to estimate time accurately.
3. Temporary mood swings, general changes in temperament, and irritability.
4. Flashbacks of the event which may be visual or may take the form of reliving the event emotionally.
5. Sleep problems and/or nightmares.
6. A change of appetite or eating patterns.
7. Emotional distress caused by events or objects that remind you of the traumatic event.
8. A desire to avoid anything that might remind you of the traumatic event.
9. Diminished interest in significant activities (work, social, or family).
10. Feeling depressed or detached or estranged from others.
11. Shortness of temper, angry feelings, or a lack of patience with yourself or others.

Effects on Children:

Frightened or traumatized children (especially very young children) express their feelings about a frightening event by means of behavioral changes. This response to trauma is expressed through behavior because most children do not possess the social, developmental, or psychological maturity to comprehend, fully, what has happened to them. In most cases, these behavioral changes will pass in two to six weeks. Adults should view the behavioral changes as the child's way of saying that he or she was overwhelmed by something very terrifying.

After a traumatic event, it is important for parents to give extra time to their children and do extra things to reassure them. It is usually best for children and adults to resume their normal routines as soon as possible. But, if a child is frightened or behaves oddly, he or she should not be reprimanded or punished. It is also a good idea to take extra time, over the next few weeks, to talk with your child about what has happened, and to encourage the child to share his or her feelings about what happened with you. Bear in mind that a child may need to have several talks with a parent before he or she can resolve an event such as the recent one.

(continued)

TABLE 9.1 (Continued)

The following is a list of symptoms that children frequently display after traumatic events:

1. Fear is the most common initial reaction. Children are often reluctant to separate from their parents; some may actually cling to their parents and need constant physical contact or reassurance.
2. Traumatized children may have nightmares, often about scary objects other than the event. Some children may refuse to sleep alone or in the dark.
3. Some children react to a traumatic event with anger and hostility. This anger is usually an expression of the child's fear and helplessness. Temper tantrums or obstinate, unruly behavior (as well as mood swings) are common in traumatized children.
4. Reluctance to go to school is often a symptom of an unresolved trauma.
5. Many traumatized children turn their emotional pain into bodily symptoms. Many complain of tummy aches and headaches that have no physical cause. They may use these symptoms as an excuse to stay home from school. Parents should respond to such unusual physical complaints in an understanding way that is reassuring to the child.
6. Traumatized children show a wide range of phobic or avoidant behavior, such as fear of being outside, being alone, or being in closed-in areas.
7. Many traumatized children regress or temporarily engage in the behavior of an earlier developmental stage. Some children will wet their beds, lose their toilet training, suck their thumbs, or generally act like younger children.
8. Changes in eating habits are fairly common in traumatized children. Frightened children may be reluctant to eat; or, they may hoard food or go on eating binges.
9. Some children feel that the traumatic event was their fault or could somehow have been prevented from happening. Children who experience guilt feelings may need considerable reassurance from their parents.

   Most traumatized children only experience symptoms for brief periods. If you have a question or a concern, please feel free to call us at any time. We are here to help.

The Staff of _____

Two major systemic issues need to be factored into the treatment equation for families. First, in a disaster everyone — including the helpers — is traumatized. In the San Francisco area, after the earthquake of 1989, many helpers and rescue workers were caught in the dilemma of seeing to the needs of their own families while still performing professional duties. (More about this subject will be found in a later chapter, "Trauma in the Workplace.") Secondly, when the event has destroyed or altered a survivor's

environment in some way, the person may have lost certain support systems on which he or she relied, or familiar surroundings that provided
comfort by "being there." For this reason, an intervention begun during the
early stages of the post-disaster period must be practical, i.e., focused upon
safety, survival, and coping with immediate consequences of the event.
The two issues converge in this way: The clinician who takes time away
from personal concerns must guard against potential countertransference
feelings in which the survivors that he or she helps become substitutes for
his or her own family members or friends.

Initial intervention should focus on restoring family unity as soon as
possible. For example, poor planning in respect to re-housing or relocation
can affect a family as an emotional aftershock. In fact, Solomon has argued
convincingly (1986, p. 238) that poorly conceived post-disaster relocation
efforts can cause lasting damage. An instance of this occurred when a small
child was sent to live with his grandparents after the family home had been
lost in a flood. The child misperceived his parents' well-intentioned desire
to send him to his grandparents, where he would be safe, as some form of
punishment. He felt banished from his parents and older siblings for somehow, magically, causing the flood. His puzzled grandparents could not
understand why this child, who was "safe" with them, developed symptoms, while his older siblings who remained with their parents at the flood
site did not.

Not only should the family be urged to join together as soon as possible,
but its members should be assisted to resume their normal roles as well.
Children should be discouraged from adopting pseudo-mature or parental
roles. Often, pseudo-mature behavior on the part of children is mistakenly
perceived as a positive sign and encouraged by the parents. Even if the
family is not able to return to the former home, family members should be
advised to return to their normal routines and behavior patterns at the first
opportunity.

Gaining Trust

In the act of drawing closer together, members of a family may follow their
natural inclination to exclude strangers at a troubled time. This may be a
vexing paradox for the therapist who would intervene on behalf of the
family: he or she must strive that much harder to gain family trust. Even
so, the path to trust may be smoother if the clinician has had first-hand
experience with a disastrous event of the same kind. Having shared a
similar experience may cause a therapist to be perceived as less threatening
and more trustworthy. In any case, trust will be essential to obtaining the
family's full commitment to participation in family therapy.

Treatment Process

We have utilized treatment approaches analogous to the five-phase process for "post-traumatic stress disorder in families" that was described by Figley (1988a, pp. 132–7). Once a commitment to therapy is made, family members are encouraged to express their feelings about what transpired during the disaster. Children are allowed to talk about their fears. Alleviating those fears is discussed as a family effort, so that the children do not feel ashamed of them; in effect, the children's fears are reframed as an issue that the family will work on together. If the children are engaging in regressive behavior, the therapist discusses this with the family, and attempts to normalize the regression by putting it into a proper context. During this reframing period, the family is helped to come to terms with any difficult decisions that its members may have been forced to make, as well as any relevant moral issues such as whether or not the event was "God's punishment," preventable, made worse by negligence, etc.

When appropriate, parents are encouraged to share their feelings with their children. This not only validates the parents' feelings but also, by extension, enables the children to understand that their feelings are also valid. During this discussion phase, the family members are encouraged to share information and to begin reconstruction as a family. In this process, the therapist fosters externalizing the disaster, so that it is seen less as a destructive force than a challenge that the family can meet by pulling together. This new frame facilitates the family's reconstruction by stimulating realistic theories about how it, as a family, will lay to rest past losses. The final phase of treatment should also include realistic discussion of how the family should meet and cope with any future disasters.

TRAUMATIC LOSS

It is true that many have demonstrated resolve and perseverance in calamitous times, but the sudden death of a family member puts these qualities to the sternest test. Walsh and McGoldrick stated this fact succinctly: "Of all human experiences, death poses the most painful adaptational challenges for families" (1991, p. 25). Often, coming to terms with this kind of trauma is not simply a matter of seeing reality clearly, but requires an acceptance of reality at its ugliest. David Rieff recounts the story of the father of a woman who was killed, along with many others, when terrorists caused a plane to crash in Ireland in 1985. As the father left the morgue after identifying his daughter's body, a group of journalists surrounded him. When one asked, "What are you going to do?" the man answered with great dignity, "Do? What do you expect me to do in this dirty world?" (1991,

p. 56). The inane question was not worthy of the man's answer, with its agonizing truth.

The grief process that this father experienced may have been long and tortuous, merely because death had been so unexpected. For example, the father may seldom have thought about what he might feel if his child died. Further, there may have been complications in their relationship that now would never be resolved. Without warning, the story ends because the final pages of the book are missing. The father's perplexity could last a lifetime.

Loss of a loved one by natural disaster can have even more drastic effects if the event has destroyed artifacts and mementos of those who were lost. When the parents of a friend of ours were killed by the Mexico City earthquake of 1985, all of their belongings (including photos, letters, family documents) were buried in the rubble that had once been their apartment house. When our friend was staring at the wreckage, he noticed, lying at his feet, a copy of his parents' marriage certificate; this was the only verification that he could find of their existence. In a matter of seconds, they had vanished into the void.

In another scenario that is common to natural disasters (or war or some such political upheaval), bodies are swept away, burned, or buried, and never found. This situation, in which a loved one is declared "missing" or "presumed dead," creates its own kind of anguish—a paralysis of emotion. One can appreciate what flights of imagination are stimulated by this form of traumatic loss, in which false hopes alternate with dreadful imaginings about the victim's fate. Long after any chance for survival has passed, these yearnings may linger. As other writers on traumatic loss have observed (e.g., Murphy, 1986, pp. 149–50), in these cases the eventual confirmation of death holds some consolation, for it enables the survivors to deal with their loss and properly grieve.

Not only does this "presumed death" keep survivors in suspense, but it prevents them from making use of rituals such as the funeral or the wake to reach closure. They may find themselves caught in tangled legal processes concerning what is to be done with the person's property while he or she is missing. In fact, their own need to survive and carry on with life may complicate their grief, causing them to feel oddly guilty toward the lost loved one.

There is trauma, as well, when a loved one is found dead by violent means. Identification of the body is one source of excruciatingly painful emotions. It is not so much the sight of the lifeless body that arouses our sorrow, but the empathic wound we feel by imagining the pain and suffering before death. Just a verbal description of what this might have been like can excite feelings such as these.

When traumatic death cuts short a young life, or when the death could obviously have been prevented, the survivors' suffering can be especially intense. Death caused by drunk driving is a trenchant example of an event that somehow should have been prevented. The mother who permitted her daughter to go for a ride with a boyfriend who got drunk and killed her in an accident experiences loss that is hopelessly tangled with self-castigation.

Homicide, another form of preventable death, is often committed by a member of the victim's own family. Family members, who are already experiencing considerable grief reactions, may also blame themselves for not preventing the death. Members may feel that the family has dishonored itself. Moreover, if a child has witnessed another family member kill his or her parent, the ultimate childhood trauma will surely follow (Eth & Pynoos, 1985, pp. 36–40).

Death of a Parent

The most frightening thought in childhood is to contemplate a parent's death. When it happens, children cannot begin to cope with its reality, because they have no cognitive framework for the experience. The dichotomy between eternal and finite is beyond comprehension, and, as a result, the child perceives a parent's disappearance as abandonment. Often, this abandonment is construed as a form of punishment. A child may ask questions such as, "What does 'forever' mean?" or "What do people eat for breakfast when they go to heaven?" The child ponders at length such subjects as where Mommy or Daddy are right now, and why they won't come back. The child may ruminate on even more disturbing questions when trying to cope with a presumed death. If there is a chance that the parent is still alive, why don't the others do more to bring him or her back? The frustration of the adults may be multiplied many-fold in the child, who wants to believe so desperately that the parent will return and the nightmare will soon be over. In times of war or natural disaster, the situation is even more fraught with anxiety for a child, because the adults may be preoccupied more with survival needs than with answering a frightened child's questions.

Magical thinking may help sustain the child through a time of loss, but it can make matters worse. For instance, a child who has been told that a parent "just went to sleep" may develop a fear of sleeping. Even worse, the child's fantasy life can lead him or her to form the belief that something he or she has done or thought caused the parent's death. Some children form the wish to "join" a parent in death, and thus are definitely at risk of committing self-destructive acts or even suicide. In addition, there is a risk factor with adolescents who have experienced earlier, in childhood, the traumatic or unresolved death of a parent or parent-figure.

The grief reactions of children differ from those of adults both in form and intensity. A child tends to fluctuate more often between periods of intense mourning and normal behavior, than does an adult. In one case, a four-year-old girl who was attending her mother's funeral was observed to be, by turns, dumbstruck and playful. When her emotions threatened to overwhelm her, she would escape into playing with a stuffed animal that she had brought with her.

The capacity of a child to grieve is regulated by the child's developmental level, in that the questions that the child wrestles with are governed by how much he or she can understand of what has happened. When a new stage of development is reached, new questions will demand answers and new issues will need to be resolved. When these matters arise, some time may have passed since the death occurred, and adults who have completed their grieving may try to suppress the child's inquiries. They may have "moved on," but the child has not. For example, a widowed parent may have found someone new to love, and may consider the child's need to reflect on his or her lost parent as an intrusion on the present relationship. The therapist needs to deal with this systemic conflict sensitively.

Some children try to compensate for the loss of a parent by incorporation, in which the child attempts to take on his or her parent's role in the family. This is not to be encouraged, just as it is not advisable to foster any pseudo-mature behavior in a child. Even so, there are many adults who seem to derive pleasure from observing this type of role-playing by children, and getting them to discourage it may require the clinician's most sensitive but persuasive powers.

TREATMENT FOR TRAUMATIC LOSS

When a family suffers the death of one of its members, the interplay of psyche and system is in a continual ebb and flow. Each person struggles with the pain, conflict, and anxiety of his or her wholly individual experience of the loss. From a systemic point of view, the structure of the family may be altered, and the roles within it may need to be reorganized to cope with the loss (McGoldrick, 1991, p. 51). Besides, the family's interactions with, and place within, the greater social system may have been temporarily or permanently changed by the traumatic event.

Even though some significant traumatic losses may never be fully resolved, the family will eventually accept and adapt to them. Some families have the internal resources to make the necessary adjustments to continue as a healthy family system, while others will require assistance. With the more extreme cases, in which the family is devastated by more than one loss caused by a single event, there is a danger that the trauma response (although homeostatic in principle) may escalate into nonadaptive behavior and, if not treated, pathology on the part of one or more family members. Examples of nonadaptive behavior include making impulsive changes to compensate for the loss(es), such as moving away or remarrying hastily. Some parents who have lost a child will conceive a new one soon after, with the best of intentions, to provide a replacement.[3] This is another instance of making things worse by trying to make them better. Here, the changes come too soon (as with a replacement child), or are so drastic (a hasty remarriage) that the family is plunged into added turmoil.

Walsh and McGoldrick (1991, p. 16) discuss two fundamental styles of pathogenic family interaction following a traumatic loss, "enmeshment" and "disengagement." The *enmeshed* family insists that each member share in the experience of the loss; those members who do not hold a shared view or reaction to the loss are silenced or pointedly ignored. The *disengaged* family is generally incapable of tolerating a shared or interactional experience of the loss: Members drift apart to experience their grief in isolation from the others. A clinician might find the enmeshed family to be quite resistive to outside intervention; i.e., even when help for every member is offered, they believe that together they can do whatever is required. If the family fits in the disengaged category, the therapist will have to be flexible, meeting with individual family members, dyads, or other subsystems; this kind of family resists meeting as a whole with an outsider present to observe its interactions.

Even within the family group, individual grief reactions may vary widely. For instance, women tend to focus on emotional aspects of the loss, while men focus on the practical aspects. The clinician should take these tendencies into account, to facilitate the understanding of each person's way of grieving by everyone in the group. No one's way is more "valid" than another's.

There should be no secrets in the traumatized family—at least none about the traumatic event. The keeping of a secret from a child is particularly dangerous, for one compelling reason: Most children can sense when adults have conspired to keep something from them, even when they haven't the slightest notion of what it might be. If they feel this sensation after a death, they will know what the subject of the secret is, but not its exact nature. They will fill this vacuum with fantasies of all sorts, even to

---

[3]This "replacement child" phenomenon has been studied extensively by the French psychologist Anne Ancelin-Schutzenberger (in press). Vincent Van Gogh was such a child; he was born on the year anniversary of the stillbirth of a child who was to have been given the same first name. In effect, he was born with the identity of a dead person. His ego belonged to someone else. The role confusion that this created followed him throughout his short, sad life.

the point of myth-making about the lost loved one. We have observed that when a child is forced to create a myth about the cause of death, there is invariably an element of self-blame.

For the adults of a family that has lost a loved one, the primary treatment objective is to help them resolve conflicts that were abbreviated by death. Their regret at not having "cleared things up" before it was too late is mixed with anger at being left behind, and confounded by pangs of guilt for not being able to prevent the traumatic event. Some can relieve this internal pressure by writing a "letter" to the lost person or by establishing a certain ritual that will help them say goodbye. In many cases, role-playing, guided fantasy, or empty-chair work proves useful. Remember that the family's history will need to be revised as a result of what has happened. As this reflective process evolves, the family may restructure itself with new relationships and alliances, and by doing so set a course toward a healthy future.

CHAPTER X

Trauma Originating Within the Family

MANY A FAMILY has worsened the effect of a traumatic event of outside origin, but some make their own trauma. Instances of the latter include incest, physical abuse, and suicide. This is by no means an exhaustive list of the tragedy that a family can inflict upon itself, but it epitomizes the more self-destructive forms. In this section, what has led up to these types of familial trauma is described less thoroughly than what can be done about them; i.e., treatment is discussed in more detail than etiology.

THREE TYPES

Incest[1]

In the house of incest, pandemonium is loose. The child-victim may experience simultaneously the loss of true fathering, her mother's betrayal, the collusion of siblings, the indifference of neighbors, relatives, and teachers — even the alienation of peers who cannot be told the secret. Moreover, the child has been ejected forcibly from childhood and the child's role. But it is not this loss of innocence by premature sexualization that causes the most damage. Worst of all, her child's trust has been cruelly misused, and the only place that she has known as sanctuary has been invaded. The gingerbread house of "Hansel and Gretel" is a metaphor for this archetype.

Treatment for a family in which incest has recently been revealed will inevitably involve the entire family.[2] As alluded to above, the entire system

---

[1]Here, treatment is discussed only for cases of father-daughter incest.
[2]Treatment methods presented here are adapted from Everstine and Everstine, 1989, pp. 117–126.

is awry. A crisis of this magnitude also involves considerable suicide potential, with no member of the family, including the incestuous father, being risk-free. A clinician bears considerable responsibility for monitoring each family member in terms of this risk.

In this kind of case, questions of family versus individual treatment are paramount, because of the origin of trauma in the father's behavior. At least in the beginning, whole-family sessions probably will not be possible. In our view, the father must accept his guilt and apologize to the child (in addition to whatever legal penalty he must pay), before he can be permitted to have contact of any duration with her.[3]

Therapy can be started along two parallel tracks. If the parents are still together, they should be seen as a couple; if not, they should be seen individually. At the same time, the child should have a therapist of her own. Eventually, the whole family can safely be united in treatment, but only after several goals have been achieved. When working with the parents of an incestuous household, the aim is to repair generational boundaries that were ruptured by abuse. This means helping husband and wife to function as a couple and to accept their roles as adults vis-à-vis their child. Further, the marital subsystem must be capable of operating separately from the parental subsystem. A clinician can expect to expend considerable time and effort before so dysfunctional a couple can regain sexual compatibility. The best path for the therapist through this dark wood is to keep the sessions structured and the interventions direct. The clinician's role is to be a model of the healthy parent. This means setting behavioral limits and enforcing acceptance of responsibility for one's actions.

Working with an incestuous father in individual treatment offers many rewarding challenges. The therapist can establish ground rules early by requiring that the father confess what he did to his daughter in full detail. He must also acknowledge that whatever took place was and is entirely his fault. In effect, any rationalization that the child was partly to blame must be contradicted; moreover, it can be used to advantage as a way to show the father that he lacks insight into what it means to be a child. When the clinician is convinced that the father has confronted himself—without reservation—about his abusive behavior and has acknowledged what the future consequences for his daughter might be, therapy of the more conventional sort can begin. Obviously, he has a lot to learn about parenting, and his education on this subject will have to be built on fundamental concepts. He should be taught that the child's need for nurturance and

---

[3]If there is more than one child in the family, there may have been more than one victim; the clinician has a duty to investigate this possibility. If the identified victim has siblings, this by itself is a compelling reason for taking steps to remove the father from the home, even if the victim has already been placed elsewhere.

2. She may herself have been the victim of severe neglect or abuse — even incest — in childhood. If this happened and scars still exist, this woman may fear that she may never become a good mother until they are laid to rest; any attention given to the child diverts attention away from her own role as victim.

3. She may wish to "contain" the current investigation into incest for some reason; for example, she may want to minimize her guilt for letting it happen, or she may want to conceal incest that is still going on with her other children. In the worst scenario, she may want the investigation to halt, the child's treatment to end, and incest by the father to *resume*.

These contingencies represent subjects that are worth exploring in the mother's individual therapy, but their importance lies only in what meaning they may have for the child's treatment. If the mother is genuinely prepared to subordinate her needs to those of the daughter, the real intervention for both can be focused on the mother-daughter dyad.

Interaction between mother and daughter should be studied, clarified, and strengthened by interpretation and advice. This can be done either in joint mother-daughter sessions or in a group of mothers and daughters. The eventual goal is to create or restore an emotional bond between the two of them that is based on respect and empathy instead of envy and antagonism. (Specific techniques that can be used in joint sessions of this kind are outlined in Everstine & Everstine, 1989, pp. 123, 124.)

Not all incest families can be put back together again. This is chiefly because the best efforts of clinicians to rehabilitate incestuous fathers have so often fallen short of success. The most likely outcome is that the parents will remain separated or get a divorce, and mother and victim will try to build a new life. For this to be successful, the mother must become capable of protecting her daughter (and other children if there are any) from future abuse. The daughter should be helped to understand the reasons for separation, so that she doesn't feel that it was somehow her fault.

Child Abuse[4]

In some countries, corporal punishment of a child by a parent is a crime. Our country has not evolved to this point, but it is illegal in every state to *beat* a child. In addition, strict laws concerning reporting now require nearly every professional who works with children to contact governmental

[4]This section concerns only physical abuse of children. Sexual abuse is addressed in complete detail by *Sexual Trauma in Children and Adolescents* (Everstine & Everstine, 1989).

protection agencies *on suspicion* that a child has been abused. It may be that these deterrents have hit their mark; for example, the *Journal of Child Abuse and Neglect* has, in recent years, devoted more of its pages to articles on child sexual abuse and newly identified forms of neglect, than on child beating per se. Nevertheless, there are still all too frequent newspaper accounts of children brought to hospitals with burns, evidence of scalding, or deep puncture wounds; there are still stories of children who suffer brain damage as a result of being shaken severely, and of some who die after long torture. These horrors are in most cases committed by parents who never venture near the reporting network; they are people who have no knowledge of the laws relating to children, or little motivation to obey them if they do.

Our concern here is with the traumatic effects of the kind of physical maltreatment that may occur in an otherwise respectable household day after day, abuse so subtle that no one outside the family knows about it. Harm of this magnitude often does not require physical treatment at a hospital, but meets the criterion of " . . . punishment [that] has caused bruises or other injury to the child" (Everstine & Everstine, 1983, p. 103). The problem for the clinician, as astutely noted by an attorney, Richard Kohlman (1974, p. 245) is one of case-finding. For example, how do we know that a child we are seeing in therapy is the victim of trauma caused by being beaten?

Any one of the following observations or clues may point to possible abuse:

1. an unexplained or unexplainable physical injury;
2. a discrepancy between the descriptions of how the child was injured that are given by the parents when each is questioned separately;
3. a discrepancy between the nature of the injury and what a parent says was the cause (e.g., "just an accident");
4. when the injury is said to have been self-inflicted;
5. when someone other than the child or a parent is said to have caused the injury;
6. when a delay occurred before the parent(s) sought treatment for the injury;
7. repeated injuries or being "accident-prone" attributed to the child (from Schmitt, 1978, *passim*).

These signs are definitive of abuse, but even though none is apparent to a therapist, abuse might nevertheless be occurring. Indicators of the emotional injury that the child is also suffering might include:

1. unexplainable mood swings being displayed in therapy sessions;
2. sudden withdrawal on the part of the child from his or her usual forms of interaction with the clinician, alternating with angry comments or destructiveness in play therapy;
3. uncharacteristic refusal to answer questions about the parent(s) or avoidance of questions such as "What's happening at home?";
4. reports, by parent(s) or teacher, of acting-out behavior at school;
5. any other major changes in deportment or level of adjustment that occur with sudden onset or adopt a cyclical pattern.

Of course, when trust has been firmly established with a child, the child may reveal the abuse directly. This is not the ideal way to find out about abuse, because when the clinician reports it, the victim will feel guilt for "turning in" his or her parents. Coping with guilt feelings will then become the main subject of the child's therapy.

A major issue for the therapist is whether or not to recommend that the child be removed from the abusive home. This is a good reason to involve the parent or parents in the victim's treatment right away; in many cases, some form of family therapy takes over completely, at least until order can be restored to the child's home.[5]

Treatment for child abuse poses logistical problems because the abusive parent may have been put in jail or may refuse to cooperate. Even a nonabusive co-parent may resist change. In general, abusive families resent any outsider's intrusion, closing ranks in a form of "damage control." They may at first deny that anything happened, and later fall back upon the position that "it wasn't that bad." If they acknowledge one instance of abuse, they may conspire to conceal other instances, in an effort to narrow the scope of any investigation currently underway. A frequent type of referral is the one in which, after a court proceeding establishing abuse, a parent is ordered to enter treatment to "get this matter straightened out" and prevent further harm to the child.

Therapy should begin with clearly stated ground rules. The clinician is not a judge, detective, or police officer, but he or she should be alert to any evidence that abuse has resumed with the identified victim, or has occurred with siblings. The message is that, even though they are being offered help, and even though most of the proceedings of psychotherapy are confidential matters, the therapist does not condone nor will he or she keep silent about any hint of continuing abuse on the part of a parent. A

[5]The treatment methods presented here are adapted from Everstine & Everstine, 1983, pp. 112–119.

major theme of this therapy will be training in ways to cope with the stresses of parenthood without striking a child.

If the parent has deep-seated psychological problems that predispose him or her to lose control in this way, those problems should certainly be brought up in treatment. In some court-mandated cases, the participant(s) will be expected to continue for a specified, minimum period of time. If this contract is breached, the clinician will report that fact to the referral source. Therapy will be coordinated with other agencies that are helping the child victim in recovering from trauma, and information about the parent's progress will be exchanged with those agencies.

In the case of a two-parent family, the most effective plan will establish weekly sessions for each parent and one couples session weekly. Family sessions including the abused child (and siblings, if any) are recommended if the child is strong enough to take part. This multifaceted treatment plan is highly labor-intensive, and the abusive family system may need at least two therapists working in tandem, especially if the child's individual needs are to be met as well. Certainly, a child victim will benefit greatly from individual sessions organized around play therapy. When resources are limited, the family can be referred to a multifamily group, if available; this will supplant family therapy sessions and is often a helpful experience for abusive parents.

The initial phase of treatment with parents usually encompasses this sequence of events:

1. In the first stage, the parents' fear and anger is expressed by the resistance and denial described above.
2. They may subsequently become quite dependent upon the therapist, sometimes calling for advice in the middle of the night. Because this form of transference contains some infantile characteristics, this dependent period can be a risky one with child abusers. Their impulse control in moments of stress might be shaky, and a responsive voice at the other end of the telephone could prevent a new episode of abuse.
3. After the dependency period has run its course and the clinician has proven to be a "good parent" to the parents, the real work of treatment can begin.

From a practical standpoint, an abusive parent needs to be taught about children: about the stages of normal child development and what form of punishment is most useful with children at differing stages. Much progress can be made by explaining techniques that a parent can use to enforce discipline without resorting to violence after a rule has been broken. The parent will realize that the therapist does not deny his or her need to control the child's behavior, but is recommending that new methods of control be tried.

Many abusive parents have a deficient sense of empathy, probably because no one taught them about it when they were young. They simply cannot conceptualize how it must feel for a child to be hit or berated or humiliated; they have no capacity for placing themselves "in someone else's shoes." Their training in this vital aspect of child-rearing must begin at the most fundamental level. They can be asked to recall moments when they were hurt by someone else, or when they felt great joy; the point of the exercise is to relive the feelings that were felt in these moments. In that way, they can practice feeling the same emotion that the child will feel, *before* the blow is struck.

Finally, the parent must learn how to express anger in new, healthier ways. The premise for fostering this change is that he or she has very likely been displacing much anger onto the child. A problem-solving approach is indicated, in which the parent makes an inventory of situations and people that arouse his or her anger; in such a list, it is inevitable that the child or the child's behavior will have only minor importance. The parent will then be guided toward finding more direct ways of expressing anger where it belongs. In addition, the parent should learn to displace free-floating anger in harmless ways, whether by hitting a punching-bag, a softball, or some other inanimate object.

In conclusion, child abuse can be brought to a halt by prompt, direct clinical intervention that involves most of the family members. It is a family crisis that must be met squarely to be overcome. Even if the abusive parent takes a vow never to strike the child again, this kind of family reconstruction is needed, for the same reason that people in Scandinavian countries have voted to abolish corporal punishment in the home: hitting a child teaches the lesson that problems can be solved by violence.

Suicide

Suicide by a member of the nuclear family may well be the most traumatic event that a family system can endure. The more close-knit the family, the more devastated it is by such an event, as each person tries to make sense of what has happened and as conflicts arise between and among family members about what or who could have prevented the death. The survivors of a suicide are, whether one person alone or part of a family group, among those at the highest risk for being traumatized. Wallace, in his highly informative book, *After Suicide* (1973, *passim*), has described the catastrophic effects that the suicide of a loved one can have on those who are left behind. In many cases, their lives are never the same.

For a family that has lost a member to suicide, the principal dilemma is to comprehend in what way their system has been altered by the event. A complicating factor will arise from their conscious or unconscious realization that the motive for self-destruction was to send a message to at least one person among the survivors (Everstine & Everstine, 1983, pp. 201–19). The content of the message was rage that the suicidal person could not express in any other way than by dying. Each family member is, in effect, "put on trial" by his or her own conscience, and each will render a verdict ranging from innocent to agent of death. The major obstacle to recovery, for a family, occurs when disagreement arises about these self-assessments of guilt, and family members begin to assign blame to each other. Clearly, this process can, in some instances, wreck a family system — which may or may not have been part of the suicidal plan.

The toughest task that a family therapist may ever face is to create a functioning family out of the chaos of suicide. This is certainly a situation in which the clinician would be well-advised not to adhere rigidly to family therapy dogma. For example, a session with the entire nuclear family present shortly after a suicide could be a traumatic experience for the therapist and might make matters worse. In these highly-charged circumstances, the best strategy might be to meet with family members individually, first, to let each one ventilate his or her feelings about what has happened.

Without question, a family in which suicide has occurred merits a high level of therapeutic concern and careful observation. Especially if there is a history of suicide, the clinician should evaluate whether or not another family member may be at risk. Another factor to consider, if there are adolescents in the family, is that many adolescents who kill themselves come from families of origin in which suicide was not unknown. It is worth noting, moreover, that the rate of adolescent suicide has increased in our culture in recent years. We agree with Walsh and McGoldrick (1991, p. 15) that thorough history-taking is a requisite when working with a family in which suicide has occurred.

PART FOUR
Trauma and Society

CHAPTER XI

Trauma in the Workplace

HIDDEN OR UNRESOLVED TRAUMA

Each day seems to bring news of more people who have decided to reveal that they were physically or sexually abused as children. The percentage of the population who have been victims of, or who have witnessed, violent acts is on the increase. When those experiences are added to the ones caused by the unusual (e.g., natural disasters) and the commonplace (e.g., car crashes), the probability that any one person is the survivor of a traumatic experience is great. Even so, many of these people have been able to mobilize their own emotional resources to overcome the effects of these events; i.e., their trauma responses have reached closure. But there are many others who have not been so fortunate, in that they retain unresolved conflicts caused by trauma; worse, some are not aware of the extent to which they are affected by long-since "buried" feelings. In terms of Freud's two stage settings for ego-functioning, home and work, it is easy to see how trauma in one sphere can influence how one functions in the other. If a person brings a lot of traumatic "emotional baggage" to the workplace, his or her performance on the job may be adversely affected.

One factor that contributes to this transfer of personal life to work life is that the workplace is analogous to a family system. An authority figure may be seen as the symbolic substitute for an abusive, neglectful parent by an employee who has been the victim of familial trauma.[1] In the beginning,

---

[1]From another perspective, we have observed that people who come from abusive families are often drawn toward professions that project a strong "family" image, such as the military, law enforcement, and fire fighting (see below, this chapter).

the employee is likely to strive hard to please this newfound "parent," in an attempt to earn the acceptance or recognition that were denied in his or her own family. When these high expectations are not met, as in most cases they are not, complications can be expected to arise. The employee who feels rejected by an authority figure who unwittingly has been cast in a parent-substitute role, will likely express his or her frustration by some form of "testing" or rebellious behavior. Misplaced scorn or resentment may rise to the surface unchecked and become directed toward supervisors who have no idea what they have done to offend.

How often is this the underlying dynamic in cases when an employee is disciplined for "insubordination"? When the clash comes, each antagonist retaliates blindly against the other, because neither has any comprehension of what the issues are: The employee has no conscious awareness of the reasons for creating a substitute parent, while the supervisor does not know that he or she is playing that role. Each responds reflexively to the "unreasonable" behavior of the other. When they are totally polarized in their perceptions of what is happening, communication stops. From that point, emotions take over and the battle escalates.

A clinician may be asked to intervene in this kind of conflict when the employee is referred by management for "counseling" or voluntarily seeks help for what is happening to him or her at work. The best policy for a therapist is to set boundaries around clear clinical objectives, to avoid being drawn into the workplace struggle. The most practical aim is to provide suggestions about how the employee can negotiate a truce at work. A long-term goal might be to help the client understand what led to this state of affairs. That will mean bringing to the surface any episodes in the client's history that will explain his or her current maladaptive way of perceiving people. If past trauma is uncovered in this process, this will also have to be dealt with.

It is well known that personal and family problems are the major cause of employee absenteeism and impaired job performance. In sum, a past or *current* problem at home may surface as a problem at work. It is the task of the clinician to sort out this possible cause of workplace conflict from that caused by prior trauma, and plan treatment accordingly.

TRAUMA IN WORKPLACES THOUGHT TO BE SAFE

When they go to work, people carry with them the same assumption that they carry when entering any public place, namely, that it is safe. Not only is it assumed that the work environment is a safe one, one takes it for granted that the people one encounters in the course of doing the job are reasonable and will not act negligently or do harmful things. That trust notwithstanding, everyone knows of at least one instance in which a normally tranquil work environment has suddenly been transformed into chaos. In one such instance, a receptionist in a real estate office was taking a message from a client, when, suddenly, an out of control car crashed through the window of the office, struck her desk, pinned her to the wall, and seriously injured her. A young attorney was working late to prepare for a case; in the next office suite, a man was showing off a gun in his collection. Two shots rang out; the bullets went through the wall, striking and nearly killing the attorney as he sat at his desk. Workers in a modern, state-of-the-art office building in a major city were seriously injured when a large piece of construction equipment at the building next door went out of control and slammed into their building. In another office building, workers were exposed to toxic fumes believed to be carcinogenic, which were produced by a fire. A saleswoman was preparing to close a candy shop located among small, elegant boutiques in an affluent neighborhood. A gunman forced his way into the shop, pistol-whipped and robbed her. The victim, a woman in her mid-40s, had taken the job thinking that it would be safe. Five years earlier, she had been the victim of a robbery when armed men held up the bank in which she worked.

The Attitude of Management

Employees look to their supervisors for support and assistance when such traumatic situations occur. A sensitive approach by management can become a major force in how swiftly and thoroughly the employees will recover. Managers who take an overly defensive, aloof, or adversarial position in these matters — due often to their fear of litigation — can make the situation far worse. Sometimes, a defensive approach will spark the employee's anger and lead him or her toward litigation. Moreover, this anger, if excessive, could serve to drain the traumatized person's energy *away* from resolution and closure.

Most traumatized employees can return to proper functioning if they are treated reasonably. This would include being given access to clinical services that can aid recovery as early as possible. These services should be confidential and presented in a way that makes the victims feel that they are genuinely meant to help them recover. Sadly, many companies, agencies, and insurance carriers are reluctant to make psychological referrals after a traumatic incident at work, fearing that each referral will lead to expanded claims against them. In our experience, exactly the converse is true.

Recommending and making available psychological services to employees who may have suffered trauma can reduce the number of stress claims (not to mention the settlement amounts), because it makes a clear statement to the employee that management is concerned about his or her well-being. Further, when an employee gets help with symptom alleviation, the person is less likely to turn to drugs or alcohol as a form of self-medication, or to "convert" emotional distress into psychosomatic symptoms. Counseling or therapy can also serve to channel feelings — especially anger — appropriately, so that the traumatized person can vent it constructively. If not, these feelings may become misdirected toward supervisors, co-workers, friends, or family members.

In our view, treatment to help an employee cope with the trauma response should be carried out by professionals who have specialized experience and training in this form of clinical work. The services offered should be designated as *relief of job-related trauma*, because people have a tendency to avoid traditional "mental health" care. The treatment services should be designed for the specific needs of each individual employee and modified to fit the specific work environment. In the ideal case, of course, the employee would be able to return to his or her job assignment and schedule, but when that is not possible therapy should facilitate the employee's reassignment or retraining.

Trauma and Level of Functioning

Although we are constantly impressed with the strength and resilience of the human spirit, there are those who must struggle to perform within the average range, even under ordinary circumstances. Hence, when a traumatic event strikes these people, it can render them virtually nonfunctional. Some suffer from past, unresolved traumas as described in Chapter VI; others have nonfunctioning support systems or lack them completely. Employers should be advised not to assume that every previously capable worker can return to a pre-trauma level of functioning, even when the traumatic incident was of moderate proportions.

THE ROLE OF MANAGER, SUPERVISOR, OR CONSULTANT

Many organizations delegate responsibility for dealing with the varied aspects of a traumatic event at the workplace to supervisors and managers. They assume that managers or supervisors will know what to do and will deal with the matter appropriately. Even so, with the exception of professions such as law enforcement, fire fighting, and emergency services, whose supervisory personnel are trained in interventions with employees after extreme events, few managers are better prepared to deal with a crisis situation than is the average person. It is true that there have been many cases of inspirational, even heroic, leadership in times of grave danger and acute loss, but the leaders probably behaved so admirably because of exceptional qualities that they themselves possessed. Seldom are supervisors and managers given thorough training in what specifically to do, as leaders, when employees experience a traumatic event. Moreover, a supervisor is just as likely as anyone else to be in a state of traumatic shock when others are in need.

Training at the managerial level should include information about the core psychological components of the trauma response. When feasible, the organization would do well to consider using outside consultants to provide this training. It is also recommended that the contract with those who do the training include a provision in which the consultants will be available to the organization when a traumatic event actually occurs; one such arrangement would be that a consultant will visit the scene of an emergency to advise supervisory personnel on the spot. When appropriate, a consultant might provide a direct service to traumatized persons, or, the consultant may concentrate attention on the larger issues of group reintegration and recovery.

As with any organizational consultation, the clinician should be sensitive toward matters concerning roles, status, and professional boundaries. In traumatic situations, tremendous pressure may be placed upon a consultant to "do everything"; in addition to consulting, he or she may be asked to do employee assessments as well as the direct clinical task of therapy with employees. These requests are often made with the best of intentions by managers, who are reacting to felt needs of the moment and may not have thought through some of the inherent conflicts of this request.

As clinicians, we make clear distinctions between the tasks of *treatment* and psychological *evaluation or assessment*. In many cases, these functions serve the same purpose, but they *can* serve conflicting purposes under some circumstances. For example, a traumatized person may have taken time off work to recuperate and have received treatment during this time. When the person feels better and seeks to return to work, his or her supervisor may ask the therapist whether or not the employee is "fit" to return. Because the clinician has been a consultant to the organization, the employer considers the request for information to be a legitimate one, but owing to the nature of the therapeutic relationship, there is a probability that the therapist is biased toward the client. Hence, the clinician may not be able to offer a wholly objective evaluation of the client's fitness to return to work. In short, there is a conflict of interest.

It is important that an employer know about this possible outcome when entering into any contractual arrangement with a mental health professional as consultant. At the outset, it is useful to establish that consultation, assessment, and treatment are distinct entities, each with its own ground rules. It may be that a clinician will contract to play only one of these roles for the organization, or that several colleagues will divide the roles among them. In any case, the organization should be made aware, in advance, of what it can expect.

ANGER, BLAME, AND RESPONSIBILITY

After a traumatic incident at a workplace, emotions usually run the gamut from numbness to terror or rage. Those directly involved in the event are probably in a state of shock or emotional paralysis, while those less directly involved may display their anger more freely. In time, the anger of those who were directly involved will emerge, often through the medium of speculation and information-gathering about who might bear responsibility for what happened. (In the wake of a natural disaster, this often takes the form of identifying those who should have given a warning.) It is one of the anomalies of traumatic injury that a victim's angry, acting-out behavior may emanate from a preconscious process in which the anger is expressed before the person is aware of feeling angry.

Because of the hierarchical structure of workplaces, in which people tend to defer to authority, there is often an impulse on the part of employees to think of their supervisors as being somehow responsible for a disastrous event. And even when most people perceive that what has happened was clearly an accident, there is no guarantee that certain employees will not feel resentment or that one of them will not blame "the brass" or "the company." It is characteristic of paternalistic systems that followers will cast their leaders into the role of "failed protector" when a crisis occurs. If there is considerable anger being felt toward top management, and especially when there is some degree of culpability among members of the managerial group, a clinician can play the role of peacemaker. The therapist as consultant may be able to defuse these feelings by means of individual counseling or, if there is more than one victim, group sessions. While it is important that anger be brought to the surface, the clinician can exert an influence on an employee to express it appropriately. In this way, an employee can achieve a catharsis of feelings without losing his or her job in the bargain. Specific techniques for helping a victim cope with angry impulses were presented in Chapter V.

THE WORK ENVIRONMENT
AND TRAUMA

Discussion Groups and Clinical Services

When a traumatic event occurs at the workplace, employers should take decisive steps to facilitate stabilization and recovery. For example, time should be set aside for employees to discuss and work through their reactions to the event; employees should not be forced, but encouraged to participate. Discussion groups for this purpose can best be organized according to the employees' degree of involvement in the traumatic event. In many instances, those who were directly involved view the participation of those who were not with suspicion; they suspect that the motives of the others for joining the group might vary from morbid curiosity to pity. Therefore, including those who were not directly involved should be done with considerable caution, lest their presence impede open discussion. Although some employee groups may choose to discuss the traumatic event only among themselves, it is recommended that employers enlist a mental health professional or trained group facilitator, to ensure that the group functions efficiently. Another reason for having professional leadership is that the leader can spot employees who may need more intensive clinical interventions.

The reason that each employee of an organization should be encouraged to participate in this group process to some degree, is that it discourages stigmatizing; it fosters a sense of community and gives employees a sense that they are valued by management. Further, those employees who exhibit signs of trauma and are unwilling to enroll in a group should be approached privately. The indications of trauma that they have given should be brought to their attention sensitively, and then they can be referred for individual counseling. In the ideal instance, a supervisor would first consult with a mental health professional about how to discuss the problem with a resistant employee. The discussion should focus upon observable, measurable behavior as opposed to "attitudes" or mannerisms. Every effort should be made to convey a sense of genuine concern lest the discussion be misconstrued as critical or punitive. An employee who has witnessed the traumatic injury of another person may have been quite traumatized by being a helpless onlooker. Hence, witnesses should be included in any program of services that the organization provides for injured employees.

After a traumatic incident, employers should give employees as much factual information as possible about the incident as well as the condition of co-workers. Often, in the confusion following a traumatic incident, misinformation and rumors abound. Although these rumors are rarely malicious in intent, they can serve to make an unfortunate situation worse. After a traumatic event, people have a deep need for information, chiefly to recapture a sense of control and to dispel the fear that random forces have been set loose. If they are not told frankly what has happened, their imaginations may run wild.

Because acquiring information is a key component of the trauma response, supplying that information is one of the important functions of the discussion groups referred to above, since they provide a structured setting in which to exchange knowledge constructively. Similarly, those employees who are recuperating at home or in a hospital will need to be supplied with accurate information as well. In many instances, there is a flurry of support and attention for injured co-workers immediately after a traumatic event, but as time passes their contact with fellow employees may dwindle, causing them to feel alienated.

Civilization is not so advanced that there are no longer superstitions about bad luck. In this context, it often takes the form of one worker avoiding another who was the victim of a traumatic event; the "logic" is that the victim's ill fortune could "rub off" on the one who is, so far, unscathed. This fear of contagion by people who have been singled out by fate can even lead to ostracism of the victim. And even when the reaction is not so primitive as this, it can generate marked friction among colleagues at a workplace. These irrational sources of conflict can be defused by group meetings, led by persons trained in aspects of the trauma response.

Any intervention that an organization can provide after a traumatic event should strive to (a) channel feelings of blame, (b) dispel magical thinking (i.e., superstition), and (c) restore group cohesion. The discussion format is by no means a substitute for psychotherapy, but it can succeed in bringing back stability among the members of an organizational team.

HIGH-RISK CAREERS

Professions that involve high-risk activities and/or constant exposure to dangerous situations — such as police work, fire fighting, emergency medical services, and some components of the military — warrant special consideration because of factors unique to these professions.

Public Prejudices

The public is shielded (and shields itself) from many of the randomly violent aspects of life. Strong defenses and rich fantasies are used by people to insulate their thoughts from these horrors. Fortunately, there are agencies and services that take up the burden of intervening when events of this kind occur. Knowing about the existence of these protective services represents our best defense against worrying about what might go wrong. Even so, we have a tendency to take these guardians for granted, and we are quick to criticize them if they do not respond as rapidly or act as efficiently as we would like. It is easy to fall back upon the commonly-held notion that the people who do this kind of work enjoy the maudlin circumstances that they encounter on the job, or that they should have known what they were getting into ("It comes with the territory."). It is true that the people who work in these professions enjoy and take pride in their work. But moments such as attempting to give CPR to a dying three-year-old, holding a dying colleague who has been your friend for ten years, or digging through the rubble of a fallen building to look for survivors among corpses can take a toll on even the most zealous and hardened professional.

Reasons for Choosing a High-Risk Profession

People choose high-risk careers for all manner of reasons. Many have a realistic sense of what the profession entails, believe sincerely that they are well-suited to the profession, and know themselves well enough to have developed good coping and defensive strategies. Nonetheless, some make this choice because of low self-esteem; these people are drawn by factors such as status, glamour, and excitement. Others are propelled by a counterphobic need to "undo" past harm or past traumatic experiences, just as some people are attracted to the helping professions because they were neglected or abused as children. No one would dispute that these are legitimate reasons for making a career of rescuing people in distress. But it is certainly preferable if the person is aware of these motives than if not aware.

Because of the physical and emotional demands of high-risk professions, we believe that people who wish to enter these professions should be screened according to psychological criteria. For example, in California, this process is mandatory for anyone who applies for a job in law enforcement. We advocate expanding this approach to hiring for professions such as fire fighting, emergency medical services, radio dispatching, and rescue work, because these workers will encounter potentially traumatic situations on a regular basis. Screening can ensure that those who are hired are prepared to cope with the emotional hazards of these professions.

Defense Mechanisms

When exposure to potential trauma is a fairly regular occurrence on the job, a professional must develop a flexible defense system that can be activated at difficult times and deactivated as needed, especially when personal life resumes at the end of the workday. This is the ideal case, but in some high-risk jobs it is viewed as unprofessional or weak to discuss feelings associated with highly-charged situations or events. Workers are encouraged to be tough and, one way or another, to "stuff" their feelings. Denial is popular in this context, in that some people cannot even acknowledge that an event was emotionally painful. Nevertheless, a growing body of research testifies to the reality of trauma in "public safety" occupations (e.g., Blackmore, 1978, p. 48; Lester, 1982, p. 1094; Levitov & Thompson, 1981, p. 167; Martin, McKean, & Veltkamp, 1986, pp. 100–101; Taylor & Fraser, 1982, pp. 8–10), even though there is still considerable resistance in these professions toward admitting its emotional toll.

Because many people who work at a high level of risk defend themselves against strong feelings routinely, they incur a further risk of entering a chronically defended state. When this occurs, they carry their work-related defense mechanisms into other spheres of their lives. And these defenses, so functional in the professional realm, can be grossly dysfunctional when extended to home and family; often, they cause considerable alienation in significant relationships. One manifestation of this state of affairs is when the worker confines his or her social interactions to fellow workers, based on the belief that only people who have shared experiences can understand or care. There has been much improvement in public awareness of the emotional hazards of professions such as these, but this glacially slow change in attitude represents a mere beginning. Of course, everyone reaches out with sympathy when a police officer or firefighter dies in the line of duty. But there is still a want of sensitivity toward the everyday travails of these protectors and restorers of community peace.

Creating an Emotionally Healthy Work Environment

The creation of an emotionally healthy work environment in high-risk professions should begin with the employees' initial training and be enhanced by subsequent training. Taking care of oneself, emotionally, should be *promoted* by the profession and advanced as an intelligent approach toward a successful career (as opposed to being for the "weak ones" who "can't handle it"). Although the media have recently made considerable strides toward changing popular stereotypes of these professions, their portrayals often sensationalize the traumatic events that they publicize. The less dramatic, more commonplace sources of trauma that the workers face routinely are, as a result, made to seem trivial. In short, we cannot expect the media to give the public a realistic view of the emotional shocks that these professionals endure.

In addition to educating high-risk professionals in skills of primary prevention, an employer should sponsor counseling services on an as-needed basis. A major theme of this counseling would be to help a worker in coping with persistent stress engendered by his or her job. Ideally, these services should be kept separate from the organizational structure itself (i.e., "out-house" instead of "in-house"), and should maintain absolute client confidentiality.[2] In other words, information about the content of treatment sessions (or even their occurrence) should not be disclosed to supervi-

---

[2]Confidentiality in psychotherapy has limits, proscribed by the duty of a therapist to warn the intended victim if a client threatens to harm someone, as well as the duty to report any suspicion that child abuse has occurred. For a thorough dissection of these issues, see Everstine and Everstine (1986, *passim*).

sors or managers without the permission of the employee. Only in this way can an employee place trust in the counselor, a trust that must be established if the counseling service is to be fully utilized by employees.

Organizational sponsorship of a clinical program means more than just making it available. An employer should actively support participation by employees who are having psychological problems. Too often, high-risk professionals deny needing help themselves, mainly because they are preoccupied with helping others. In addition to providing a clinical program for everyday stresses and emotional difficulties, a progressive organization will arrange for emergency services on stand-by status. If there were a disaster or serious traumatic incident, counselors would be on-call to respond to the scene of the event, to the workplace, or to the homes of victims.

Emergency Interventions

People in high-risk professions should be offered clinical intervention — if only one session — following a serious traumatic event; even those who were on the periphery of it should be seen at least once. Individual screening of employees to find out who needs assistance the most should be carried out as soon as possible after the event. Preferably, screening would be done by clinicians who are known and trusted by the staff, because unknown mental health professionals may be viewed with suspicion and receive a guarded response.

Group therapy following a traumatic incident can be very helpful, but before forming a group a clinician should individually screen the people who were directly involved in the incident. For some, meeting in a group may be inappropriate and contraindicated: For example, a person may be too distraught or fragile to tolerate the group process. Not everyone behaves as others think they should during a crisis and, subsequently, there may be strong negative feelings on the part of some people about how another person reacted; this, in turn, could cause the group process to become confrontational. In addition, there could be litigation that affects those who were involved. If this is likely, it may be better to substitute individual counseling for those who might conceivably be affected, because group therapy is not protected by the confidentiality privilege.

Once pre-screening of participants has been completed, it is a good idea to wait from 24 to 48 hours (since the event concluded) before holding the first group meeting. That will permit the survivors to have some time for rest and reflection. We have found that group sessions for traumatized people proceed more smoothly when there is a "time out" period before starting.

The focus of the group experience should not be merely on catharsis, because workers very likely will be returning to the same conditions that produced the traumatic event. For this reason, ventilation of feelings alone is not much help to them. Groups for these employees should be organized around a structure that validates feelings through understanding, putting what happened in perspective, and accepting that they did the best they could under the circumstances. These strategies are aimed at achieving a measure of closure, so that the group members can take up their professional duties again as soon as possible. When feasible, the group may meet for as many as six times, depending on the severity and complexity of the traumatic situation.

This group approach is so often effective with workers in high-risk professions because—apart from funerals—there is no standard ritual that provides for the release, working-through, and resolution of feelings aroused by a traumatic incident.[3] For example, losing and grieving for a fellow worker is not represented by a provision of the union contract. A clinician who works with organizations such as police or fire departments or the military is often struck by how their funerals are fraught with emotion, some thinly suppressed and some overflowing. People who normally, in the course of their work, face tragedy with calm and control, may find themselves expressing feelings of which they were scarcely aware. These funerals offer a setting in which the unstated rule is that it's all right to show bereavement and sorrow. They fulfill an absolute need imperfectly, and by doing so demonstrate how strong the need is. The focused group for traumatized workers is a more direct means to the same end, and individual counseling the most direct of all.

Even when an employee has benefitted from attendance at group sessions, he or she may find it useful to enter psychotherapy concurrently or after the sessions have ended. High-risk professionals may, in fact, require intensive treatment for a considerable period following a traumatic event. An advantage of therapy of this kind is that it can include members of the traumatized person's family, when appropriate.

Individual Therapy

Clinicians should be very sensitive to the fact that people in high-risk professions may come to therapy with complaints other than those related to a traumatic event. They may seek treatment for family problems or

---

[3]At the recent gatherings in memory of the attack on Pearl Harbor, there were many instances in which survivors demonstrated that they still had pent-up feelings from a traumatic event that occurred fifty years before. Probably few of these veterans had sought treatment during or after their terms of service, and it is likely that few had any idea that their trauma responses had been unresolved for so long.

other emotional issues such as unexplained anxiety, job dissatisfaction, depression, sleep dysfunction, or excessive drinking. Not unlike other traumatized people, they may have resisted seeking treatment because of the stigma that is associated with mental health care. Or, they may have attributed their problems to "weakness." Conversely, they may see, in therapy, some form of threat to an already-weakened defensive structure.

In some cases, treatment is sought because a spouse has insisted upon it; external motivation of this kind is not a good prognostic sign. The dilemma is complicated if the person is reacting not only to a recent, known traumatic event but also to an accumulation of past traumatic situations; in such cases, a victim's defenses may have been sufficiently strong to prevent a severe trauma response, but the most recent event has proven too much for these defenses. Often, when emotions from accumulated traumas do erupt, they follow a divergent path toward some "safe" aspect of the person's life, such as marriage or family. This is another instance in which the iron might of the defenses deployed earlier is a disadvantage, because the person is unable to see the connection between his current outpouring of emotion and what happened in the past. The significant others are themselves unable to perceive the connection, because the person convinced them, in the past, that what happened had done no harm. For their part, the outbursts that are presently occurring may not seem justified by the recent traumatic event. To them, it may seem as though "All of a sudden he just fell apart," or "He blew up for no reason."

This perplexity of the loved ones and family members of workers in the high-risk professions is an artificial condition that the worker creates in them unwittingly. In the belief that it is best to protect them from the harsh realities of his or her working life, the professional spares them the details; some have a rule never to talk about it at home. This attempt to shield the loved ones is misguided in many instances, because it requires a degree of self-deception to succeed. The subconscious fear is that, by revealing how they felt today at work, their defenses would fail them and they might "break down." In some walks of life, that kind of display is taboo.

For therapy with trauma victims in this category, the significance of these personality traits is that the emotions emerging in treatment may be detached from the incident that jarred them loose. In fact, they may have "migrated" a considerable distance away from their center. Confusing matters even further, grief may masquerade as anger, fear as the compulsive retelling of an account of the event, or self-doubt as bravado.

Once an event has been accepted as trauma-producing and a victim has acknowledged traumatic feelings, therapy to guide the trauma response can begin. Strategies for this treatment are presented in Chapter V. To recapitulate a major theme of the approach recommended here, providing information to the victim is a key element. By means of supplying facts about what happened, and helping the person reinterpret what he or she remembers of the event, one can stimulate defense mechanisms into renewed activity. For example, a statement of belief such as, "I failed to save the child" can be re-structured into, "I did everything possible to save the child." Some clients will be able to make transformations such as these straightforwardly, while others will respond more favorably to the structured hypnosis process that was described previously in Chapter V.

WORKERS' COMPENSATION

When a client becomes traumatized by an event at the workplace, it is likely that the clinician will sooner or later be asked to interact with the workers' compensation system. In most cases, the client will have little prior knowledge about this system, but most will have an attorney who specializes in this kind of case and should be the person's best source of advice. A client who does not have an attorney should be strongly encouraged to get one, because an application for workers' compensation is an especially complex form of insurance claim. (If denied, the claim can become an equally complicated type of law suit.) The client should be urged to interview more than one attorney to be sure that the person chosen has experience in cases in which psychological trauma is a factor.

Many lawyers who take workers' compensation cases have considerable understanding of physical injuries, but do not comprehend emotional injury. For example, the middle-aged woman described previously (p. 188), who was pistol-whipped and robbed while at work in a boutique, was told by the first workers' compensation attorney she consulted that she had no case; the reason given was that, because her physical injuries were relatively minor, she was capable of returning to work and therefore would require no compensation. This attorney did not even give consideration to her emotional trauma. Her symptoms included panic attacks, fear of strangers to the point that she was practically agoraphobic, sleep disturbances, and hypervigilance. He ignored the fact that she had been on antidepressant medication since the attack, as well as the probability that she would never be able to work with the public again. Fortunately, she was able to find a lawyer who understood emotional trauma, and her case was favorably resolved.

Clinicians should be cautious when a client, because of anger about what he or she has suffered, develops an inflated sense of the righteousness of the case or exaggerates symptoms. In a situation like this, a therapist should encourage the client to talk realistically with his or her attorney; certainly one should refrain from giving any form of legal advice.

As with the legal processes described in the chapter to follow, a workers' compensation case is inherently adversarial. Therefore, a therapist should maintain careful boundaries and stick to the clinical role. If the therapist's function is treatment, only this function should be performed; i.e., he or she should *not* attempt to conduct an evaluation for either the client's attorney or the workers' compensation system. The evaluation should be done by a different clinician hired for that purpose.

Often a treating therapist will be asked to make a "report of first injury" about a worker, so that the worker can open a claim. This report should be written objectively from the therapist's viewpoint, without judging the merits of or advocating the client's claim. This approach can prevent the clinician's being drawn into a position that could compromise the therapeutic process at a later time.

The report of first injury and subsequent, follow-up treatment reports are not normally reviewed by people with clinical training, and thus should be written in clear terms that a layperson can understand. The worker's symptoms should be described in behavioral terms, and conclusions about dynamics should be supported by behavior. It is wise to keep reports of this kind brief, being careful not to include observations not directly relevant to the injury being claimed. The kind and amount of treatment the worker will need in order to recover from trauma should be estimated, with reasons for the choice of treatment mode and projected duration discussed.

In some cases, a workers' compensation insurer will choose to accept the claim on receipt of the report of first injury; in others, the claim will be rejected at this early stage. One can advise the client not to overreact to this or to take it personally. Instead, one can point out that this often occurs as a part of the process of workers' compensation litigation. The client can confirm this with his or her attorney.

WORKPLACE TRENDS

Winds of change sweep across this field. In some states, legislation is planned to "curb the excesses" of claims for emotional injury suffered on the job. These laws are designed to make it more difficult for employees to be compensated for "stress," chiefly by raising the standard of proof required to establish that an injury has occurred. Those who propose this kind of legislation are encouraged by the lobbyists of business, industry, and insurors who indemnify companies and public organizations. Their arguments are persuasive because there has been a marked increase in lawsuits and workers' compensation claims in recent years. We can understand their motives, even as we observe that they are *unclear on the concept.*

Why is it that cases of emotional injury in the workplace are increasing nationwide? For the same reason that more and more instances of child abuse are revealed. Is there perhaps more of this abuse in our country than there was at the turn of the century? More likely, the trend is a result of increased reporting of these crimes, itself the result of increased awareness of this social problem.

There has been an evolutionary raising of consciousness about workplace trauma. We have become aware that the workplace can be an oppressive environment, in ways that go far beyond such hazards as radiation from computer terminals or blocked fire exits. As we are learning from the proliferation of cases of sexual harassment, *interpersonal relationships* can be injurious, in a setting where most people spend at least 40 hours of the 168 that there are in a week. We have achieved the insight that relationships on the job can be as rewarding or as vexing as they are in family life.

We know now that our experience in a job can be crazy-making. Because we are sensitized to the issue, it is understandable that more symptoms will be noticed and more demands be made for compensation from those who are responsible. This represents a significant but temporary statistical elevation in the incidence of a social phenomenon. It is not an "alarming trend" but rather a corrective process. When existing wrongs are righted, the experience will act as a deterrent to prevent new outrages. Our workplaces will improve in the bargain.

CHAPTER XII

Trauma and the Law

P SYCHOTHERAPISTS ARE NOT attorneys, nor do they aspire to be. From
the standpoint of temperament, they are poles apart, in that lawyers
tend to be good talkers, and therapists good listeners. Under most circumstances, the two disciplines do not meet, with the exception of clinicians
who specialize in forensic work.[1]

The vast majority of therapists prefer to talk with people in the sanctity
of their offices. Their wish, *inter alia*, is to be as far away from a courtroom
as possible. In respect to law enforcement, their wish is to have as little to
do with the police as possible. What an irony it is for them when, as a part
of their jobs, clinicians are thrust into situations that are anathema to
them. Yet this is often their lot when doing trauma work. In so many
instances when a person experiences a traumatic event, court action may
not be far behind.

Few clinicians are prepared to cope with the vagaries of the legal world.
They receive no formal instruction in legal procedures during graduate
school or medical school, and few texts are available to supplement their
training. The typical trauma victim is even less informed about what role
he or she will play in whatever formal disposition there will be to a traumat-

---

[1]The authors are licensed in, and practice in, California, and for that reason have
first-hand knowledge only of legal requirements pertaining to that state. They
have read extensively in literature that pertains to both nationwide requirements
and those which differ in spirit from state to state. In this chapter an attempt is
made to describe and interpret general principles of conduct that are appropriate
in any setting. Some discrepancies between what is set forth here and the most
recent laws applying in certain regions are inevitable, and we recommend caution
on the part of the reader.

ent. This pertains especially to the client who is being asked to partici-
te in any criminal proceeding that may arise out of the event. As will be
discussed below, the victim is not assigned an attorney in a criminal case,
and unless he or she hires one for the purpose, there will be no advocate or
guide. Often, the therapist of a trauma victim is asked to play the part of
legal counsel in respect to a client's questions about what is going to
happen, why that is necessary, and what are the probabilities of one outcome or another. This chapter is intended to inform clinicians about what
they will need to know to take on this uncharacteristic therapeutic duty.

THE VICTIM AND THE LAW

When a person falls prey to a traumatic event, the experience may include
one or more encounters with the justice system. Many factors determine
the outcome of these legal processes, but the least that can be expected is
that no further harm will be done. Sometimes, this expectation is not met.
Part of the job of the clinician is to ensure that, by seeking justice, the
client is not in danger of being victimized again. The law has not always
been kind to the victims of trauma. Suffice it to say that, in recent years,
this indifference has been softened, mostly because police officers and
attorneys and judges have received training in the effects of trauma, and
because understanding often leads the way to empathy. Helping victims to
cope with law enforcement agencies and the courts is one of the functions
that therapists may be asked to perform, as a part of trauma work.

Three major arenas of legal process in which a victim may become
involved are the criminal courts, the civil courts, and the Workers' Compensation system. Some clients will have occasion to seek justice from all
three, such as a person who was intentionally injured by another employee
while at work: The victim may decide to bring criminal charges against the
person who caused the injury, may choose to bring a civil suit against that
person for damages, and may wish to be compensated for any loss of wages
while on leave from the job.

THE CRIMINAL PROCESS

When trauma has been inflicted by another person, the victim may feel
that the perpetrator should be punished. There are sound social reasons
for doing this, not the least of which is to keep the perpetrator from
causing harm to anyone again; another is the fervent wish that others will
be deterred from doing that kind of thing. The police are called, a statement is given, and witnesses to the event are requested to give evidence.
That represents only an igniting spark of the complex machine that now,
having been set in motion, moves on its own tracks.

When a victim reports to a police officer that a crime has been committed, the officer is acting as a representative of the local community and, by extension, the state where the crime occurred. In the legal system, a criminal act is committed against the *community*, and it is dealt with by the justice system in such a way as to protect the community against further damage. One may gather from this description that the victim is *not* the central figure in this process. The criminal justice system has its own goals and priorities, and the fact that a victim's psyche has been devastated by the crime is not its major concern.

The justice system operates according to very specific procedural rules. The police officer who takes a report is supposed to find answers to questions such as: Was a law broken? Who is believed to have broken the law? Where can that person be found, and what is the best way to apprehend him or her? It is often imperative to the success of an investigation that the officer gets answers to these questions immediately; this may give a victim the false impression that the officer is preoccupied by facts and uncaring about what the victim has suffered.

Even if the officer is especially thoughtful, the system contains many potential roadblocks to the prosecution of a crime, which can further traumatize a victim. For example:

1. The officer may decide that there is a lack of evidence that a crime was committed and write a report to this effect. This has happened more than once in cases of child sexual abuse that only later were substantiated and reported anew.

2. The report, if written, may contain substantial errors of omission or may reflect the officer's biased view of what happened. In one instance, when a woman claimed that a physical therapist attempted to rape her, the officer wrote that the fondling of her breasts was only "illegal touching," a charge that was later dropped. Another example is a case in which ten children in two families were molested by a teenaged neighbor; the officer who interviewed both families wrote a report concluding that no crime could be substantiated. The report served to halt an investigation that, only months later, had to be revived.

3. It may be that the accused perpetrator cannot be found; until the perpetrator *is* found, the criminal process will be totally suspended. In the case of a woman who was brutally raped and tortured, four years passed before her assailant was identified. By this time, the man was serving a prison term for an unrelated crime—his being linked to the rape was entirely fortuitous.

4. Even though the police may find a perpetrator, the person could go free because the victim and/or a witness might not be able to identify the suspect correctly in a police "lineup." Even if the police were sure they had found the right suspect, they would be obliged to let him or her go for lack

of positive identification. In one case, a woman who had been assaulted was hit on the head so violently that she suffered temporary brain damage. At the lineup, she became confused and could not make an identification with certainty.

5. A district attorney may review the police report, weigh the available evidence, and, even though a suspect has been found and properly identified, decide not to prosecute the case. This may occur for any number of reasons: lack of physical evidence proving that a crime was committed or linking the alleged perpetrator to the crime, lack of an independent witness to the crime who has no connection with the victim, or improper police procedures in the investigation of the crime or in arresting the suspect. In one of the most controversial aspects of our current criminal justice system, a district attorney can decide that a victim might not be capable of withstanding the rigors of court questioning, and for that reason the case will not be prosecuted. This often happens when the victim is a child; the younger the child, the more frequently this occurs. In short, a district attorney has virtually unlimited authority to decide whether or not a case will find its way to court.

Any one of the obstacles mentioned above may thwart the goal of the victim to obtain justice. A victim needs to be warned of these eventualities in advance.

If the district attorney chooses to proceed with a prosecution against the accused, it will be done on the grounds that a law was broken, that the accused person broke it, and that the available evidence will convincingly prove these allegations true. The district attorney is not concerned so much with the acts themselves but the laws governing those acts, and is *not* a representative of the victim but rather the state, through its laws. When a victim becomes aware that the district attorney does not represent him or her but an abstract entity, it is often an added shock. The clinician can greatly lessen this impact by explaining the district attorney's role to the victim well in advance.

A matter of principal importance to a district attorney is the potential effectiveness of the victim as a witness in the eventual trial of the case. Naturally, the victim is the key witness to what happened, but the concern of the district attorney is focused on whether or not he or she will be a "good" witness, namely one who can calmly, credibly, and thoroughly describe exactly what happened in the event. Hence, the clinician can be of much assistance as someone who helps prepare the victim for the new role of giving testimony under oath.

A criminal trial is literally a public rite. It embodies the best aspects of our open society, but it also has elements in common with the Roman circus. The defendant, innocent until proven guilty beyond a reasonable doubt, is granted certain rights by the rules of court procedure. Among them is the right to face his or her accuser in the courtroom. This right may be waived by the defendant, but its purpose is to honor the shibboleth that an accuser will be more likely to tell the truth about the person accused, when that person is staring him or her in the eyes.

There are two stages in a criminal trial. The first, a "pre-trial hearing," is conducted by a judge without a jury being present. The district attorney argues that the case against the defendant should go forward, while the defense attorney (or public defender) argues that the evidence against his or her client is insubstantial and does not merit a trial. The victim will be questioned under oath, often at length. The questions may require an-swers in minute detail, and the victim may be harangued *ad nauseam*: i.e., merely because there is no jury, a defense attorney may choose to confuse or intimidate the victim as a means to discredit his or her testimony. The only protection on which a victim, acting as witness, can rely, is the inter-vention of the district attorney by raising objections to certain questions or by pointing out that the defense attorney is badgering. If the judge decides that the evidence is sufficient for the state to mount a case against the defendant, a jury trial will be ordered. (The preparation of the victim for this and later stages of the court process is discussed below in "Helping a Client Prepare For The Criminal Trial.")

The actual trial is informed by the prior experience of the pre-trial hearing, in that both sides will be more thoroughly prepared. Before it occurs, the arcane maneuvers of plea bargaining may take place. In this *gavotte*, opposing attorneys reveal elements of their thinking about what the jury's eventual verdict will be. Each tries to persuade the other that the opposing case is lost; as a result, a defendant may plead guilty to the lesser of the charges and the state will not ask for more. If agreement is reached, there will be no trial as such. If the district attorney feels empathy for the victim, he or she will probably consult him or her about a plea bargain before it is done. There is no guarantee, even if this consultation takes place, that the victim's wishes will prevail. If no bargain is struck, the case will proceed to trial and the victim will be called upon to testify under oath again.

The actual trial, with so much at stake, can be an enormously painful experience for a victim. Months may have passed since the preliminary hearing, but this prior testimony can be used by the defendant's attorney to discredit a witness; for example, after the victim has answered a ques-tion, the attorney may say: "According to the transcript of your previous testimony, what you said then is not what you are saying now. Which is the truth?" In some instances, what the attorney claims to be reading from this transcript may be deliberately false. Any indecision or apparent contradic-tion on the part of the witness can be used to attack his or her credibility and thus raise doubt, in a jury, that the crime was done by the person accused.

Once the ordeal of testifying in a public place has ended, the victim must prepare for a verdict or, if the jury can't decide, possibly *another* trial. If the accused person is convicted, the victim may have an opportunity (at least in California) to attend the sentencing hearing. There, he or she can make a statement about what punishment might fit the crime. The judge may or may not take the victim's statement into consideration.

This sentencing hearing is not always a victorious occasion for a victim, even if permitted to speak out about the wrongs that have been suffered. In one instance, a defense attorney learned that a woman who was beaten by her boyfriend had entered psychotherapy shortly after the event occurred. While he did not question her about this psychotherapy during the boyfriend's trial itself, he introduced the subject in his arguments before the judge prior to sentencing. He persuaded the judge to issue a subpoena for the complete record of her treatment, and this record would have been made public in open court if the therapist had not claimed the privilege of confidentiality for his client. Even so, the judge ordered that the record be given to him so that he could read it *in camera*.[2]

This case reached an apt conclusion when the judge decided that the fact that the victim needed psychotherapy was further proof of long-lasting consequences from the boyfriend's assault. As it turned out, the clinical record influenced the judge to impose a maximum sentence on the assailant. What the defense attorney had, presumably, tried to do in this case was to show — on the basis of some statement he might find in the record — that the woman had been disturbed before the traumatic incident. If he had accomplished this, he might have obtained a light sentence for his client, even though the client had been convicted by a jury. By calling for the treatment record, this attorney was striving to (a) re-try the case, (b) discredit the victim once again, and (c) sway the judge to excuse the crime when a jury had not. That these tactics met with total failure is the cream of the jest.

Helping a Client Prepare For a Criminal Trial

A therapist whose client is involved in the criminal justice process must clearly understand the functions of the process and the various roles that people play within it, as well as its essential goals. Above all, the clinician must accept that the function of the criminal court is *not* to redress the wrongs inflicted upon the traumatized person. Because, in the eyes of the law, a crime is committed against the state, when a traumatized person appears in court he or she is testifying as a witness for the state. Suffice it to say that there may be times during this process when the victim feels

---

[2]This legal maneuver will be described in more detail in the section on "When a Therapist Receives a Subpoena" below.

both used and abused. We have observed many instances when a court was insensitive and even cruel toward victims, especially children and adolescents.

Because the client's involvement in the trial may be limited to providing proof of the occurrence of a crime and identifying the perpetrator, guiding him or her to a tolerant point of view may be difficult. A victim may ask plaintive questions such as: "[The perpetrator] has someone there to defend him [her]; why is there no one to defend me?" or "Why does [the perpetrator] have so many rights, so many protections by the law; what kind of law is that?"

If the client is especially fragile, a therapist can ask for the client's consent to telephone the district attorney in order to seek advice about the best way to prepare the client for court. Even so, one should not assume that the district attorney will understand the victim's emotional ordeal; some do not even meet a victim prior to the day of the hearing or trial.[3] In general, we believe that a meeting between prosector and victim can be beneficial, in that a victim can have a clearer idea of what to expect. Very likely, such a meeting will have to be encouraged by the clinician, whose presence at the meeting as a facilitator will be desirable.

Although a therapist should under no circumstances tell a client what to say in court, one can aid the client in reviewing what he or she experienced during the event. In this way, a victim may be better able to report calmly on what happened, with more precise organization of the details. The clinician can counsel the victim to speak slowly when being questioned by the defense, to permit the district attorney time to object to a question if necessary. It will help if the client repeats silently, "Take a deep breath and you will be fine" before responding to any defense question; this self-enhancing phrase can be reassuring when the person feels pressured to say something.

A victim is not compelled to look at the perpetrator in the courtroom if he or she would rather not. If a support person is present at the trial, the victim can focus his or her gaze on that person, on the judge, or on the jury. The victim should be made aware that a defense attorney may ask why the victim will not look at the accused; without being defensive, the victim can tell the truth about his or her feelings. Some are reluctant to say "He [she] frightens me" or "He [she] hurt me and I don't want to look at him [her]" or "If I look at him [her] it will remind me of what he [she] did to me." Each reply would be valid and probably force the defense attorney to move on to another question. A good reason for telling a client that it is not necessary to look at the perpetrator is that sometimes the latter will look at

[3]In some cases, a different district attorney prosecutes the preliminary hearing than the one who prosecutes the trial.

the victim in a menacing way or make some threatening gesture; this is done, in some instances, with the encouragement of the defense attorney. A judge who sees this taking place will probably put a stop to it, although a clinician cannot always count on this happening.

Further, the client can be forewarned that the judge may often read or leaf through documents while testimony is being given. This doesn't necessarily mean insensitivity on the part of the judge—this may be the judge's way of maintaining "distance" from the more distressing aspects of the case.

At the outset of the trial, a therapist can warn the client that there may be many delays ("continuances" in court parlance); these are inherent to the system, but they can be infuriating to victim and clinician alike. Many such delays are occasioned by an overcrowded court calendar or by an attorney being involved in another case simultaneously. These factors are beyond anyone's control. To a victim, such detours may signify that the case is in trouble, and he or she may not believe whatever excuse is given for the continuance. The clinician can help the client to deal with these fears realistically. In addition, it should be made clear to the victim that even when a verdict has been rendered and the perpetrator convicted, a lengthy appeals process may forestall the final resolution of the case.

As introduced above, the participation of a victim in the sentencing hearing can be beneficial to the person's recovery process. When the client's condition is thought to be too fragile for this kind of public appearance, one can advise the person to write a letter to the judge, expressing his or her feelings about an appropriate sentence. Into such a letter can be poured the victim's emotional pain, and to express it in this way has proven cathartic in many cases.

When A Therapist Receives a Subpoena

A subpoena is a form of request or invitation that has legal sanction. Some documents of this type are more compelling than others, and the wise clinician will know the difference. Of the various participants in the criminal court drama, it is the attorney who can issue a subpoena. But when a judge makes the same request or invitation, it takes the form of a "court order" and must be obeyed—as will be discussed later in this section. When a subpoena is issued concerning the records of a client who is involved in a criminal case, it usually arrives in the form of a one-page document that has the words *duces tecum* prominently displayed. This Latin phrase means "bring with you," and, like most archaic phrases, doesn't always mean what it says. In some instances, this invitation is for the case records only, and in others the clinician must accompany them in person.

The first thought of a therapist who receives a subpoena should properly be for the client's welfare. The therapist should ask himself or herself the following questions:

1. What is in the record and should this information be revealed?
2. What are my client's wishes in this regard?
3. What are my client's rights in this matter?

Because the client is also a victim and must be protected from becoming a victim again through the court process, the appearance of a subpoena becomes a clinical issue by itself.

As soon as it is propitious in treatment, the client should be told about the subpoena. This request for records is above all a challenge to his or her privilege of confidentiality in psychotherapy. The term "privilege" is used because confidentiality is not an inherent right, and the term is also apt because there are many exceptions to that confidentiality. (For example, there is no privilege when a client threatens to kill another person, as in the famous *Tarasoff* case.) A good reason for the confidentiality of case records is that, if the client has been candid about his or her thoughts and feelings in therapy, these are facts that he or she would least like to reveal in a public forum. And it was the very promise of confidentiality that encouraged him or her to speak freely from the start. In short, confidentiality is a key component of therapy, and many believe that therapy would be incapacitated without it. For these reasons, our duty of care to the client implies that what is in the best interest of the client to be kept secret, must be kept secret.

In recent years, we have come to a new awareness of the implications of the ancient art of clinical charting (see Everstine & Everstine, 1989, pp. 177–9). We perceive that a chart is more than just a private repository for the thoughts and musings of a therapist about a case; it is intrinsically a legal document and can be a public document if someone chooses to compel disclosure. The guiding principle should be whether or not the clinician would be willing to read a chart note aloud in a courtroom.

When the client is a victim, he or she quite naturally may have a different agenda from most clients in traditional practice, namely, to seek justice for what was done. That is why some limited exposure of the clinical record may, in trauma cases, be quite appropriate under the circumstances. Nevertheless, the clinician who is asked to send client records to an attorney can decide to resist the request. If his or her client wishes to assert the confidentiality privilege, the therapist can claim the privilege (withhold the records) for the client.

Claiming the privilege can be a looking-glass adventure for a clinician who has no prior experience in the matter. He or she can write a letter to the attorney who issued the subpoena (defense attorney or public defender), letting the attorney know that the privilege will be claimed for the client. Or, he or she can telephone the district attorney with the news that the privilege will be claimed; in some cases, a district attorney can have the subpoena "quashed" (nullified) by the judge. In any case, the district attorney will know in advance that part of the defense strategy is to find out what is in the clinical record concerning the victim. If the privilege is under heavy siege, and the therapist is convinced that revealing the records would endanger the client's well-being, he or she can hire an attorney as a personal representative; this attorney would present to the judge an argument for the merit of honoring the client's privilege. The latter tactic, or course, is not often employed by therapists, but it has been done. The countermeasure to any one of these maneuvers, on the part of a defense attorney, may be to ask the judge for a specific order requiring the clinician to appear in court with the records. And because judges in our legal system have almost unlimited power to force people to serve the court's needs, this order cannot be ignored.

Upon arriving at the court hearing, a clinician may be asked by the judge whether or not the records were brought along, whether or not the records are complete (nothing that was put in writing omitted), and whether or not the privilege is being claimed on behalf of the client. In the vast majority of cases, the answer to each question will be "yes," and the judge will then decide if the records must be given directly to him or her. When a judge takes the records for personal review, the purpose is to find out whether or not they are pertinent to the case and should be made public in court at a later time. In either event, the therapist can expect that the records will be returned when the judge has no more use for them.

These oddly ritualistic procedures should be explained to a trauma victim before the fact. It is a routine detour in what must already seem a demeaning and exhausting journey. Even so, the more one knows in advance, the better defended one will be. The victim can only wish that what is found in the record will be read with sensitivity, or that the reader who cannot be sensitive will at least be wise.

THE CIVIL PROCESS

By contrast with a criminal case that is brought by the state against a suspected lawbreaker, a civil case is initiated by a private citizen against another person or against an institution. The role of the civil attorney is to act as an *advocate* for the alleged victim's case. The purpose of the case is not to prove guilt but to establish that the person or institution being sued has, in some way, damaged the person who is bringing the suit, and that an amount of money is owed to the victim in compensation. The specific kind of case referred to here fits within the general category of personal injury law.

Historical Background

There has always been some degree of social sanction for revenge, as expressed, for example, by the Law of Talion ("an eye for an eye . . . ") or the principle that a person might be excused for killing someone if his or her own life were threatened. But it took many centuries for people to accept that the harm caused by one person to another should be "compensable"; this belief implies that there is a responsibility on the part of the one who damages to restore the person who was damaged to the condition that the person enjoyed before the damage occurred.

The concept of "being made whole" is the cornerstone of modern legal thought on personal injury. Of course, this concept is not a simple one to apply, especially when the injury in question is catastrophic. If a person, for instance, develops cancer as a result of working with asbestos, the "injury" amounts to a shortened life. When a person is turned into a quadriplegic by an accident resulting from another person's negligence, the "injury" affects every aspect of the victim's life. Fortunately, it is possible to calculate some assessment of the physical damages incurred, and to obtain some recompense, however symbolic. It is much more difficult to measure the damage that has been done to a persons' *psyche* by a traumatic event.[4]

A key dilemma in testimony before a court on psychic injury is inherent in legal process itself. A court, embodied by a judge and jury, strives to decide a case on strict *matters of fact*. That is, it seeks precise information on topics such as these:

1. What happened in the so-called "traumatic event"?
2. Who did what to whom?
3. Was there intent to harm or was harm inflicted negligently?
4. What damage was incurred, preferably in quantitative terms?
5. What will be needed to repair the damage done?

---

[4]No less a keen observer of mental process than Charles Dickens wrote about a personal experience in which he was traumatized by being a passenger in a train that had an accident; even though he was not hurt, Dickens felt unmistakable symptoms of emotional distress (Mendelson, 1987, p. 48). As far as is known, Dickens did not sue for his injuries, but if he had he would have learned how hard it can be to substantiate their existence in a court of law — even harder to establish what "being made whole" might mean.

While the judge will not be the one who renders a verdict, the judge is responsible for seeing to it that the case is fairly argued. What the judge decides to permit in evidence, and the rulings on the points of procedure that arise as the case develops, will strongly influence what the attorneys do and say on behalf of their clients.

One small advantage for the person who is suing (the plaintiff) is that the jury can decide in his or her favor on the grounds of only a preponderance (majority) of the evidence—unlike the criminal case, the verdict does not have to be "beyond a reasonable doubt." This factor may contribute to the trauma victim's decision about whether or not to sue.

No matter what the outcome of any criminal case that occurs after a traumatic event, one may sue for personal injury.[5] One deterrent to doing this is that much more can be revealed about one's personal life in the civil as opposed to the criminal case; in effect, any confidentiality pertaining to mental health records is waived when a person files a suit in which damage to one's mental health is claimed. Another deterrent is that the person being sued may not have the means to compensate a victim even if the victim's suit is won. In regard to these considerations, the judgment of the attorney should guide the victim when deciding if the possible benefits outweigh the possible risks.

The clinician who is providing treatment is another advocate for the victim, and it is vitally important for therapist and lawyer to be sure that they are working in the best interests of the client throughout each phase of the suit. Several ways in which a therapist can be of help are outlined in the sections below.

Helping a Client Prepare for Civil Litigation

The fact that civil litigation is not primarily focused on issues of right or wrong as much as it is on damages, may be puzzling to a client. As introduced above, the rationale for a civil process is to "right the wrong" that was allegedly done to a victim, by means of financial compensation; to do this, one needs to establish measurable damages. But quantifying trauma and suffering is not always easy. Too often, traumatized people become overly focused upon how unfair, wrong, or evil the traumatic event was. Therefore, the purpose of helping a client prepare for being questioned is to enable the person to give a rational explanation of how the traumatic event has altered or diminished his or her life and well-being.

For example, a victim will be called upon to describe his or her life before the traumatic event, preferably in ways that can be verified by other

---

[5]In many instances, there is no criminal proceeding in connection with a traumatic injury—before or after the civil proceeding.

sources. Then, the victim will be required to describe what changes have occurred since the event—also subject to corroboration by others. Some clients will be too young or too vulnerable to accomplish either of these tasks; ironically, some may be too damaged to describe what injury was done to them. In these cases, an expert witness may be retained by the victim's attorney to inform the court about the nature and extent of the traumatic injury. The part played by an expert witness is described in a separate section below.

In civil litigation, as in a criminal case, the victim may have to testify twice under oath. The first time occurs when the victim's deposition is taken by opposing counsel. Preparation for this event and follow-up are important tasks for the treating clinician. Both deposition and court testimony are elicited under oath, and a person may face charges of perjury if it is thought that he or she has lied. If the case is settled out of court, of course, the victim will avoid being asked the same questions in a public forum.

The defense against a claim for emotional injury is often an attempt to establish that a victim's problems existed before the traumatic event. Another approach is to reveal aspects of the person's life prior to the event that would make a jury unsympathetic. The first line of defense implies that the victim has fabricated or exaggerated his or her current emotional condition to obtain compensation fraudulently. The second implies that the victim is fundamentally an immoral or flawed person who is unworthy of being compensated. Both tactics derive from a basic strategy of persuading the plaintiff (victim) to withdraw the suit or accept an out-of-court settlement.

Especially if the compensation sought is substantial, the victim should know that any record kept on him or her may come under scrutiny by the opposing counsel. In this category are medical records, academic or employment history, or financial dealings. Professional as well as personal relationships will be examined for possible flaws. Naturally, one's client will resent this and will require considerable support to endure it. In one case, a woman who had been severely hurt in an automobile accident was asked to provide details of an abortion that she had had four years before the accident. Her therapist had prepared her for this line of questioning and she was able to cope with her angry feelings when the inquiry was made in court. She was not defensive about it, and was able to reply calmly that the two events were totally unrelated.

A clinician should prepare a victim for the likelihood that, in respect to a claim for emotional damages, he or she will be subjected to an Independent Medical Examination (IME) by the opposing side. The client should cooperate fully with this necessary procedure and, again, try not to take a defensive stance. If the clinician is concerned about how this examination might be conducted, the client's attorney can be asked to request that the interview be audiotaped; this usually ensures that the victim will be treated appropriately by the examiner. Unfortunately, some practitioners conduct this kind of examination like an inquisition or deliberately attempt to mislead or manipulate examinees.

Just as in the criminal process, there can be long delays in the process by which a civil case is resolved. Some require years to run their course. The only factor that can intervene to hasten resolution would be if the opposing (defending) side were to offer an award of damages that the victim could accept as sufficient. When this happens, the client's attorney can negotiate a settlement of the case that makes an actual trial unnecessary. Usually, when such an offer is made, the victim will be in considerable turmoil, even if the amount of compensation offered is generous. Issues of pride may enter here, and a victim must weigh the monetary offer against the need to have the proverbial "day in court." This decision is solely the client's to make, but the therapist can be a powerful ally in helping him or her to act with enlightened self-interest.

When a Therapist Receives a Subpoena

Because a civil case is a joust between hired legal adversaries, the therapist must carefully stay within the appropriate clinical role; one's goal is to ensure that the victim does not suffer more emotional trauma during the court battles. Some clients should *not* sue, even though they have been severely wronged or damaged. The first consideration is that of stamina: Can the victim, who has suffered a traumatic event and its aftermath, and who may have experienced a harsh criminal trial since then, face another bout with the legal system? A second issue is directly related to the topic of confidentiality: Is the victim willing to reveal the psychological pain that he or she has felt since the traumatic event (feelings of lessened self-worth, shame, or powerlessness)? Does the victim understand that any aspect of his or her personal life (including medical history) or professional life can be laid bare in this process? Third, does the victim expect more of the outcome of the civil case than can reasonably be expected? In effect, what does "being made whole" mean to the client, and is there a realistic chance that the suit will bring this about?

If a trauma victim is determined to carry forward a civil suit, the clinician can explain that the next step will entail giving the entire therapy record (past and present) to his or her attorney. The opposing attorney will issue a subpoena for the same information, and it will very likely be to the client's benefit if the therapist does not resist this request. Still later, the opposing attorney can be expected to invite the therapist, by subpoena, to appear for a deposition. This development should be revealed to the client in advance, and discussing its implications can become a part of the therapeutic process. The client should be reminded that, having placed his or her "mental state" at issue by bringing this lawsuit, he or she has waived any right to confidentiality of matters pertaining to that "state."

A deposition is the pretrial questioning of a witness, in this instance the therapist, under oath, in a setting such as the therapist's office or the office of the attorney who issued the subpoena.[6] Here, the clinician is a witness on behalf of the victim and can be asked any question pertaining to the client that the opposing attorney believes is relevant to the case. This can include questions of opinion, even opinion about the client's moral character. The attorney for the victim will invariably be present throughout the deposition, and can raise objections to questions that seem vague or irrelevant. What is said in the deposition is taken down, word for word, and can be quoted in the actual trial. Because of this, a clinician should review this transcript carefully to ensure that it does not contain errors of omission or misquotation.

If the case is actually tried in court, the therapist may be called again as a witness. Because any conceivable question could be asked once he or she has taken the oath, many professionals prefer that the client *not* be present in the courtroom during this testimony. Instead of feeling intimidated by being asked to testify, the clinician can look upon it as an opportunity to give the jury an opinion about the impact of the traumatic event on the victim. To do this properly, the therapist should be able to support the opinion by objective facts such as behavioral observations, test results, or actual repetition of statements made during therapy sessions. One should be ready to recount interviews with relevant third parties such as physicians, supervisors, teachers, co-workers, etc. Throughout, it will be advisable to let the client know in advance what will be said about him or her. In this regard, a clinician may be better able to articulate the client's suffering than the client can. Many victims are so immersed in their traumatic pain that they cannot give clear explanations of the full impact of the trauma on their lives. The therapist's objective view may assist the court in forming an accurate opinion about what harm the traumatic event has caused and what the victim will need for healing.

THE INDEPENDENT MEDICAL
EXAMINATION (IME)

When a claim for emotional injury is lodged, through the filing of a civil suit, the person or institution that is accused of causing the trauma ("defendant") has the right to order an evaluation of the claim. Three purposes are

---

[6]The term "deposition" refers to the formal questioning of a witness in a place other than a courtroom. Theoretically, anyone whose testimony might be relevant to the case can be deposed.

to be served: (1) to establish the validity or lack of validity of the person's allegation of damage; (2) to quantify the severity of the damages; and (3) to obtain a reasonable estimation of the kinds of treatment that will be required to alleviate the trauma, as well as the cost of the treatment.

When conducting an IME, a clinician should be sure to conform to his or her role as a clinician who seeks to (1) understand the plaintiff's psychological condition; and (2) advise defendant's counsel of the nature of the damages and how best to proceed in a defense against the claim. Unfortunately, some experts mistakenly believe that they have a duty to trick, "lead," or even intimidate a plaintiff into making statements that will discredit his or her case. An expert who indulges in such tactics takes a dangerous step toward unethical conduct and does not serve the defense well. When such conduct is later revealed — and it almost always is — it will discredit the entire evaluation. And, if there *are* valid damages, the defense attorney needs to know this to decide how to proceed with the case. Information of this complexity cannot be obtained in one hour; therefore, the defense attorney should be told in advance that to limit an evaluation to one hour is being penny wise, pound foolish.

Evaluations should be conducted thoroughly, systematically, and sensitively. Ideally, the examination will be done in two-hour segments, but many plaintiffs request that it be done in one day, to "get it over with." A prolonged session may be more stressful than the person realizes, and is not advised, even though some plaintiffs or their attorneys will insist. If possible, it is best to interview the person both before and after psychological testing so that, if something significant comes forth during the testing, the evaluator will have an opportunity to explore it more fully.

Before the interview, the examiner should review any records that pertain to the traumatic event or to the plaintiff's level of functioning before and after the event. During the course of the interview, the examiner seeks to compile a structured developmental, personal, social, educational, and medical history. In respect to this history, one should consider whether or not it is consistent with what was found previously in the records, and if not, why not?

As far as symptoms are concerned, one should not ask direct questions, taking care not to lead the plaintiff in one direction or another. Instead, the examiner should ask open-ended questions that will allow the plaintiff to mention a symptom if it was experienced. Next, the plaintiff should be asked to describe each symptom in his or her own words. In this way, the examiner can determine whether or not the examinee's description of the symptom is consistent with the actual disorder.

During the interview, the examiner should also look for information that will aid in understanding how the person coped with pain, illness, or injury in the past, as well as how members of his or her immediate family coped with the same problems. Here, one can look for patterns of responsible versus irresponsible health care, exaggeration versus minimizing symptoms, blaming versus accepting responsibility. The examiner also needs to establish what the plaintiff's level of pre-trauma functioning was. It is not a good idea to rely exclusively on information provided in the interview or existing records for this purpose: such information should, if possible, be corroborated by outside sources. For example, an examiner may ask the person being examined to describe a typical day of work and a day of leisure that occurred a year before the traumatic event. These reports can be substantiated by independent sources such as friends, co-workers, employers, etc.

An IME should include a full battery of psychological tests because such tests can provide objective data on the person's level of functioning since the traumatic event occurred. Psychological tests can also indicate any longstanding conditions that may have been present before the event occurred. The authors use the following battery for evaluating adult plaintiffs:

- PROJECTIVE TESTS
- Rorschach Inkblot Test
- Thematic Apperception Test (TAT)
- Sentence Completion Test
- Draw-a-Person Test
- OBJECTIVE MEASURES
- Everstine Trauma Response Index

When work impairment is claimed, these tests can augment those noted:

- Bender Gestalt Test
- Weschler Adult Intelligence Scale (Revised)
- Quick Neurological Screening Test

When both objective and projective psychological tests are part of an evaluation, the evaluation is less vulnerable to the criticism that it merely represents a subjective opinion.

As noted earlier, even if the person being evaluated is blatantly malingering, it is unwise to conduct the evaluation in an adversarial, heavy-handed way, or to engage in attempts to mislead or confuse the plaintiff. If the plaintiff *is* malingering or exaggerating symptoms, he or she can be confronted with the fact appropriately and professionally.

When the Plaintiff is a Child

When conducting an independent medical examination of a child, the clinician should be extremely sensitive to the child's needs as well as those of the parents. It is not uncommon, nor is it indicative of malingering, for parents to be suspicious or reluctant to have their child examined. It may be that their child was traumatized at the hands of another adult, and they may be struggling with the fact that they were not able to protect the child from the traumatic event. Many such parents act defensively in an attempt to immunize themselves against their own feelings of failure. Hence, an evaluator should try to put the parents at ease rather than get into a power struggle or confrontation with them.

As with an adult evaluation, the evaluation of a child should be based upon as much outside, objective data as can readily be obtained: e.g., school and pediatric records should be reviewed. Parents and significant caretakers should be interviewed, if possible. The evaluator will need all these sources of information to establish the child's pre-trauma level of functioning. From that perspective, an evaluator can proceed to assess the child's post-trauma level of functioning, using the same sources as well as interview, observation of the child's behavior, and a battery of psychological tests. The authors currently utilize the following battery for children:

- Wechsler Intelligence Scale for Children (Revised)
- WIPPSI
- Rorschach Inkblot Test
- Thematic Apperception Test (TAT) or Children's Apperception Test (CAT)
- Draw-a-Person Test
- Sentence Completion Test
- Bender Gestalt Test

We prefer using the TAT instead of CAT except for very young children, because we have found that the TAT yields more information that is relevant to the child's experience of a traumatic event.

It is worth noting that the school performance of some traumatized children drops significantly, but, in other cases, school behavior and performance continue to be normal. In the latter situation, the child is usually clinging to the consistency and structure of the school environment as a defense against traumatic feelings. For this reason, one cannot assume that, if a child's grades remained stable, he or she was not traumatized.

Because many traumas that children suffer are developmentally "beyond" them, they do not possess the cognitive skills that are necessary to explain their traumatic feelings or sense of loss. Even so, they frequently express their responses to trauma behaviorally, and an evaluation may have to rely upon indirect sources of information to measure the response fully.

An example of this is that of a little girl who witnessed her mother's death in an automobile accident; she said that the accident was "scary" and that she felt bad because she missed her Mommy. This statement, although poignant, does not convey the depth of the trauma that a child of six must suffer when her mother dies before her eyes. The more valid approach to clinical evaluation in such a case is to utilize the outside, indirect sources of information referred to above.

In summary, the independent medical examination must be undertaken with great care and sensitivity. An examiner needs to weigh every aspect of alleged injury, whenever possible, utilizing outside, objective data to quantify the degree of trauma that was suffered and rule out what was not suffered.

MALINGERING

Unlike physical injuries, whose effects are normally directly conveyed to pain receptors, emotional injuries are more subtly instilled. The fact that "psychic pain" has no known neurological correlates is a source of consternation to those who dream of making direct measurement of traumatic effects. Their lack of success is mocked by the lay belief in concepts such as "mental toughness" that suggest a quantity as measurable as the strength of a handshake.

There are countless instances when an event that most people would consider traumatic produces no trauma whatever. In terms of assessment, this means that there is a real possibility of making an error of the *false positive* type, in which a person is incorrectly thought to have been traumatized. This type of error is addressed in the section that follows. (Errors of the *false negative* category, in which a person's real trauma is not detected, are believed to be avoided by the use of instruments such as ETRI and other techniques described previously.)

A first step in pursuing a suspicion of symptom amplification or malingering is to make a differential diagnosis of whether or not the symptoms constitute psychogenic pain disorder (a form of conversion disorder). This is done because, with psychogenic pain disorder, the person genuinely believes himself or herself to be ill. This is a true psychological disorder, whereas in malingering the person consciously falsifies the symptoms of a disorder. The differentiation between the two situations is critical to the independent medical examination (see above).

As noted earlier, there is considerable misunderstanding of, as well as prejudice against, those who claim traumatic injuries. When one raises the question in the legal community there is an almost automatic suspicion of malingering. According to Resnick (1988a, p. 87), actual statistics on the malingering of psychological symptoms vary from 1% to 50% of cases, depending upon who is funding the research (i.e., insurance companies or plaintiffs' attorneys). Our experience is consistent with that of Resnick (1988a), namely that malingering rarely occurs in reaction to a traumatic event, but that symptom amplification is quite common. In our view, the adversarial nature of both the civil and workers' compensation systems, focused as they are on proving or defending damages rather than fostering timely and appropriate treatment, may be to blame, in part, for much of this problem of amplification. In the research of Kelly (1975), it was found that when treatment was applied early and effectively, noncompensated and compensated cases did not differ in recovery time.

All too often, plaintiffs are sent to one specialist after another for evaluation, and treatment becomes secondary to the legal fray. By contrast, when the person is in therapy with a reasonable therapist who is knowledgeable in treating the response to trauma, he or she will make a more reasonable claim and have less symptom amplification. The reason is that the person has found someone who can attend to his or her emotional needs, as well as help in focusing anger and frustration appropriately.

Another source of accusations of malingering is that of physicians who are frustrated by difficult patients who do not respond to medical interventions. Many such cases are time-consuming, demanding, and cause the physician to blame the patient for "making the whole thing up" rather than to accept that the person suffers from an emotional injury. In fact, many physicians and medical professionals who work with traumatized people on a daily basis are not trained in the diagnosis and treatment either of traumatic reactions or conversion disorder and, as a consequence, draw erroneous conclusions.

We have found, as did Resnick (1988, *passim*), that instances of the malingering of *psychotic* reactions to a traumatic event are extremely rare. Few malingerers are sufficiently knowledgeable in the true symptoms of psychosis, nor are they willing to risk the indignity of psychiatric hospitalization. Even so, this kind of malingering would very likely be detected in short order by psychiatric inpatient staff.

When a psychotic break does occur as a reaction to a traumatic event, there usually is a serious underlying psychological condition that may be chronic or that predated the event for a considerable period of time. A psychotic reaction to trauma may also represent the emergence of symptoms that the person suffered from a serious traumatic experience occurring in the past. In this kind of case, the past traumatic event most likely occurred during childhood or adolescence and may be diminished in the conscious memory by defenses such as disassociation or denial. It may take considerable effort to uncover this original trauma response, but it will be essential to the successful treatment of the person that the early trauma be dealt with and worked through in treatment.

The seriously flawed research of Miller (1961), who claimed that 48 out of 50 plaintiffs recovered spontaneously after a civil settlement with no treatment, has continued to encourage the belief that those who claim emotional damages are malingerers. By contrast, Thompson, who studied 190 persons who had traumatic reactions (1965), found that only 15% of the subjects showed improvement after their claims were settled. More recently, Miller's research has been challenged as having been biased, and the results contradicted by subsequent findings. For example, the work of Kelly (1975), Kelly & Smith (1981), Mendelson (1981), and Resnick (1988a) also supports the conclusion that the majority of people who are unable to work at the time of a settlement do not return to the same job later on. These refutations notwithstanding, attorneys (and some clinicians) still quote Miller's work because it bolsters their view that symptoms, particularly those of a psychological nature, are more motivated by thoughts of compensation than genuine.

Differentiating Between Psychogenic Pain (Conversion) Disorder and Malingering

The major diagnostic criteria for malingering, according to Resnick (1988a), are:

1. avoidance of an independent medical examination; in many cases, having to be forced to take the examination;
2. unwillingness to admit past problems or personal flaws, in many cases ascribing all current difficulties to trauma;
3. defensiveness, sullenness, lack of cooperation with the examination, aloofness;
4. a history of noncompliance with treatment or recommended diagnostic procedures;
5. current or past treatment with medical or mental health professionals who are known to overtreat or whose approach to treatment is considered questionable by the professional community, or who are known to have a bias in favor of plaintiffs' claims;
6. the ability to give a clear, consistent, well-detailed account of the traumatic event, its aftermath, and an organized catalog of symptoms;
7. description of a pattern of dreams in which the event is relived.

By contrast, the person who is suffering from a psychogenic pain (conversion) disorder may present quite a different picture upon examination:

1. appears friendly and cooperative, sometimes even asking for the examiner's opinion;
2. admits flaws and past problems, not ascribing all current difficulties to the traumatic event;
3. is generally cooperative with diagnostic procedures and treatment recommendations, i.e., exhibits a wish to be "cured";
4. seeks an organic explanation of symptoms and is even willing to accept an organic diagnosis that would frighten most people;
5. has received treatment from responsible practitioners who have been baffled by the person's condition and may have suggested possible malingering;
6. prefers not to discuss details of the traumatic event, avoids the subject when possible; when speaking of the event, is vague, leaves gaps in the account, or is inaccurate and inconsistent; paradoxically, the person may seem less credible in this respect than the malinger;
7. reports a pattern of dreams whose themes are representations of the traumatic event, but are not literal recreations.

The evaluation of a person for emotional damages permits other factors to inform the evaluator's conclusions. For example, it is useful to ask, "What does this person seek to gain by making this claim?" Has a healthy productive life been rudely interrupted by the event, or has the person already received social or financial advantage from the event and is desirous of more? In the case of most genuine trauma victims, there has been serious alteration or damage to at least one major sphere of life, i.e., social, personal, or occupational. Little or no pleasure or reward has been obtained from these limitations.

Another identifying characteristic of those who amplify symptoms or malinger is that they have unstable or inconsistent work records, with prior injuries (especially compensable ones) or long leaves of absence for illnesses of uncertain authenticity. By contrast, a typical trauma victim is ashamed of his or her emotional condition, and may even make an effort to hide problems and to resume normal functioning—including attendance at work—as soon as possible.

Many people who feign emotional trauma are incapable of returning to work but quite capable of enjoying recreational activities. It is not uncommon to find that those who malinger have engaged in other forms of acting-out such as substance abuse or criminal activity or have problematic driving records. Nevertheless, the clinician should be cognizant of the fact that some antisocial behavior, especially the kind that is essentially self-destructive, may be an indication that the person has suffered trauma in the past, *before* the most recent traumatic event. (This subject of undisclosed, prior trauma is presented in detail in Chapter VI.)

A related caution for the examiner is not to let his or her own social or cultural biases intrude upon the task at hand. In fact, people who have different values may behave in ways that are compatible with those values but seem, to the observer, to be incompatible with genuine responses to trauma. Far from being blinded to this possibility, a responsible examiner will consult with professionals who know other cultures, to find out how the expression of pain is perceived and what the cultural viewpoint is on people who seek psychotherapy. The latter is important because in some cultures it is considered cowardly to speak of emotional difficulties, and in some only "crazy" people enter into therapy. It may be more acceptable, according to these social mores, for emotional pain to be expressed through psychosomatic ailments or susceptibility to illness.

Finally, it is worth noting that chronic physical pain can have a deleterious effect on the functioning of the personality and can adversely affect personal relationships. In our experience, pain sufferers can develop regressive tendencies or become emotionally labile, especially quite angry. Persons in this category tend to "turn up the volume" on their reports of symptoms. This is not a conscious attempt to falsify the extent of their trauma, but instead an expression of frustration best considered a "cry for help."

Epilogue

TRAUMA WORK IS an extremely difficult yet immensely rewarding variant of conventional practice. A clinician who does this kind of work can be of as much help to others as one who admits a seriously disturbed person to a psychiatric hospital or one who persuades a suicidal person perched on a window ledge to come back inside.

We have seen that working with trauma victims can lead a therapist far afield—from the office to a hospital emergency room, to a courtroom, to the site of a natural disaster. The work is not programmed for the nine-to-five hours of ordinary clinical practice. The intake of new clients cannot be planned. The victim cannot be offered an appointment next month or put on a waiting list. Trauma happens. The need cannot be ignored.

A trauma victim is, unlike many traditional therapy clients, totally innocent of his or her symptoms. This is not the terminal neurotic who inhabits most waiting-rooms and whose tribulations are perhaps the best rationale for brief therapy. Trauma clients are the walking wounded, whose injuries have been visited upon them by a hostile environment as opposed to an inner flaw or "dysfunctional family background."

The Book of Job is a parable telling us that even a virtuous man can be made to suffer. It teaches the lesson that earthly misfortune does not signify a sinful heart. *This* book shows that healthy men and women can become trauma victims. Therefore, it is no longer necessary to think of the trauma response as the mirror of a sick mind.

With some passion, the authors believe in the adage that strength comes from adversity. But how can we be sure, in real terms, that the trauma response is potentially a positive force? How can be *prove* that the glass is half full?

215

For this we draw inspiration from the logic of St. Anselm, the 11th-century theologian whose mission was to prove the existence of God. To Anselm, there is a God because human beings can conceive of one. Because people are acutely aware of their imperfections, it occurs to them that there could be a perfect being. That being is God, no matter what language describes His countenance. From a practical standpoint, there is a God because we need there to be one; having a God is useful. As Voltaire observed, "If God did not exist, it would be necessary to invent Him."

Since trauma is a fact of life, it is not a question of having it or not, but what to do with it. In the wake of the most searing tragedy, we are most comforted when we can say, "Life goes on." Then we are ready to search for a way to make what has tested us to the limit into a life-enhancing experience. That's when the glass will appear half full. Then will become clear that what has happened is one of life's abundant beginnings.

References

American Psychiatric Association. (1987). *Diagnostic and statistical manual of mental disorders* (3rd ed., rev.). Washington, DC: Author.

Ancelin-Schutzenberger, A. (in press). *Psychogénéalogie, le génosociogramme, les secrets de famille, l'enfant de remplacement, le syndrome d'anniversaire.* Paris: La Méridienne.

Blackmore, J. (1978). Are police allowed to have problems of their own? *Police, 1*(3), 47–55.

Bugen, L. (1977). Human Grief: A model for prediction and intervention. *American Journal of Orthopsychiatry, 47,* 196–206.

Caplan, G. (1964). *Principles of preventive psychiatry.* New York: Basic.

Elmer, E. (1977). A follow-up study of traumatized children. *Pediatrics, 59,* 273–279.

Erickson, M. H. (1980a). The nature of hypnosis and suggestion. In E. L. Rossi (Ed.), *The collected papers of Milton H. Erickson on hypnosis* (vol. 1). New York: Irvington.

Erickson, M. H. (1980b). Hypnotic alteration of sensory, perceptual and psychophysical processes. In E. L. Rossi (Ed.), *The collected papers of Milton H. Erickson on hypnosis* (vol. 2). New York: Irvington.

Erickson, M. H. (1980c). Hypnotic investigation of psychodynamic processes. In E. L. Rossi (Ed.), *The collected papers of Milton H. Erickson on hypnosis* (vol. 3). New York: Irvington.

Erickson, M. H. (1980d). Innovative hypnotherapy. In E. L. Rossi (Ed.), *The collected papers of Milton H. Erickson on hypnosis* (vol. 4). New York: Irvington.

Eth, S., & Pynoos, R. S. (1985). Developmental perspective on psychic trauma in childhood. In C. R. Figley (Ed.), *Trauma and its wake* (vol. 1) (pp. 36–52). New York: Brunner/Mazel.

Everstine, L. (1989). *Manual for administrators: Everstine Life Stress Index.* (Available from Affiliated Psychologists, 555 Middlefield Road, Palo Alto, CA 94301.)

Everstine, D. S., & Everstine, L. (1983). *People in crisis.* New York: Brunner/Mazel.

Everstine, D. S., & Everstine, L. (1989). *Sexual trauma in children and adolescents.* New York: Brunner/Mazel.

217

Everstine, L., & Everstine, D. S. (1986). *Psychotherapy and the law.* Orlando, FL: Grune & Stratton.

Everstine, L., Everstine, D. S., Heymann, G. M., True, R. H., Frey, D. H., Johnson, H. G., & Seiden, R. H. (1980). Privacy and confidentiality in psychotherapy. *American Psychologist, 35*(9), 828–840.

Fairbairn, W. R. D. (1943). The war neuroses: Their nature and significance. *British Medical Journal, 1,* 183–186.

Figley, C. R. (1983). Catastrophes: An overview of family reactions. In C. R. Figley & H. I. McCubbin, *Stress and the family* (vol. 2) (pp. 3–20). New York: Brunner/Mazel.

Figley, C. R. (Ed.). (1985). *Trauma and its wake: The study and treatment of post-traumatic stress disorder* (vol. 1). New York: Brunner/Mazel.

Figley, C. R. (1988a). A five-phase treatment of post-traumatic stress disorder in families. *Journal of Traumatic Stress, 1*(1), 127–141.

Figley, C. R. (1988b). Post-traumatic family therapy. In F. M. Ochberg (Ed.), *Post-traumatic therapy and victims of violence* (pp. 83–109). New York: Brunner/Mazel.

Figley, C. R., & McCubbin, H. I. (1983). *Stress and the family* (vol. 2). New York: Brunner/Mazel.

Green, B. L., Wilson, J. P., & Lindy, J. D. (1985). Conceptualizing post-traumatic stress disorder: A psychosocial framework. In C. R. Figley (Ed.), *Trauma and its wake* (vol. 1) (pp. 53–72). New York: Brunner/Mazel.

Holmes, T. H., & Rahe, R. H. (1967). The social readjustment rating scale. *Journal of Psychosomatic Research, 11,* 213–218.

Horowitz, M., Wilner, N., & Alvarez, W. (1979). Impact of Event Scale: A measure of subjective stress. *Psychosomatic Medicine, 41*(3), 309–318.

Jones, D. R. (1983). Secondary disaster victims: The emotional effects of recovering and identifying human remains. *American Journal of Psychiatry, 142,* 303–307.

Kaltreider, N. B., Wallace, A., & Horowitz, M. J. (1979). A field study of the stress response syndrome: Young women after hysterectomy. *Journal of the American Medical Association, 242,* 1499–1503.

Kaplan, H. S., & Kaplan, H. I. (1967). Current concepts of psychosomatic medicine. In A. M. Freedman & H. I. Kaplan (Eds.), *Comprehensive textbook of psychiatry* (pp. 1039–1044). Baltimore, MD: Williams & Wikins.

Keane, T. M., Malloy, P. F., & Fairbank, J. A. (1984). Empirical development of an MMPI subscale for the assessment of combat-related post-traumatic stress disorder. *Journal of Consulting and Clinical Psychology, 52,* 888–891.

Kelly, R. (1975). The post-traumatic syndrome: An iatrogenic disease. *Forensic Sciences, 6,* 17–24.

Kelly, R., & Smith, B. N. (1981). Post-traumatic syndrome: Another myth discredited. *Journal of the Royal Society of Medicine, 74,* 275–278.

Kohlman, R. (1974). Malpractice liability for failing to report child abuse. *The Western Journal of Medicine, 121*(3), 244–248.

Kramer, M., Schoen, L. S., & Kinney, L. (1984). Long term effects of traumatic stress. In B. A. van der Kolk (Ed.), *Adult psychic trauma: Psychological and physiological sequelae* (pp. 51–96). Washington, DC: American Psychiatric Press.

Krauthammer, C. (1992, Feb. 11). Invasion of the pseudo-shrinks. San Jose *Mercury News,* p. 7B.

Kubler-Ross, E. (1969). *On death and dying.* New York: Macmillan.

Lear, M. W. (July 31, 1988). Redefining anxiety. *The New York Times,* pp. 30, 31.

Lester, D. (1982). Subjective stress and sources of stress for police officers. *Psychological Reports, 50*, 1094.

Levitov, J. E., & Thompson, B. (1981). Stress and counseling needs of police officers. *Counselor Education and Supervision, 21*, 163–168.

Lindy, J. D., Green, B. L., Grace, M., & Titchener, J. (1983). Psychotherapy with survivors of the Beverly Hills Supper Club fire. *American Journal of Psychotherapy, 37*, 593–610.

Lindy, J. D., Green, B. L., Grace, M., & Titchener, J. (1986). Long-term psychotherapy following disaster. *Journal of Preventative Psychiatry, 3*, 21–33.

Lister, E. D. (1982). Forced silence: A neglected dimension of trauma. *American Journal of Psychiatry, 139*(7), 872–875.

Lyons, J. A. (1978). Post traumatic stress disorder in children and adolescents: A review of the literature. *Developmental and Behavioral Pediatrics, 8*(6), 349–356.

Martin, C. A., McKean, H. E., & Veltkamp, L. J. (1986). Post-traumatic stress disorder in police and working with victims: A pilot study. *Journal of Police Science and Administration, 14*(2), 98–101.

McCubbin, H. I. (1976). Coping repertoires of families adapting to prolonged war induced separations. *Journal of Marriage and the Family, 38*, 461–471.

McCubbin, H. I., & Figley, C. R. (1983). Bridging normative and catastrophic family stress. In H. I. McCubbin & C. R. Figley (Eds.), *Stress and the family* (vol. 1) (pp. 218–228). New York: Brunner/Mazel.

McFarlane, M. B. (1986). Post-traumatic morbidity of a disaster: A study of cases presenting for psychiatric treatment. *The Journal of Nervous and Mental Diseases, 174*(1), 4–14.

McGoldrick, M. (1991). Echoes from the past: Helping families mourn their losses. In F. Walsh & M. McGoldrick (Eds.), *Living beyond loss* (pp. 50–78). New York: W. W. Norton.

Mendelson, G. (1981). Persistent work disability following settlement of compensation claims. *Law Institute Journal (Melbourne), 55*, 342–345.

Mendelson, G. (1987). The concept of post traumatic stress disorder: A review. *International Journal of Law & Psychiatry, 10*, 45–62.

Miller, H. (1961). Accident neurosis. *British Medical Journal, 1*, 992–998.

Mollica, R. F. (1988). The trauma story: The psychiatric care of refugee survivors of violence and torture. In F. Ochberg (Ed.), *Post-traumatic therapy and victims of violence* (pp. 295–314). New York: Brunner/Mazel.

Murphy, S. A. (1986). Health and recovery status of victims one and three years following a natural disaster. In C. R. Figley (Ed.), *Trauma and its wake* (vol. 2) (pp. 133–155). New York: Brunner/Mazel.

Newman, C. J. (1976). Children of disaster: Clinical observations at Buffalo Creek. *American Journal of Psychiatry, 133*, 306–312.

Ollendick, D., & Hoffman, M. (1982). Assessment of psychological reactions in disaster victims. *Journal of Community Psychology, 10*, 157–167.

Pepys, S. (1972). September. In R. Latham & W. Matthews (Eds.), *The diary of Samuel Pepys* (vol. 7) (pp. 267–285). Berkeley: University of California Press.

Pynoos, R. S., & Eth, S. (1985). Children traumatized by witnessing acts of personal violence: Homicide, rape, or suicide behavior. In S. Eth & R. S. Pynoos (Eds.), *Post-traumatic stress disorder in children* (pp. 19–43). Washington, DC: American Psychiatric Association.

Quarantelli, E. L. (1985). An assessment of conflicting views on mental health: The consequences of traumatic events. In C. R. Figley (Ed.), *Trauma and its wake* (vol. 1) (pp. 173–215). New York: Brunner/Mazel.

Resnick, P. J. (1988a). Malingering of post-traumatic disorders. In R. Rogers (Ed.), *Clinical assessment of malingering and deception* (pp. 84–103). New York: Guilford.

Resnick, P. J. (1988b). Malingered psychosis. In R. Rogers (Ed.), *Clinical assessment of malingering and deception* (pp. 34–53). New York: Guilford.

Rieff, D. (1991, October). Victims all? *Harper's*, pp. 49–56.

Rodale, J. I. (1978). *The synonym finder.* Emmaus, PA: Rodale Press.

Rosenthal, D., Sadler, A., & Edwards, W. (1987). Families and post-traumatic stress disorder. In T. C. Hansen & D. Rosenthal (Eds.), *Family stress* (pp. 81–95). Rockville, MD: Aspen.

Sarason, I. G., Johnson, J. H., & Siegel, J. M. (1978). Assessing the impact of life changes: Development of the Life Experiences Survey. *Journal of Consulting and Clinical Psychology, 46*(5), 932–946.

Schmitt, B. D. (1978). The physician's evaluation. In B. D. Schmitt (Ed.), *The child protection team handbook* (pp. 39–57). New York: Garland STPM Press.

Selye, H. (1950). *The physiology and pathology of exposure to stress.* Montreal, Canada: Acta.

Solomon, S. D. (1986). Mobilizing social support networks in times of disaster. In C. R. Figley (Ed.), *Trauma and its wake* (vol. 2) (pp. 232–263). New York: Brunner/Mazel.

Spiegel, H. (1974). *Manual for hypnotic induction profile: Eye-roll levitation method.* New York: Soni Medica, Inc.

Summitt, R. C. (1983). The child sexual abuse accommodation syndrome. *Child Abuse and Neglect, 7,* 177–193.

Symonds, M. (1970). Emotional hazards of police work. *American Journal of Psychiatry, 30,* 155–160.

Taylor, A. J. W., & Fraser, A. G. (1982). The stress of post-disaster body handling and victim identification work. *Journal of Human Stress, 8,* 4–12.

Terr, L. (1983). Chowchilla revisited: The effects of psychic trauma four years after a school-bus kidnapping. *American Journal of Psychiatry, 140,* 1543–1550.

Terr, L. (1990). *Too scared to cry.* New York: Harper & Row.

Terr, L. (1991). Childhood trauma: An outline and overview. *American Journal of Psychiatry, 148*(1), 10–20.

Thompson, M. R. (1965). Post-traumatic psychoneurosis—A statistical survey. *American Journal of Psychiatry, 121,* 1043–1048.

Vail-Williams, W., & Polak, P. R. (1979). Follow-up research in primary prevention: A model of adjustment in acute grief. *Journal of Clinical Psychology, 3,* 35–44.

van der Kolk, B., Blitz, R., Burr, W., Sherry, S., & Hartmann, E. (1984). Nightmares and trauma: A comparison of nightmares after combat with lifelong nightmares in veterans. *American Journal of Psychiatry, 141,* 187–190.

Wallace, S. E. (1973). *After suicide.* New York: Wiley.

Walsh, F., & McGoldrick, M. (1991). Loss and the family: A systemic perspective. In F. Walsh & M. McGoldrick (Eds.), *Living beyond loss* (pp. 1–29). New York: W. W. Norton.

Watzlawick, P. (1984). *The invented reality* (pp. 325–332). New York: W. W. Norton.

Watzlawick, P., Beavin Bavelas, J., & Jackson, D. D. (1967). *Pragmatics of human communication.* New York: W. W. Norton.

Wilson, J. P., Smith, W. K., & Johnson, S. K. (1985). A comparative analysis of PTSD among various survivor groups. In C. R. Figley (Ed.), *Trauma and its wake* (vol. 1) (pp. 142–172). New York: Brunner/Mazel.

Index